Literature, Spoken Language
in Second Language Learning

CW01431589

The use of literature in second language teaching has been advocated for a number of years, yet despite this there have only been a limited number of studies which have sought to investigate its effects. Fewer still have focused on its potential as a model of spoken language or as a vehicle to develop speaking skills. Drawing upon multiple research studies, this volume fills that gap by exploring how literature is used to develop speaking skills in second language learners. The volume is divided into two parts: literature and spoken language and literature and speaking skills. Part I focuses on studies exploring the use of literature to raise awareness of spoken language features, while Part II investigates its potential as a vehicle to develop speaking skills. Each part contains studies with different research designs and in various contexts including China, Japan and the UK. The research designs used mean that the chapters contain clear implications for classroom pedagogy and research in different contexts.

CHRISTIAN JONES is a Senior Lecturer in TESOL and Applied Linguistics at the University of Liverpool. His main research interests are connected to spoken language, and he has published work on spoken corpora, lexis, lexicogrammar and instructed second language acquisition. He is editor of *Practice in Second Language Learning* (Cambridge, 2018).

Literature, Spoken Language and Speaking Skills in Second Language Learning

Edited by

Christian Jones

University of Liverpool

CAMBRIDGE
UNIVERSITY PRESS

CAMBRIDGE
UNIVERSITY PRESS

University Printing House, Cambridge CB2 8BS, United Kingdom

One Liberty Plaza, 20th Floor, New York, NY 10006, USA

477 Williamstown Road, Port Melbourne, VIC 3207, Australia

314-321, 3rd Floor, Plot 3, Splendor Forum, Jasola District Centre, New Delhi - 110025, India

103 Penang Road, #05-06/07, Visioncrest Commercial, Singapore 238467

Cambridge University Press is part of the University of Cambridge.

It furthers the University's mission by disseminating knowledge in the pursuit of education, learning and research at the highest international levels of excellence.

www.cambridge.org
Information on this title: www.cambridge.org/9781108460798
DOI: 10.1017/9781108641692

© Cambridge University Press 2019

This publication is in copyright. Subject to statutory exception and to the provisions of relevant collective licensing agreements, no reproduction of any part may take place without the written permission of Cambridge University Press.

First published 2019
First paperback edition 2022

A catalogue record for this publication is available from the British Library

Library of Congress Cataloging in Publication data
Names: Jones, Christian (Linguist), editor.
Title: Literature, spoken language and speaking skills in second language learning / edited by Christian Jones.
Description: New York, NY: Cambridge University Press, [2019] | Includes bibliographical references and index.
Identifiers: LCCN 2019018396 | ISBN 9781108472944 (alk. paper)
Subjects: LCSH: Language and languages — Study and teaching. | Literature — Study and teaching. | Language awareness. | Fluency (Language learning) | Reading.
Classification: LCC P53 .L539 2019 | DDC 407.1—dc23
LC record available at https://lccn.loc.gov/2019018396

ISBN 978-1-108-47294-4 Hardback
ISBN 978-1-108-46079-8 Paperback

Cambridge University Press has no responsibility for the persistence or accuracy of URLs for external or third-party internet websites referred to in this publication, and does not guarantee that any content on such websites is, or will remain, accurate or appropriate.

Contents

Figures and Tables

Figures

Tables

Contributors

SHELLEY BYRNE, University of Central Lancashire, UK. Shelley has been involved in English teaching and research for the last ten years and currently works as a lecturer in the Centre for Excellence in Learning and Teaching (CELT). Having conducted research into second language acquisition and spoken language, her recent PhD in Applied Linguistics from UCLan fuelled her interest in learner corpora and lexicogrammar and their contributions to debates surrounding definitions of successful language learning. This continuing area of interest formed the basis of a co-authored book: Successful spoken English: Findings from learner corpora (Routledge, 2017).

JANE CLEARY, University of Central Lancashire, UK. Jane Cleary is a senior lecturer in English language teaching at the University of Central Lancashire. She has been involved in English teaching and teacher-training for over twenty years and has worked in the UK, Spain, Hungary, Hong Kong, Thailand and Japan as well as teaching online. Jane is interested in using literature, stories and drama to develop language learning as well as technology-enhanced teaching, learning and teacher-training.

GARY G. FOGAL, Sophia University, Japan. Gary Fogal is an Associate Professor of Applied English Language and Linguistics at Sophia University. His primary research examines developmental processes informing L2 writing and draws from a complex dynamic systems theory account of additional language development. His work also explores the interface between emergentism and Vygotsky's sociocultural theory as well as the utility of literary texts for developing L2 proficiency. He has published in journals such as *Applied Linguistics* and *Language and Sociocultural Theory,* and is co-editor (with Marjolijn H. Verspoor) of *Complex Dynamic Systems Theory and L2 Writing Development* (forthcoming, with John Benjamins).

ATSUSHI IIDA, Gunma University, Japan. Atsushi Iida is an Associate Professor of English and the Chair of Foreign Language Education at Gunma University in Japan. He was awarded his Ph.D. in English

(Composition and TESOL) at Indiana University of Pennsylvania. His research interests include second language writing, poetry writing, and literature in second language education. He has published his work in various journals including *Assessing Writing, System, Qualitative Inquiry, Scientific Study of Literature, English Teaching Forum,* and *Asian EFL Journal.*

CHRISTIAN JONES, University of Liverpool, UK. Christian Jones is a Senior Lecturer in TESOL and Applied Linguistics at the University of Liverpool. He has been involved in English language teaching for over twenty five years and has worked in China, Japan, Thailand and the UK, as a teacher, teacher-trainer and researcher. His main research interests are connected to spoken language and he has publish research related to spoken corpora, lexis, lexico grammar and instructed second language acquisition. He is the co-author (with Daniel Waller) of Corpus Linguistics for Grammar: A guide for research (Routledge, 2015), Successful Spoken English: Findings from Learner Corpora (with Shelley Byrne and Nicola Halenko) (Routledge, 2017) and editor of Practice in Second Language Learning, a collection of research on this area (Cambridge University Press, 2018). He is currently a member of the editorial panel for ELT Journal (Oxford University Press).

JIANGFENG LIU, Jiangsu University of Technology, China. Jiangfeng Liu is currently a lecturer in the School of Foreign Languages at Jiangsu University of Technology in China. She has been involved in English language teaching for over fifteen years and has taught both Chinese and international students. Jiangfeng completed her MA TESOL dissertation research in 2016; and since then she has been working actively on the pedagogical deployment of authentic materials to cultivate Chinese learners' communicative competence. She has published in several academic journals in China, such as Theory and Practice in Language Studies and Journal of Language Teaching and Research.

TARA MCILROY is an Associate Professor at Meiji University in Tokyo, Japan. She has a background in secondary English education with a focus on young adult literature and L2 literacy development. She recently developed the following content-based language courses using literature: Global Issues Through Literature; Linguistic Creativity in Poetry; and Literature for Language Teachers. Her ongoing research into poetry in the language classroom helps connect her interests in language education, learner autonomy in second language acquisition, and creative writing.

RICHARD S. PINNER, Sophia University, Japan. Richard Pinner is an associate professor at Sophia University in Tokyo with over 15 years of experience as a language teacher and teacher trainer. He holds a PhD in ELT and Applied

Linguistics and has published several articles on language teaching, most recently in *Language Teaching Research, English Today* and *Applied Linguistics Review*. He is the author of three research monographs and is particularly interested in the areas of authenticity and motivation in ELT and Content and Language Integrated Learning.

SCOTT J. SHELTON-STRONG, Kanda University of International Studies, Japan. Scott is a Learning Advisor and Lecturer at Kanda University of International Studies, in Chiba, Japan. His research interests include Learner Autonomy, Advising in Language Learning, the Psychology of Language Learning and Self-Access. He holds an MA in TESOL from the University of Nottingham and has been involved in English language teaching and learning for more than 25 years. He has published and presented work in a number of areas, including affect in language learning, learner autonomy, advising in language learning (ALL), learning strategies and literature circles in ELT. He is an active member of the Research Institute for Learner Autonomy Education (RILAE) and on the editorial team for the Relay Journal.

PAUL SIMPSON is a Professor of English Language and Head of the Department of English at University of Liverpool, UK. He works in a number of areas of English language and linguistics, including Stylistics, Pragmatics, Critical Linguistics and English Language Pedagogy. His books include: *Stylistics; Language through Literature; Language and Power; On the Discourse of Satire;* and *Language, Ideology and Point of View.* He is currently developing a full-length monograph on the discourse of irony, and is editing for John Benjamins a collection entitled *Style, Rhetoric and Creativity in Language.* He has been the Editor of the journal *Language and Literature*, and was recently Chair of the international Poetics and Linguistics Association.

BRIAN TOMLINSON has worked as a teacher, teacher trainer, curriculum developer, film extra, football coach and university academic in Indonesia, Italy, Japan, Malaysia, Nigeria, Oman, Singapore, UK, Vanuatu and Zambia, as well as giving presentations in over seventy countries. He is Founder and President of MATSDA (the international Materials Development Association), an Honorary Visiting Professor at the University of Liverpool, a Professor at the Shanghai International Studies University and a TESOL Professor at Anaheim University. He has over one hundred publications on materials development, language through literature, the teaching of reading, language awareness and teacher development, including Applied Linguistics and Materials Development, SLA Theory and Materials Development for Language Learning and The Complete Guide to the Theory and Practice of

Materials Development for Language Learning (with Hitomi Masuhara). He is currently working with Hitomi Masuhara on SLA Applied: Applying Second Language Acquisition Research to Language Learning for Cambridge University Press.

YAN ZHAO, Xijao-Liverpool University, China. Yan Zhao is a lecturer in Applied Linguistics in the Department of English at Xijiao-Liverpool University. She has taught Linguistics, Discourse Analysis and Research Methods modules to Chinese undergraduate and MA TESOL students. Before joining Xijiao-Liverpool University, Yan had taught English for Academic Purposes in the UK, making particular use of creative writing and literature as resources for language learning. Her current research project (as PI), funded by the National Social Science Fund of China, is an action research study which examines Chinese students' identity issues in EAP, ESP, Disciplinary and General English classrooms and subsequently looks for ways to incorporate the gained insights into the design and implementation of classroom instruction in these classrooms.

Foreword

Paul Simpson

Writing in the second half of the twentieth century, the Prague School structuralist Roman Jakobson declared that a linguist deaf to the poetic function of language and a literary scholar unconversant with linguistic methods were equally flagrant anachronisms. The second part of Jakobson's aphoristic parallel might seem the more readily demonstrable by today's criteria; after all, a scholar of literature declaring themselves uninterested in language and linguistic methods is like an academic chemist affirming that they have no interest in atoms, elements or molecules. The other side of Jakobson's formula raises a different question, of course. The assumption here is that the study of linguistics cannot be complete without some understanding of the linguistic patterns that comprise literature, or of how language functions 'poetically' in genres of discourse outside literature or even of how the striking compositional features of literary texts invite ways of reading and understanding that transcend the familiar or the routine. In another famous contribution from the second half of the twentieth century, Chomsky invokes the sequence 'Colorless green ideas sleep furiously' as a grammatically well formed, but semantically anomalous sentence. Chomsky clearly did not have literature in mind here, simply because such 'anomalous' language is often the very mainstay of creativity in literary writing. For example, the structurally very similar sequence 'Whispering lunar incantations dissolve the floors of memory' (from T. S. Eliot's 'Rhapsody on a Windy Night') presents a clear challenge for interpretation and understanding if it is not to be dismissed as simply anomalous language. Indeed, readers are tasked with working out not only what semantically complex language like this means, but also *how* it means. And as the insightful contributions in this volume make clear, literary discourse asks very important questions about language and about the learning of language.

In the decades since Jakobson and Chomsky made their observations, the rationale for the scholarly integration of language and literary study has been widely accepted, and literary-linguistics programmes are well established around the world on many university syllabuses in language, literature and linguistics. That said, these programmes are orientated in the main towards native speakers. As Christian Jones observes in his introduction to this book, whereas the theoretical significance of literary-linguistic pedagogies for second language (L2) speakers is reasonably well understood, there remains a paucity of empirical research that investigates the effectiveness of using literary texts in the second language classroom. In this respect, this collection is timely because its overarching focus is precisely on the role literature can play in non-native speakers' learning of language and in their experiences of thinking and talking about literary texts. Another ground-breaking feature of this book is its sustained focus on the ways in which the use of literary texts can enhance the awareness and development of spoken language and of speaking skills. Commendably, the chapters that comprise this collection incorporate the full gamut of literary composition, covering poetry, drama and fiction, as well screen and television adaptations thereof. The book moves from the compositional minutiae of the seventeen-syllable haiku poem, through the dramatised exchanges in the plays of Harold Pinter, to the corpus-assisted analysis of dialogue in a very large body of prose fiction. This material is supplemented elsewhere in the book by the productive use of screenplays, such as the television dramatisations and film adaptations of, respectively, the writing of Arthur Conan Doyle and of J. K. Rowling. The volume illustrates convincingly not only how a balanced literary-linguistic pedagogy can capture well the nuances of textual composition in literary texts, but also how such tools can help teachers to make informed choices about best practice pedagogically. And as the chapters in his book demonstrate consistently throughout, using literary texts in the second language classroom can improve learners' oral proficiency, communicative competence, linguistic-pragmatic awareness and spoken language skills.

Acknowledgements

This book is dedicated to the late Ron Carter, who helped and inspired so many people in the field of applied linguistics and English language teaching. We hope that the work here is in some small way a tribute to his legacy.

We would like to thank the following people for their help, inspiration and support in the past and present: Svenja Adolphs, Marco Antonini, Ruth Bavin, Nick Carter, Ron Carter, Jane Cleary, John Cross, Isabel Donnelly, James Donnithorne, Andy Downer, Graham Ethelston, Patrycja Golebiewska, Nick Gregson, Nicola Halenko, Douglas Hamano-Bunce, Simon Hobbs, Stuart Hobbs, Tania Horak, Josie Leonard, Jeannette Littlemore, Jeanne McCarten, Michael McCarthy, Fergus Mackinnon, Michaela Mahlberg, Hitomi Masuhara, Marije Michel, Alan Milby, Carmel Milroy, Clive Newton, David Oakey, Sheena Palmer, Simon Pate, Raymond Pearce, Lesley Randles, Karen Smith, Ivor Timmis, Michael Toolan, Daniel Waller, Neil Walker, Nicola Walker, Andy Williams, Jane Willis.

Thanks to Rebeca Taylor and Stephanie Taylor and all at Cambridge University Press for their help and guidance.

Finally, thanks to our families for all their support.

1 Introduction

Christian Jones

This book is about using literature – defined in this book as plays, poetry or novels or texts adapted as screenplays in film or television – in the second language classroom. There have been a number of publications in favour of using literature for language learning since the 1980s (e.g. Brumfit and Carter 1986; Duff and Maley 1990; Carter and McRae 1996; Chan 1999; Hall 2005; Paran 2006; Teranishi, Saito and Wales 2015). There have also been a number of activities and materials developed for using various forms of literature in the second language classroom (e.g. Maley and Moulding 1985; Collie and Slater 1987; McRae and Vethamani 1999). It has been argued that literature can develop language awareness (e.g. Brumfit and Carter 1986; Jones and Carter 2011), help students to develop the 'fifth skill' of thinking in the second language (McRae 1991) and help to develop competences from the Common European Framework of References for Language (CEFR) (Jones and Carter 2011), which are used to measure proficiency in a number of second languages (Council of Europe 2001).

Alongside such theoretical arguments, there have been a small number of studies that have produced evidence which suggest that literature can be beneficial in improving communicative competence, language awareness and language acquisition. Gilmore (2011), for example, found that authentic materials in general can be more beneficial than textbooks in developing several key aspects of communicative competence among English as a Foreign Language (EFL) learners when tested using a variety of quantitative measures. Although Gilmore's study was not focused on literature exclusively but authentic materials in general, we can certainly argue that, as a form of authentic material, literature may be similarly beneficial, if selected carefully. Lao and Krashen (2000) is one of many studies which present clear evidence that using literature in the form of graded readers for extensive reading has demonstrable benefits in terms of vocabulary acquisition and reading speed when compared with control groups that do not undertake extensive reading. Lin (2010) demonstrates how the use of Shakespeare's texts can develop language awareness in Taiwanese EFL learners, when using pre- and post-test measures in addition to qualitative data in the form of learner diaries. Other studies have sought to investigate the effect of specific types of instruction, from an experimental, learner or teacher perspective. Yang (2002), for example, found a student-centred approach to literature to be more effective than a teacher-centred one, when measured on a pre- and post-test. Schmidt (2004) also found that German learners of English were more positive about the use of Shakespeare in their English lessons when teachers employed a more learner-centred approach. Surveys show that learners can have reservations about the importance of literature when learning a second language (e.g. Martin and Laurie 1993) but that they can also see real value in it for learning language (e.g. Bloemert et al. 2019). Teachers themselves can also express reservations about the benefits of using literature and can demonstrate a lack of awareness of different options available to them in terms of methodology (Paran 2008). This sometimes results in approaches whereby teachers resort to teaching literature as a subject rather than as an aspect of second language learning, which we believe it can be.

Despite the evidence mentioned in the studies reviewed above, Paran (2008) and Fogal (2015) note that in general there is still a lack of empirical research which investigates the effectiveness of literature for second language learning in general (see Teranishi et al. 2015 for a recent exception to this). Of the studies that do exist, even fewer have sought to investigate the effectiveness of literature either as a tool for developing awareness of spoken language or as a tool for developing speaking skills. Although at first glance it may seem odd to discuss literature in terms of its relation to spoken language and speaking skills, we wish to argue that this is a gap in the research. We do so for several connected reasons. Firstly, as mentioned previously, it is often claimed that many second language learning courses are closely linked to the CEFR. The CEFR contains expected competences at each level, and many of these are connected to literature. One such example is 'I can understand contemporary literary prose' (Council of Europe 2001: 5) from the B2 self-assessment grid reading descriptor. In order to show such understanding, learners are likely to need to be able to talk about literature and, to at least some degree, understand the representations of spoken language within it. Therefore, we can argue that there is a clear value in research which informs teachers about how they might use literature to work on CEFR competences such as the one mentioned.

Secondly, conversation is a major part of the daily language use undertaken by people (Thornbury and Slade 2006), and in addition, the development of speaking skills and awareness of spoken language are often of primary importance to learners of English as a second or foreign language (Meddings and Thornbury 2009). However, it can be challenging for teachers to access recordings of unscripted conversations to analyse or discuss in class and, unedited, they may not always make interesting or engaging texts for language learning (Cook 1998). Therefore, it has long been suggested (e.g. McCarthy and Carter 1995; Carter and McRae 1996; Carter 1998) that dialogues from literature could provide interesting and useful models of spoken English that can also be used to develop speaking skills. This is because learners who are engaged with literary texts already have an interest in what characters are saying and in discussing the themes and ideas writers express as they interact with each other. Once engaged, there are also opportunities to encourage learners to notice features of the conversations within these texts. There is evidence that motivation (in this case via engaging texts), noticing and interaction are all important factors in language acquisition (Schmidt 1990; Long 1996; Dörnyei 2012).

Finally, it is important to acknowledge that conversations in literature are not, of course, identical to unscripted conversation. Literature, by its nature, aims to create an illusion of reality, and the purpose of literary dialogues are not the same as the transactional and social functions of conversations in the real world. However, it is also true that conversations in literature contain many features we find in the spoken language used by real speakers, and this, combined with their potential to provoke discussion as engaging texts, makes them useful as classroom material.

Despite such arguments, as noted previously, little research exists which provides evidence to support or refute them. Teachers may therefore understand such arguments in theory but wonder if they work in practice. Research can help to provide such an evidence base and either support or refute such theoretical positions. This volume seeks to address these gaps in the research by presenting a collection of studies focused upon the ways in which literature can enhance awareness of enhance awareness of spoken language and develop speaking skills. We have sought to produce evidence from studies which take a qualitative, quantitative, or mixed-methods approach to data analysis and which have been undertaken in a range of English as a second or foreign language settings. This is in order to make the data more robust and also to allow readers to find studies which are linked to a context with which they are familiar. All chapters are linked by a common question: how can literature enhance awareness of spoken language or develop speaking skills?

The studies in Part I of the book explore literature as a vehicle for developing awareness of spoken language. In this section, Byrne and Jones examine dialogues from a literature corpus in comparison with a spoken corpus in order to understand the extent to which literary dialogues offer a plausible and useful model of conversation. Tomlinson then examines how literature can be used as part of a text-driven approach in order to develop an awareness of pragmatic uses of spoken language. He does so by asking teachers in a range of contexts to evaluate materials taking this approach. Jones and Cleary examine the effects on input enhancement when using televised literature (Sherlock) to develop students' awareness of common features of spoken language. Iida continues the work from Chapter 2 on corpora but instead focuses on students' composed haiku poems and the features of spoken language they contain. Iida argues that haiku can play an important role in enhancing awareness of spoken language. For the last chapter in this section, Zhao and Liu report on a classroom-based action research study which employed screenplays. They use such materials to test the extent to which such films can develop awareness of pragmatic features of spoken English.

Part II explores the use of literature as a means of developing speaking skills. McIlroy examines the effects of discussing poetry at different levels of familiarity with learners in Japan. Her results show the potential which poetry can have as an aid to discussion and development of conversation strategies in class. Shelton-Strong analyses group discussion from literature circles, whereby learners discuss texts they have read. His research shows the potential for such group discussions to contain many language learning opportunities. Finally, Fogal and Pinner examine the language-related episodes produced by students to measure changes in lexical complexity on the speech of learners as they discussed literature.

While we recognise that many activities could involve both raising awareness of spoken language and developing speaking skills, the division of chapters into these parts will be one that many teachers and researchers recognise and that allows readers to find chapters which most relate to their interests quickly and easily. Explicit links are made between the chapters within each section and between different sections so that readers can see how each relates to the central theme. For example, the skill of noticing can be developed by analysing spoken language in literary dialogues (Chapter 4) and via discussion of literary texts (Chapter 9). Following all chapters, conclusions and implications are given for both teaching and research.

We hope that taken together, the studies will provide evidence which can inform teachers as they make choices in the classroom as well as furthering the research in this area.

References

Bloemert, J., Paran, A., Jansen, E. and Grift, W. V. D., 2019. 'Students' perspective on the benefits of EFL literature education', *The Language Learning Journal* 47(3): 371–384.

Brumfit, C. and Carter, R. 1986. *Literature and Language Teaching*. Oxford: Oxford University Press.

Carter, R. 1998. 'Orders of reality: CANCODE, communication, and culture', *ELT Journal* 52(1): 43–56.

Carter, R. and McRae, J. 1996. *Language, Literature and the Learner: Creative Classroom Practice*. London: Longman.

Chan, P. K. 1999. 'Literature, language awareness and EFL', *Language Awareness* 8(1): 38–50.

Collie, J. and Slater, S. 1987. *Literature in the Language Classroom: A Resource Book of Ideas and Activities*. Cambridge: Cambridge University Press.

Cook, G. 1998. 'The uses of reality: A reply to Ronald Carter', *ELT Journal* 52(1): 57–63.

Council of Europe, 2001. *Common European Framework of Reference for Languages: Learning, Teaching, Assessment*. Cambridge: Cambridge University Press.

Dörnyei, Z. 2012. *Motivation in Language Learning*. Shanghai: Shanghai Foreign Language Education Press.

Duff, A. and Maley, A. 1990. *Literature*. Oxford: Oxford University Press.

Fogal, G. G. 2015. 'Pedagogical stylistics in multiple foreign language and second language contexts: A synthesis of empirical research', *Language and Literature* 24 (1): 54–72.

Gilmore, A. 2011. '"I prefer not text": Developing Japanese learners' communicative competence with authentic materials', *Language Learning* 61(3): 786–819.

Hall, G., 2005. *Literature in Language Education*. Basingstoke: Palgrave Macmillan.

Jones, C. and Carter, R. 2011. 'Literature and language awareness:Using literature to achieve CEFR outcomes', *Journal of Second language Teaching and Research* 1 (1): 69–82.

Lao, C. Y. and Krashen, S. 2000. 'The impact of popular literature study on literacy development in EFL: More evidence for the power of reading', *System* 28(2): 261–270.

Lin, H. W. 2010. 'The taming of the immeasurable: An empirical assessment of language awareness', in Paran, A. and Sercu, L. (eds.), *Testing the Untestable in Language Education*. Bristol: Multilingual Matters, 191–216.

Long, M. 1996. 'The role of the linguistic environment in second language acquisition', in Richie, W. and Bhatia, T. K. (eds.), *Handbook of Second Language Acquisition*. San Diego: Academic Press, 413–468.

Maley, A. and Moulding, S. 1985. *Poem into Poem: Reading and Writing Poems with Students of English*. Cambridge: Cambridge University Press.

Martin, A. L. and Laurie, I. 1993. 'Student views about the contribution of literary and cultural content to language learning at intermediate level', *Foreign Language Annals* 26(2): 188–207.

McCarthy, M. and Carter, R. 1995. 'Spoken grammar: What is it and how can we teach it?', *ELT Journal* 49(3): 207–218.

McRae, J. 1991. *Literature with a Small 'l'*. London: Macmillan.

McRae, J. and Vethamani, M. E. 1999. *Now Read On: A Course in Multicultural Reading*. London: Routledge.

Meddings, L. and Thornbury, S. 2009. *Teaching Unplugged: Dogme in English Language Teaching*. Surrey: Delta Publishing.

Paran, A. 2006. *Literature in Language Teaching and Learning*. Alexandria, VA: Teachers of English to Speakers of Other Languages Inc.

2008. 'The role of literature in instructed foreign language learning and teaching: An evidence-based survey', *Language Teaching* 41(4): 465–496.

Schmidt, I. 2004. 'Methodische vorgehensweisen und schülerinteresse: Bericht über ein empirisches forschungsprojekt' [Methodological approaches and pupil interest: Report on an empirical study], in Schabert, I. (ed.), *Shakespeare Jahrbuch* 140. Bochum: Verlag und Druckkontor Kamp Gmbh, 196–211.

Schmidt, R. 1990. 'The role of consciousness in second language learning', *Applied Linguistics* 11: 129–158.

Teranishi, M., Saitō, Y. and Wales, K. 2015. *Literature and Language Learning in the EFL Classroom*. Basingstoke: Palgrave Macmillan.

Thornbury, S. and Slade, D. 2006. *Conversation: From Description to Pedagogy*. Cambridge: Cambridge University Press.

Yang, A. 2002. 'Science fiction in the EFL class', *Language, Culture and Curriculum* 15(1): 50–60.

Part I

Literature and Spoken Language

2   The Realism of Conversation in Literature

Shelley Byrne and Christian Jones

This chapter analyses conversations from a corpus of literature in order to uncover the extent to which these conversations contain typical features of spoken language, such as vague language and discourse markers. Such features have long been identified as key features of spoken language in corpora based on unscripted conversations (Carter and McCarthy 2017). The extent to which naturally occurring spoken language is similar to and different from literary conversations has been researched within the field of stylistics (e.g. Hughes 1996; Semino and Short 2004), but the extent to which conversations in literature could provide a useful model for learners of English as a Foreign Language and English as a Second Language (EFL/ESL) is less clear. Drawing upon corpus data from the CLiC Dickens corpus (Mahlberg et al. 2016) and the BYU-BNC spoken corpus (Davies 2004), this chapter seeks to explore how often common features occur and whether the frequency of occurrence is significant in comparison to data from unscripted conversations. We also explore the data qualitatively to examine whether the functions of common spoken language features differ or are similar. In doing so, we hope to uncover the extent to which conversations in literature can offer a plausible model of spoken English for EFL or ESL learners.

Introduction

Research in corpus linguistics has helped to describe common features of conversational language. We now commonly talk of spoken as well as written grammar (e.g. Biber et al. 1999; Leech 2000; Carter and McCarthy 2006; Rühlemann 2007; Timmis 2013), and there is an understanding that conversations cannot realistically be compared with written language on identical terms. To give examples of such differences, conversation is normally co-constructed (McCarthy 2010), it can contain forms which function differently from those in writing such as vague language, and it is often subject to rapid topic shifts (Carter and McCarthy 2006). It is clear that to develop an understanding and ability to take part in conversations, learners need a realistic model of them. While dialogues feature in almost all coursebooks, at times, the reality of such conversation is compromised in order to illustrate a particular language point. As a result, the dialogues they contain can seem contrived and unnatural (e.g. Jones, Byrne and Halenko 2017). One alternative to this is to base dialogues on data from spoken corpora (see McCarthy and McCarten 2018 for examples of this in practice). Another possible alternative model is to draw upon dialogues found in literature (see also Chapter 3, this volume, for an example of working with literary conversations in a text-driven approach), a model which seemingly is promising given the increased accessibility of large, free and online literature repositories such as Project Gutenberg (Hart 2019). Such example dialogues, if they can be shown to contain at least some common features of speech, have the potential to be both interesting and motivating when viewed from a pedagogical perspective (McRae 1991; Carter and McRae 1996). Many learners read literature in their first and second language (either in the original or a simplified form), and we thus assume that many will have an interest in the dialogues contained within novels, short stories or plays. Conversations in literature and in real life do, of course, have a fundamentally different purpose, something we discuss further in the next section. In literature, a dialogue may be pushing the plot forward, telling us something about a character or developing a theme. In real life, conversation is likely to have either a predominantly transactional or social purpose and frequently a mixture of both (see Carter and McCarthy 1997 for examples). The aim of this chapter is, therefore, to investigate the extent to which dialogues in literature contain some typical features of conversations and how these function. In doing so, we hope to discuss whether such dialogues offer a plausible model of conversation for learners of English although we exercise caution in drawing identical, 'like-for-like' comparisons between literature and speech given the diachronic changes spoken language use undergoes over time and are conscious not to assume that features of modern-day speech are fully replicated and modelled in older literary texts.

Although arguments have previously been made for the use of literary dialogues to teach spoken English (e.g. Carter 1998), we are not aware of any studies which have drawn upon large corpora of literature to analyse the features of spoken English these dialogues contain in order to assess the model they provide for English language learners. This chapter attempts to address this by examining data from CLiC (Corpus Linguistics in Context 2018), a large corpus containing both Dickens' novels and a large nineteenth-century corpus and, one which allows us to look at both quoted data (character speech) and non-quoted data (text which is not character speech). We also make comparison to the spoken (conversation) section of the BYU-BNC corpus (Brigham Young University–British National Corpus, Davies 2004).

Previous Research

There have been a number of studies which have compared dialogues in fiction to unscripted conversation. Such research has uncovered both differences and similarities between such texts. We will first discuss key differences found.

Short (1996) analyses dialogues in plays in comparison with unscripted conversations. One key difference he notes is that performance features such as hesitation marked by filled pauses ('er') or unfilled pauses and false starts are in general more frequent in unscripted conversation. When they do occur in fictional dialogues, they tend to have a different function. Pauses in conversation buy speakers time, mark pauses and/or hold the floor, while in literature, Short argues, they often function differently. A pause by a character may, for example, be used to build up tension between speakers or to tell us that a character is hesitant and nervous. Leech and Short (2007: 128–134) provide a useful analysis of conversation and dialogue in fiction. They also discuss hesitation and suggest that because in unscripted conversation, participants will tend to overlook (and probably expect) this, such features may be omitted from fictional dialogues without too much impact upon the realism of dialogues expected by readers. They also suggest that other features, such as discourse marking or the tendency for conversation to use fewer complex sentences, may occur with less frequency in fictional dialogues. This is because, in general, writers do not aim for a fully realistic representation of conversation but rather an 'illusion of real conversation' (Leech and Short 2007: 132), which serves a purpose in the fictional world they create. Dialogues are in fiction to tell us about characters or to signal a plot or thematic development and not to fulfil what Halliday and Matthiesen (2013) suggest are ideational, textual or interpersonal metafunctions. In other words, speakers use language to express some content, to link it to the ongoing conversation and to express it in a way that helps to oil the wheels of a conversation, depending on who the interlocutor is. Short (2012: 21) also shows that, in the fictional world, an author has many more options when representing what speakers say, which are unlikely to be employed by speakers in conversations. When writers report speech, Short shows that an author is able to use:

direct speech ('Just go now' he said grumpily), free indirect speech (She should get out now), indirect speech (grumpily he told her to leave) narrator's presentation of a speech act (grumpily he ordered her out) or a narrator's presentation of voice (He spoke grumpily).

Although speakers in conversations could, in theory, use similar options, it is far more likely that they will simply report what others have said directly (He said 'go now'), indirectly ('He said I needed to go now') or in summary ('He was saying I should go') and add comments or views on what they are reporting (see Carter and McCarthy 2006 for a discussion of this in spoken corpora).

More recently, work in corpus stylistics has enabled researchers to examine large bodies of fiction and explore the characteristics of the language used by writers in dialogues and other areas. Researchers undertake such analysis in order to uncover what we can find intuitively or to find evidence for our intuitions about a writer and her/his fiction (Stubbs 2008) and often to explore the fictional worlds writers create. Such analysis can uncover how language is used and this in turn gives us information about how a writer represents speech and dialogues in their work. Mahlberg and Smith (2012), for example, examine the use of suspended quotations – the interruption of a character's speech by at least five words from the narrator. Examining a corpus of Dickens' work, Mahlberg and Smith show how suspensions can be used by an author to contribute to characterisation. Focusing on the character, Mrs Sparsit, their analysis shows how Dickens uses suspensions to paint a picture of a character who is lofty. This also shows, as mentioned previously, a marked dissimilarity to unscripted conversation which would not feature the authorial voice of a narrator. Jones and Waller (2015) also discuss characterisation and speech when they explore a corpus containing a number of Sherlock Holmes stories. They show the tendency of Sherlock Holmes to say the lexical chunk 'I have no doubt that' with significantly greater frequency when compared to its occurrences in a larger fiction corpus. This chunk also tends to be used in a sentence- or turn-initial position. They argue that this usage suggests that the speech of Holmes is produced by a person who is rational, intelligent and authoritative. It is also interesting to note that 'I have no doubt that' only has one occurrence in the conversation sub-corpus of the BYU-BNC (Davies 2004), and this also illustrates the point made previously that writers, in aiming for the illusion of realism in their dialogues, may compromise this in order to create their own fictional world. Segundo (2016) also explores a corpus of Dickens in order to examine his use of reporting verbs ('he muttered', etc). His findings show that there are over a hundred types used, not including 'say', across the corpus and that there is, in general, a tendency for Dickens to choose more literary verbs such as 'reply' and 'return' instead of 'asked', which we would expect to be more frequent in unscripted conversations. He also shows that certain verbs are used much more frequently with particular characters, as they help to build a picture of a character. One example of this is the frequent use of verbs such as 'croaked' to underline the moody and sullen nature of the villain Daniel Quilp.

Overall, the studies reviewed illustrate some key differences between the unscripted conversations and dialogues we can find in literature. Table 2.1 summarises some of the key general differences discussed so far.

Despite these clear differences, there are of course also similarities between dialogues in fiction and unscripted conversations. As discussed in Chapter 4 (this volume), Short (1996) shows that ellipsis is one feature of unscripted

Table 2.1 *Key differences between dialogues in fiction and unscripted conversations*

Dialogues in fiction	Unscripted conversations
Characters	Participants
Used to develop the plot/theme(s)/character(s) in some way	Interpersonal/transactional goals
Constructed by the author	Co-constructed by participants
Topics chosen by the author	Topics chosen and developed by participants
Features of spoken English such as hesitation and false starts may be used to inform us about a character or to contribute to the theme. They may also contribute to the overall style of the literature	Features of spoken English such as hesitation and false starts are a standard 'performance feature' of conversations
Language choices of speakers are used to create a reality which fits within the fictional world the author has created	Language choices of speakers are related to the ideational, textual or interpersonal metafunctions (Halliday and Matthiesen 2013) they wish to fulfil

conversation which can be found in dramatic dialogues, whereas certain other features such as hesitation devices may be absent. Carter (1998) makes a similar argument, suggesting that dialogues from plays often contain many features of spoken English found in spoken corpora, such as those summarised in Table 2.1, and gives an example of a dialogue from Pinter to illustrate this point. Alongside illustrating the differences between fictional dialogues and conversations, Leech and Short (2007: 128–134) also show how they can have similarities. They give examples such as the use of contracted forms and informal lexical items, which can and do feature in fictional dialogue. If such features are common, we would argue that fictional dialogues could then be useful for classroom use. We know that dialogues in fiction are not the same as conversations in the real world, but we wish to uncover whether they could offer a plausible model of conversation. A key reason for this, as argued throughout this volume and elsewhere (e.g. McRae 1991), is that dialogues in fiction may provide a motivating and interesting source of materials for learners. We would hope, for example, that learners could be motivated to explore dialogue from stories and characters they are also interested in. We would also concur with McRae's (1991: 3) argument that representational language, that which 'in order that its meaning be decoded by a receiver, engages the imagination of the receiver' is often contained in such dialogues. This decoding can, we would argue, in itself be motivating and interesting and, if the dialogues also contain common features of unscripted conversation, potentially useful. Unedited transcripts of conversations taken from a corpus can of course be used as the basis for useful classroom materials (see McCarthy and McCarten 2018 for a recent discussion and examples) but may not always be as motivating, and so dialogues from literature could at least offer an alternative for teachers.

Before presenting the research questions central to this chapter, it is necessary to outline the conversational features selected for analysis. To fully explore the merits of literature as a useful teaching aid for realistic conversation, we considered the variable nature and contexts of interpersonal communication and the needs and goals of EFL/ESL learners aiming to interact appropriately with others. Firstly, spoken interaction is rarely 'neat, tidy, and predictable' but is instead incomplete and composed of numerous interruptions (Carter 1998: 47); they require active listenership in the 'speaker–listener world' and careful turn-taking management (Adolphs and Carter 2013: 32). Secondly, research into formulaic language has previously identified that the most common chunks in conversational speech often function to organise and monitor discourse or to ensure it is effectively co-constructed by the speakers involved (O'Keeffe et al. 2007; Buttery and McCarthy 2012; Adolphs and Carter 2013). Being of an interpersonal nature, such co-construction is also vital in expressing social identities and maintaining speaker–listener relationships in shared, real-time contexts (Thornbury and Slade 2006). Finally, with descriptors of learners' interactive abilities depicting the differences across levels (e.g. those outlined in the Common European Framework of Reference for Languages, CEFR (Council of Europe 2001: 26–29)), it is clear that models of realistic conversational features could be highly valuable for those aiming for success in their spoken English (Jones et al. 2017) because they allow for more proficient interaction on an organisational and interpersonal level. The decision was thus taken to concentrate on vague language and discourse markers, as they both play vital roles in these aspects and, to the best of our knowledge, nobody has examined them within literature with EFL/ESL students in mind. For these reasons, we seek to answer the following research questions in this chapter:

> RQ1: What are the frequencies of occurrence and significant collocations of *or so, stuff* and *kind of* in dialogues from a literature corpus, and how does this compare to usage in unscripted conversations?
>
> RQ2: What are the frequencies of occurrence and significant collocations of *now, oh* and *I mean* in dialogues from a literature corpus, and how does this compare to usage in unscripted conversations?

Methodology

In answering the research questions set, we adopted a predominantly corpus-based approach using the 3,835,807-word DNov sub-component of the CLiC corpus (Mahlberg et al. 2016). Containing the works of Charles Dickens, the data are divided into five sub-corpora: all text, short suspensions, long suspensions, direct quotes and non-quotes. Owing to our focus on spoken conversation, we predominantly analysed data from the 1,369,029 token quote sub-corpus, with the 2,456,944 token non-quote sub-corpus used as a point of comparison. The DNov quote sub-corpus was chosen simply to provide an example of conversation in literature and how these can be analysed. We recognise that the age and characteristics of Dickens' work may not be suitable for every learner, so research based on more modern novels, should they become available for analysis in the future, would be extremely useful.

Though distinctions between corpus-based and corpus-driven approaches have been deemed somewhat 'over-stated' (McEnery et al. 2006: 8), they are nevertheless helpful in introducing the methodology we followed. Essentially used to explore and exemplify previously formulated theories, hypotheses or descriptions of language structure or use, corpus-based methodologies allow researchers to test previously held theories about language (Tognini-Bonelli 2001; Baker 2010; McEnery and Hardie 2012). With corpus-driven techniques alternatively allowing hypotheses to emerge from the chosen corpus texts themselves, it could be said that corpus-based analyses are susceptible or limited to the researcher's own intuition or the parameters of previous descriptions. The approach adopted was more typical of a corpus-based analysis; however, to minimise the potential negative influences on our analysis, we based our research on descriptions of informal, unscripted conversation originating from in-depth corpus studies such as those conducted by Carter (1998), Carter and McCarthy (2006), and O'Keeffe et al. (2007). As is highlighted by Amador-Moreno (2010: 532), such comparison of literature with 'real spoken data' is thus thought to reveal much in terms of the accuracy of speech representations in literary texts. With this in mind, it is necessary to remember that in this chapter we seek to determine not simply how well literature could replicate or imitate natural speech but the extent to which it could potentially act as a useful model of spoken interaction for learners of English.

The first stage of examination involved analysing the DNov corpus data quantitatively to refine our focus further and ascertain which vague language and discourse markers warranted closer qualitative comparison. A list of vague language items and discourse markers (DMs) were hence retrieved from Carter and McCarthy (2006) as a focus for initial quantitative analysis (see Table 2.2), but since the online CLiC corpus software affords users only four functions – concordance, subsets, Ngrams and keywords (Wiegland et al. 2017) – obtaining word frequencies had to be performed manually. Using the concordance tool, which retrieves lexis with a frequency below 10,000 occurrences, each item in Table 2.2 was searched for raw frequency in both the quotes and the non-quotes sections. A minimum frequency threshold of 50 was set for the DM

Table 2.2 *Vague language items and discourse markers identified for preliminary quantitative analysis* (Carter and McCarthy 2006)

Vague language	Discourse markers
THING	ANYWAY
STUFF	COS
OR SO	FINE
OR SOMETHING	GOOD
OR ANYTHING	GREAT
AND SO ON	LIKE
OR WHATEVER	NOW
KIND OF	OH
SORT OF	OKAY
LIKE	RIGHT
	SO
	WELL
	YOU KNOW
	I MEAN
	AS I SAY
	FOR A START
	MIND YOU
	YOU SEE
	INCIDENTALLY
	BY THE WAY
	WHILE I THINK OF IT
	SPEAKING OF WHICH
	AH WELL
	AS IT WERE
	IF YOU LIKE
	FIRST
	NEXT
	AND THEN
	SECOND
	LISTEN
	THIRD
	IN GENERAL

lexis in the DNov quote data due to the number of items available for analysis. The same process was then followed using the BYU-BNC Conversation sub-corpus (Davies 2004). However, it is important to note at this stage that because all uses of a particular word are captured in raw frequency figures, any multiple meanings conveyed or functions performed by it would not be distinguished. A raw frequency of 70 for NOW, for instance, simply shows its occurrence; it is unable to convey how it is used.

The next stage called for more meaningful comparison of the DNov and BYU-BNC data; normalised frequencies were therefore calculated. Normalised frequencies allow comparisons to be made across corpora of different sizes; word occurrence is divided by the overall corpus size and then multiplied by a common base (in this case 1 million words) to demonstrate how frequently a word can be expected to appear across corpora (McEnery and Hardie 2012). These normalised frequencies were then used to calculate percentage increases or decreases in usage between the chosen lexis across: (i) DNov quotes and the BYU-BNC conversation corpus, and (ii) DNov quotes and DNov non-quotes. To add a statistical comparison, log-likelihood scores were also computed using Rayson's (2018) UCREL log-likelihood online calculator to compare the use of lexis between DNov quotes and BNC Conversation. Log-likelihood scores are useful as they do not assume a normal distribution of the item in question within a text while increasing the confidence of a researcher's assumptions about their investigations and allowing them to extend beyond simple descriptions of phenomena (McEnery and Hardie 2012).

To check that the selected words functioned as vague language and DMs and to enhance understanding of their usage, we also examined the collocations they occurred in. Collocations are fundamental in language as meaning extends beyond the realms of the single word (e.g. Firth 1957; Lewis 1993; Adolphs and Carter 2013). Therefore, greater insight about a chosen word, or node, can be obtained by examining the words co-occurring with it. It should be remembered, though, that while collocations consist of co-occurrences of words which can satisfy statistical significance (Hunston 2002; Greaves and Warren 2010; McEnery and Hardie 2012), they are only able to reflect tendencies in language rather than unequivocal, fixed bonds (Wray 2002). They are nevertheless essential for identifying which patterns of use are meaningful or may be of importance to learners, since words primed to occur together act as a 'driving force behind language use, language structure and language change' (Hoey 2005: 12).

Concordancers are vital in the pursuit of such collocational data in corpora. By placing node words in a central position within a particular window of words appearing before and after them, their patterns of use can be retrieved, tested for significance and analysed (Hunston 2002). While CLiC's software does possess a useful concordancer, which retrieves all uses of a particular node word, it is unable to calculate or list collocations unless the researcher knows which word pairings they are already interested in. Consequently, BYU-BNC's online software was used to extract potentially useful collocations of the selected vague language and DMs to see if their use in real, unscripted communication mirrored or contrasted with those in the DNov literature. To do so, the BNC Conversation sub-corpus was searched for collocates with a minimum frequency of 5 sorted according to their relevance, or Mutual Information (MI) score; a maximum window of four words to the left and right of the node word was also established. MI is 'a statistical measure of the degree of relatedness of two elements' (Oakes 1998: 253). The probability of co-occurrence is ultimately compared to the probability that the words occur independently of each other in a corpus, with a figure of 3 or more being considered significant (Hunston 2002). The frequency threshold of 5 was imposed as MI can inadvertently retrieve collocates seemingly significant and high in degree of co-occurrence despite their rare overall occurrence in the corpus. Significant collocations were then searched using CLiC software with their MI scores calculated using the online Lancaster Stats Tool (Brezina 2018). Similarly, in an attempt to combat potentially exaggerated inferences about strong collocations with low frequencies, t-scores for DNov quote data were incorporated into the analysis (Barnbrook 1996). These helped determine how much evidence existed in the DNov corpus for particular pairings and thus scores above 2 were deemed significant.

Finally, due to the rich amount of data and the additional context of use displayed by the CLiC concordancer, analysis was completed in two ways. As mentioned earlier, the frequency of a word fails to recognise the polysemy of words (Schmitt 2010); similarly, searching only for known, or suspected, collocates of interest could have resulted in other useful observations being overlooked. We therefore made use of concordance lines to check that vague language and DMs remained the sole focus of our analysis and to identify other possible avenues to explore. Ultimately, intuition in corpus analysis still has an important role to play in corpus linguistics, since the evidence presented requires interpretation to see what else is present, absent or indeed salient in the data.

Results

Preliminary Quantitative Analysis

As per the methodology discussion, the first stage of data analysis consisted of identifying which items from Table 2.2 would be selected for further investigation. It involved observation of raw frequencies, normalised frequencies, percentage differences and log-likelihood scores for data from DNov quotes, DNov non-quotes and the BNC Conversation corpus. See Tables 2.3 and 2.4 for vague language and DM statistics, respectively. We discuss this first, before showing how the data answer the research questions set.

Initial analysis of the data in the two tables allowed us to identify the following vague language and DM items as a focus for in-depth analysis:

Vague Language

- OR SO – The most significant vague language item showing more usage. Representing the fourth most frequent normalised frequency in the DNov

Table 2.3 *Quantitative analysis of vague language items*

Vague language item	Raw frequencies			Normalised frequencies (basis per million)			Percentage (%) comparison of normalised frequencies		Log-likelihood (LL)		
	DNov quotes	DNov non-quotes	BNC Conv.	DNov quotes	DNov non-quotes	BNC Conv.	DNov quotes vs BNC Conv.	DNov quotes vs DNov non-quotes	LL score	Used more/ Used less in DNov quotes	Significant?
THING	1112	547	5247	812.255	222.634	1307.678	−37.89	264.84	229.86**	Less	Yes
SORT OF	328	307	4116	239.586	124.952	1025.805	−76.64	91.74	973.66**	Less	Yes
KIND OF	221	479	466	161.428	194.958	116.138	39.00	−17.20	15.58**	More	Yes
OR SO	91	162	76	66.470	65.936	18.941	250.93	0.81	63.59**	More	Yes
STUFF	45	19	1680	32.870	7.733	418.696	−92.15	325.05	692.58**	Less	Yes
OR ANYTHING	34	26	358	24.835	10.582	89.222	−72.16	134.69	72.16**	Less	Yes
OR SOMETHING	29	24	1712	21.183	9.768	426.671	−95.04	116.85	789.53**	Less	Yes
OR WHATEVER	25	13	389	18.261	5.291	96.948	−81.16	245.13	108.02**	Less	Yes

Note: ** = $p < 0.0001$.

Table 2.4 *Quantitative analysis of discourse markers*

Discourse markers	Raw frequencies			Normalised frequencies (basis per million)			Percentage (%) comparison of normalised frequencies		Log-likelihood (LL)		
	DNov quotes	DNov non-quotes	BNC Conv.	DNov quotes	DNov non-quotes	BNC Conv.	DNov quotes vs. BNC Conv.	DNov quotes vs. DNov non-quotes	LL score	Used more/ Used less in DNov quotes	Significant?
SO	7634	9641	24209	5576.215	3923.980	6033.460	-7.58	42.11	36.54**	Less	Yes
NOW	4636	3306	11803	3386.342	1345.574	2941.589	15.12	151.67	64.62**	More	Yes
WELL	3956	1506	35778	2889.639	612.957	8916.731	-67.59	371.43	6079.33*	Less	Yes
LIKE	2607	3048	21887	1904.269	1240.566	5454.763	-65.09	53.50	3380.91**	Less	Yes
OH	2588	226	41542	1890.391	91.984	10353.257	-81.74	1955.13	11773.82*	Less	Yes
GOOD	2511	2082	8178	1834.147	847.394	2038.153	-10.01	116.45	21.76**	Less	Yes
YOU KNOW	2032	67	15529	1484.264	27.270	3870.197	-61.65	5342.91	2096.56**	Less	Yes
RIGHT	1330	892	14980	971.491	363.053	3733.373	-73.98	167.59	3220.23**	Less	Yes
FIRST	1127	2288	3056	823.211	931.238	761.628	8.09	-11.60	4.92*	More	No
GREAT	1108	3776	1066	809.333	1536.869	265.673	204.64	-47.34	646.28**	More	Yes
YOU SEE	739	28	3386	539.799	11.396	843.872	-36.03	4636.63	132.81**	Less	Yes
NEXT	451	961	2629	329.431	391.136	655.210	-49.72	-15.78	212.84**	Less	Yes
I MEAN	448	46	9905	327.239	18.722	2468.562	-86.74	1647.84	3351.96**	Less	Yes
AND THEN	427	1539	5308	311.900	626.388	1322.880	-76.42	-50.21	1245.75**	Less	Yes
FINE	326	281	765	238.125	114.370	190.656	24.90	108.21	10.95**	More	No
SECOND	159	382	755	116.141	155.478	188.164	-38.28	-25.30	33.84**	Less	Yes
LISTEN	115	129	780	84.001	52.504	194.395	-56.79	59.99	86.31**	Less	Yes
IF YOU LIKE	78	2	164	56.975	0.814	40.873	39.40	6899.18	5.59**	More	No
MIND YOU	67	5	691	48.940	2.035	172.214	-71.58	2304.85	136.15**	Less	Yes
THIRD	60	197	299	43.827	80.181	74.518	-41.19	-45.34	15.77**	Less	Yes
IN GENERAL	52	75	30	37.983	30.526	7.477	408.02	24.43	52.27**	More	Yes

quote data, it occurred substantially more often in the quoted data than it did in DNov non-quoted data.

- STUFF – The third most significant vague language item showing reduced usage. Ranked in the middle of the DNov quote normalised frequencies, but again, it seemed a much more frequent feature of quoted than unquoted language.
- KIND OF – Exhibited the third most frequent normalised frequency and was one of only two vague language items to show significantly greater use in the DNov quote data. Interestingly though, it was used 17 per cent less frequently in quoted data than it was in non-quoted data.

Discourse Markers
- NOW – The second highest DM in DNov quotes for raw and normalised frequency figures. With its normalised frequency in BNC Conversation ranking in seventh position, this was the only statistically significantly DM to show overuse apart from GREAT (GREAT was discounted from analysis as it functioned as an adjective in every occurrence). The increase in occurrence between DNov quotes and non-quotes stood at 152 per cent.
- OH – The most frequent DM in BNC Conversation's normalised frequency but only the fifth highest in DNov quote data. It represented the most statistically significant DM to show underuse, but it nevertheless had the biggest percentage difference between quoted and un-quoted data (a difference of nearly 2,000 per cent).
- I MEAN – This DM was ranked 13th in the normalised frequency figures for DNov data, whereas it appeared in 8th position for BNC Conversation figures. Its log-likelihood score showed a highly significant underuse, and once again, it revealed a much-increased usage in quoted DNov data than DNov non-quoted data.

In the following section, we discuss each research question. Answers for the questions are integrated into the discussion of results and then summarised at the end of this section.

Further Quantitative and Qualitative Analysis

RQ1: **What are the frequencies of occurrence and significant collocations of OR SO, STUFF and KIND OF in dialogues from a literature corpus, and how does this compare to usage in unscripted conversations?**

Or So

Or so appeared in the DNov quote corpus on 91 occasions; it was also the most significantly 'overused' vague language item when compared with

Table 2.5 *Significant OR SO collocates from BNC Conversation*

Position to node		L4–L1			L1		
		Collocate	Freq.	MI	Collocate	Freq.	MI
Left position collocates	1	HOUR	25	8.30	NONE		
	2	MONTHS	5	6.67			
	3	WEEK	16	6.02			
	4	MINUTES	5	5.99			
	5	AN	22	5.90			
	6	HALF	9	5.25			
	7	YEAR	5	4.81			

Table 2.6 *Collocational significance of OR SO in DNov quotes*

	L4–L1		
Collocate	Freq.	MI	t-score
HOUR	13	10.51	3.60
MONTHS	1	8.28	1.00
WEEK	10	10.62	3.16
MINUTES	1	8.11	1.00
AN	14	7.70	3.72
HALF	6	8.98	2.45
YEAR	2	8.22	1.41

BNC Conversation. Table 2.5 displays the significant left-hand collocates found in the BNC Conversation corpus; no significant collocates were found in the R1 nor R1–R4 positions. With a minimum frequency threshold of 5 occurrences imposed, collocates are sorted according to MI score and according to their position to the node (L4, for instance, is the fourth word to the left of the node *or so*). Since no significant co-occurrences were found in the other positions, the L4–L1 position was the sole focus for analysis here.

The data showed that *or so* was a useful end-position vague language item for reducing the precision or directness of a statement in unscripted conversation. Similarly, its usage seemed to revolve mostly around time durations. The collocates in Table 2.5 were therefore used as a basis for exploring the DNov quote data to see if the same function was performed. The findings are presented in Table 2.6.

As can be seen, there are several significant collocations shared across BNC Conversation and DNov quotes: *hour or so, week or so, an (x) or so* and *half or so*. The use of *or so* to hedge the duration of events was thus a function common across both corpora, which suggests that the literature in this corpus, for this vague language item, could provide a useful and reliable model of real spoken language use. However, the full flexibility of *or so* in the DNov literature was somewhat neglected in the collocational data presented. *Or so* was used with 11 different words concerning duration or time (*hour, minute, minutes, week, weeks, year, years, month, months, day, at first*), 4 words relating to money (*pounds, guineas, shilling, shillings*), 2 different words denoting distance (*mile, point*) and a vast array of nouns for quantity and other miscellaneous categories (see Extract 1). In total, *or so* was used with 29 other words to soften the exactness of character utterances. While significant collocations showed how DNov's quoted language was similar to that in the BNC Conversation corpus, and despite the limited currency of some lexis (e.g. *guineas*), this high number of collocates could, to some extent, explain the overuse found in the literary texts. Combined with the fact that DNov non-quoted data offered 57 different pairings containing *or so*, the literature could demonstrate to learners how adaptable some vague language can be in conversation, but it could also raise the saliency of some forms, helping learners to notice them.

Extract 1: 'a dozen *or so* of bottled ale, and a noggin or two of whiskey to close up with.' (PP255159)

Stuff

Stuff appeared on only 45 occasions in the DNov quote corpus. As such, it represented the third most significantly 'underused' vague language item in the study. With *stuff* being described as 'one of the most frequent nouns in spoken English' (Carter and McCarthy 2006: 149), already, the particular type and age of this literature suggests it has limited potential as a model of current-day conversation. However, the significant collocates revealed in the BNC Conversation analysis (see Table 2.7) did uncover one particular colligational pattern: that it was common for *stuff* to be qualified by an adjective or noun before it. In spite of the low frequencies exhibited, just over a quarter of all DNov quote occurrences (12/45) of *stuff* were accompanied by an adjective or noun. In terms of form, such utterances did therefore display some parallels with usage in unscripted conversation. There were also some similar functions in the DNov data. For instance, Extract 2 shows how *stuff* can be used as a substitute for multiple items of equipment; Extract 3 shows how *stuff* can be employed to save time on listing individual items; and Extract 4 illustrates how *stuff* can be used in exclamations to portray a speaker's satisfaction or joy.

Table 2.7 *Significant collocates of STUFF from BNC Conversation*

Position to node		L4–L1			L1		
		Collocate	Freq.	MI	Collocate	Freq.	MI
Left position collocates	1	SKI	5	6.12	FROZEN	7	7.49
	2	FROZEN	8	5.68	AMERICAN	5	6.39
	3	AMERICAN	5	4.39	SALAD	5	6.23
	4	COLLECT	5	4.23	THICK	6	5.70
	5	SALAD	5	4.23	GREEN	6	4.38
	6	LOADS	15	4.20	WHITE	8	4.37
	7	THICK	7	3.93	HOT	5	4.15
	8	LOAD	8	3.72	GREAT	7	3.97
	9	USING	7	3.60	OWN	9	3.96
	10	EXPENSIVE	6	3.16	CHRISTMAS	9	3.89
	11	PLENTY	5	3.10	NEW	13	3.88
	12	BUYING	5	3.06	BLACK	6	3.84
	13				SOME	36	3.46
	14				BUY	8	3.44
	15				GOOD	36	3.39
	16				MUCH	20	3.34
	17				THIS	84	3.33
	18				OUR	10	3.09
		R1			R1–R4		
		Collocate	Freq.	MI	Collocate	Freq.	MI
Right position collocates	1	IN	6	3.83	NONE		
	2	LIKE	88	3.26			
	3	FROM	24	3.24			
	4	AROUND	5	3.23			

Extract 2: Does he shed even legs of mutton for you in any decent proportion to potatoes and garden s*tuff*? (DNov quotes, ID: MC8549)

Extract 3: cambric, cloth, crape, stuff, carpet, merino, muslin, bombazeen, or woollen s*tuff* (DNov quotes, ID: OT137364)

Extract 4: 'Leave him alone,' said the green-coated stranger; 'brandy-and-water—jolly old gentleman—lots of pluck—swallow this—ah!—capital s*tuff*.' (DNov quotes, ID: PP15980)

That being said, it was apparent that some of the more common collocations and uses of this vague language item, e.g. *loads of stuff* and *stuff like* were noticeably absent from the DNov data. Though helpful in many informal contexts (Carter and McCarthy 2006), especially with younger speakers (Lin 2013), such collocations allow for approximations and comparisons to be made in which the speaker does not want to seem overly exact and pedantic (see Extract 5), or when the speaker may

Table 2.8 *Significant collocates in BNC Conversation for KIND OF*

Position to node		L4–L1			L1		
		Collocate	Freq.	MI	Collocate	Freq.	MI
	1	DIFFERENT	11	3.98	DIFFERENT	10	5.84
	2	SAME	14	3.67	SAME	11	5.32
	3				VERY	18	4.57
Left position	4				SOME	21	4.53
collocates	5				WHAT	59	3.72
	6				ANY	8	3.68
	7				THOSE	5	3.60
	8				THIS	20	3.11
		R1			R1–R4		
		Collocate	Freq.	MI	Collocate	Freq.	MI
Right position	1	NONE			PERSON	12	5.32
collocates	2				THING	52	4.42
	3				THINGS	15	3.25

perhaps want to sound hyperbolic (see Extract 6). Overall, *stuff* was therefore found to be inadequately represented and modelled in the DNov corpus in terms of its frequency and its more modern-day uses.

Extract 5: got to revise for my erm science test tomorrow and I've got loads of *stuff* to do (BNC Conversation ID: KD0)

Extract 6: We bought loads of *stuff*! (BNC Conversation ID: KB2)

Kind Of

As Table 2.3 showed earlier, *kind of* appeared with a raw frequency of 221 in the DNov quotes and showed significant overuse. Analysis of its collocates and functions was needed to discover whether it functioned as vague language and what the meanings behind its usage were. The collocates in Table 2.8 were extracted from BYU-BNC's conversation sub-corpus.

Using the data above, the collocates in the L1 and R1–R4 categories were chosen for comparison with DNov frequencies to see if there was a significant co-occurrence (MI) or sufficient evidence (t-score) to suggest the word pairings were of interest.

It would appear that while all left-hand collocates of *kind of* in the DNov quote data were significant in their collocational strength, t-scores for many of the pairings revealed that they were infrequent in the corpus. The collocations *very kind of, what kind of, any kind of* and *this kind of* showed both significant MI and t-scores but evidently, *kind of* in these examples did not always function as a vague language device, for example, 'You have abetted him in it, and very

Table 2.9 *Collocate comparison for KIND OF in DNov quotes*

L1			
Collocate	Freq.	MI	t-score
DIFFERENT	3	8.23	1.73
SAME	2	5.31	1.38
VERY	25	6.45	4.94
SOME	1	3.22	0.89
WHAT	23	5.45	4.69
ANY	8	5.51	2.77
THOSE	0	N/A	N/A
THIS	8	4.15	2.67

R1–R4			
Collocate	Freq.	MI	t-score
PERSON	1	4.90	0.97
THING	19	8.21	4.34
THINGS	2	5.72	1.39

kind of you it was to do so' (DNov quotes, ID: BR82110). Likewise, the potential formation of noun phrases using *different kind of* or *same kind of* (see Extract 7), while significant in BNC Conversation, was not as evident in the DNov quote data. Attention was thus paid to the right-hand collocates, despite them being few in number.

Extract 7: I thought it was a different *kind of* brochure that's all (BNC Conversation ID: KBL)

Though *kind of* can collocate with many different nouns, the DNov data in Table 2.9 show clear distinctions between those that are considered significant. It is at this point that *thing* becomes woven into the discussion. In both the BNC Conversation and DNov quote data, *kind of thing* was the most frequent collocation following the node word. Carter and McCarthy (2006: 148) highlight that constructions such as those formed by grouped vague language items 'refer vaguely to categories, on the assumption that the listener will understand what is included in the category'. Not only do they act as ways to avoid being overly precise in speech, but they can emphasise the shared knowledge that speaker–hearers in the same contexts possess, an interaction strategy seen in Extract 8. To some extent, therefore, the DNov quote data show some replicability with real examples of unscripted conversation, though they are somewhat limited.

Extract 8: I will only say that it is an additional proof of what one knows from experience; that this *kind of* thing never answers (DNov quotes, ID: LD213484)

The next stage of analysis involved manually examining concordance lines to see if any functions other than those revealed by observation of the collocations could provide further insight. Interestingly, there was one particular usage which could prove especially helpful to learners. It was found that there were approximately 40 examples in the DNov corpus in which speakers hedged their vocabulary choices in their utterances to signal to the listener that the words used were not the most exact for the descriptions needed (see Extract 9).

Extract 9: 'What sort of a noise?' Asked the cook. 'A *kind of* busting noise,' replied Mr Giles (DNov quotes, ID: OT77731)

As a model, DNov literature, in respect of vague language overall, demonstrates how it can be used not only as a tactic for maintaining speaker–hearer relationships via the avoidance of overly pedantic dialogue, but also as a signal to listeners that the imprecise vocabulary or missing detail provided by a speaker will need to be interpreted by them.

RQ2: **What are the frequencies of occurrence and significant collocations of NOW, OH, and I MEAN in dialogues from a literature corpus, and how does this compare to usage in unscripted conversations?**

Now

Upon comparing DNov quotes and BNC Conversation, it was found that *now* exhibits a significant overuse; its usage in quoted language increased by 152 per cent when compared to unquoted usage. As such, the data implied it was used as a prominent feature of spoken dialogue in the literature. Analysis of *now*'s collocates in BNC Conversation (see Table 2.10), however, did not prove fruitful, as it seemed to operate mostly as an adverb of time rather than as a DM (see Extract 10).

Extract 10: I thought you might have recovered by *now*. (BNC Conversation ID: KBW)

Closer examination of the concordance data was therefore required to see if, and how, it was used as a DM in literary speech. Though the polysemic nature of *now* presented a mixture of uses, we were able to identify two noticeable functions: that of beginning a turn and getting the listener's attention, and that of giving commands.

In approximately a third of all concordance lines (37.53 per cent), *now*, in sentence-initial position, was accompanied by a character's name or by a noun or noun-phrase referring to them. Totalling over 1,700 occasions, proper nouns were joined by nouns or noun phrases such as *boy, brother, darling, gentlemen, ma'am* and *old chap* in getting a listening character's attention in the conversation. Clearly, some of the associated nouns are outdated (*old chap* alone only

Table 2.10 *Significant collocates of NOW in BNC Conversation*

Position to node		L4–L1			L1		
		Collocate	Freq.	MI	Collocate	Freq.	MI
	1	RECOVERED	5	4.92	HAPPIER	6	6.35
	2	HAPPIER	8	4.77	BOOM	6	4.14
	3	BOOM	12	3.14	RAINING	5	4.04
	4				FORGOTTEN	9	3.77
	5				LATE	26	3.73
Left position	6				CLOSED	6	3.50
collocates	7				TIRED	12	3.47
	8				WHEREAS	5	3.45
	9				STAGE	7	3.35
	10				RECORDING	11	3.33
	11				HAPPENS	10	3.30
	12				PUDDING	5	3.20

Right position collocates		R1			R1–R4		
		Collocate	Freq.	MI	Collocate	Freq.	MI
	1	NONE			NONE		

appears on 14 occasions in the BNC Conversation), but importantly, the meaning behind the utterance could also be considered antiquated and, quite simply, inappropriate. Take the following extract as an examples:

Extract 11: '*Now*, Clara my dear,' said Mr Murdstone. 'Recollect! Control yourself, always control yourself! Davy boy, how do you do?' (DNov quotes, ID: DC16945)

The addition of a name or noun phrase after the DM works to gain not only the attention of those listening but the attention of a particular person. This could happen whether there is one person or multiple people present at the time of the character's speech. What is even more palpable in such uses of *now* is the authority with which a character speaks and the feelings about that character that are generated. In Extract 11, for instance, '*Now*, Clara my dear' might sound rather caring, but the imperatives which follow create a more tangible sense of prosody. Given that Mr Murdstone is directing the discourse at his wife, the reader may detect a tone of condescension in what he is asking her to do. Such authority and attitude are similarly portrayed when *now* is accompanied not by a name, but by a reporting verb in the non-quoted language. With literature aiming to tell a story, reporting verbs can be neutral or they can be used to create a sense of drama or tell us something about characterisation, as noted in our review of previous research. Incidentally, though *now* and *said* in Extract 11 could be considered rather neutral, the character's authority, through either status, knowledge, gender or power, is still easily conveyed. Alternatively, as in Extract 12, they can seem more emotive. DNov quote analysis showed 28 different reporting verbs used with *now* including *added, exclaimed, remonstrated, says, screamed* and *sobbed.* Interestingly, therefore, though *now* when used for this particular function may be an inappropriate model for much of today's interpersonal communication, it is the first item investigated which gives an explicit sense of prosody and the way something is said.

Extract 12: '*Now,*' he pursued, 'concerning Miss Havisham. Miss Havisham, you must know, was a spoilt child. Her mother died when she was a baby, and her father denied her nothing.' (DNov quotes, ID: GE67327)

To finish discussion of *now,* and to once again emphasise that this DM was used mostly to convey the difference in authority between characters, the second function identified saw *now* co-occurring with imperative forms. On approximately 7 per cent of occasions, *now* in sentence-initial position preceded a command. However, in contrast to the previous discussion about negative power imbalances, *now* was likewise used to show more caring relationships, for instance between a parent or guardian and child (see Extract 13).

Extract 13: Affery had never dreamed her to be capable, drew down the face of her little seamstress, and kissed her on the forehead. '*Now* go, Little Dorrit,' said she, 'or you will be late, poor child!' (DNov quotes, ID: LD140185)

Oh

Upon comparing the DNov quotes and BNC Conversation frequency data, it was discovered that *oh* was significantly less frequent in the literary data. Despite this observation, however, comparison between DNov quotes and non-quotes showed a stark difference in that *oh* was clearly used as a feature of spoken dialogue in the novels.

Preliminary collocational analysis of *oh* in the BNC Conversation corpus revealed some unusual collocations in the left-hand position. For that reason, investigation concentrated on collocates occurring in the R1 position. As can be seen in Table 2.11, a wide range of exclamations of different strengths were evident.

Though many of the collocates from the BNC Conversation did not occur at all in the DNov quotes corpus, Table 2.12 does show those that did feature.

The collocates listed do not display the same variety as those from the BNC Conversation corpus, but they do demonstrate shared co-occurrences in which *oh* functions as a DM. *Oh* signals a listener's response at turn boundaries to new information, and combined with a collocate, it can express stronger feelings such as surprise, pain and disappointment (Carter and McCarthy 2006). Such usage was clearly evident in the DNov data. For simple affirmations, *oh yes* showed significant collocational strength as well as the highest t-score of all the

Table 2.11 *R1 collocates of OH from the BNC Conversation*

	Collocate	R1 Freq.	MI
1	DEAR	1193	5.86
2	CRIKEY	23	5.56
3	GAWD	5	5.46
4	CAROLINA	13	5.21
5	CRUMBS	11	5.01
6	GOD	846	4.98
7	GOLLY	9	4.86
8	STREWTH	5	4.67
9	CHRIST	73	4.58
10	GOSH	50	4.57
11	SHIT	139	4.31
12	BLIMEY	27	4.30
13	AYE	426	4.18
14	GEE	9	4.09
15	HECK	17	4.01
16	EY	6	3.97
17	JESUS	39	3.96
18	WOW	30	3.80
19	FUCK	71	3.59
20	LORD	17	3.53
21	GOODNESS	25	3.42
22	SHUT	98	3.32
23	BLESS	9	3.30
24	YES	1710	3.21
25	SOD	13	3.14

R1 collocates. *Oh certainly* and *oh indeed*, performing a similar function, were also found upon reading the concordance data to be significant with MI scores of 5.288 and 4.732, and t-scores of 6.239 and 6.730, respectively. Similarly, *oh dear* occupied top position in MI ranking for both the BNC Conversation and DNov quotes, but *oh god* was substituted for *oh lord* in the literature. As can be seen in Extract 14, *oh* as a DM does portray similarities with its usage in real examples of unscripted conversation in that other emotions such as agreement, gratitude and shock can be conveyed. However, more modern-day collocations such as *oh god* (frequency of 846) and *oh my god* (frequency of 328), found in the BNC Conversation, were almost non-existent.

Table 2.12 *Collocates of OH from BNC Conversation that appeared in DNov quotes*

		R1		
	Collocate	Freq.	MI	t-score
1	DEAR	205	4.486	13.679
2	GOD	2	1.259	0.823
3	AYE	2	1.79	1.005
4	LORD	18	4.07	3.99
5	GOODNESS	3	2.666	1.459
6	BLESS	9	3.09	2.648
7	YES	208	5.371	14.074

Extract 14: 'When you wouldn't give me nothing. But the gentleman, he give me something! *Oh*, bless him, bless him!' mumbled the old woman. (DNov quotes, ID: DS233867)

As was identified in analysis of *now*, prosodic features were once again noticeable. Whereas *now* occurred with numerous reporting verbs to portray a character's tone, e.g. murmured, *oh* instead frequently occurred with commas and exclamation marks to suggest volume and pausing. In the concordance data 27 per cent of concordance lines contained *oh!* and 46 per cent contained *oh*. When combined, nearly three-quarters of all uses depicted some type of pausing by a character. Once again, in increasing dramatic effect, learners can envisage more accurately how this DM was employed in speech.

I Mean

Comparisons of DNov quotes and BNC Conversation data demonstrated a highly significant underuse for *I mean* in the literary texts. Despite this finding, it was clearly a feature of spoken discourse in Dickens' novels, as it was used considerably less often in non-quoted data.

Investigation of significant collocations in the BNC Conversation retrieved only two statistically significant collocates, both in the R1–R4 position: *ideally* and *majority*. Their occurrence was, however, very low and neither co-occurred with *I mean* in the DNov quote data. Attention was therefore paid to some of the most frequent, rather than the strongest, collocates in the BNC Conversation corpus to appear to the left of the node. Table 2.13 shows the comparison of these collocates with data from DNov quotes.

Though none of the above collocates were significant in their MI score, some of the t-scores demonstrated that there was nevertheless sufficient evidence for

Table 2.13 *Comparison of frequent I MEAN collocates in BNC Conversation and DNov quotes*

		BNC Conversation L4–L1		DNov quotes L4–L1		
	Collocate	Freq.	MI	Freq.	MI	t-score
1	BUT	938	1.78	23	0.981	2.366
2	KNOW	773	1.31	34	1.996	4.338
3	WHAT	641	0.76	94	2.970	8.458
4	WELL	489	0.47	7	0.435	0.689
5	YEAH	678	0.23	0	0.000	0.000
6	YOU	821	−0.70	73	*	*
7	AND	330	−1.44	38	*	*

*Could not compute due to collocate frequency being greater than 10,000 in DNov quotes.

the groupings in DNov quote data. *I mean* is used for a variety of purposes including elaboration, expansion, clarification and self-correction; it can also be used to signal hesitation, hedge statements, resolve misunderstandings and corroborate shared knowledge in conversation (Carter and McCarthy 2006). Using the collocates in Table 2.13, only some of these functions were apparent, for instance elaboration in Extract 15 and clarification in Extract 16.

Extract 15: 'I don't, indeed, my dear boy,' he returned; '*but I mean* to say that they are managed and decided by the same set of people, down in that same Doctors' (DNov quotes, ID: DC139986)

Extract 16: 'It's very gratifying, Arthur,' he said, 'after all, to look back upon.' 'The past?' said Clennam. 'Yes – *but I mean* the company' (DNov quotes, ID: LD166598)

There was instead more evidence to suggest that *I mean* in the literary texts was used most often to confirm or establish shared knowledge between speakers. Occurring frequently in the expression *(you) know what I mean* (Carter and McCarthy 2006), significant t-scores indicated that *know* and *what* appeared with the DM often in the DNov quotes. Though log-likelihood comparisons of *you know I mean* and *you know what I mean* between the two corpora showed significant underuse in the literature texts, it could still be seen that *I mean* was deployed to show attempts by characters to maintain a shared understanding of the contexts, people or topics being discussed:

Extract 17: 'But, young men,' resumed Mrs Merdle, 'and by young men *you know what I mean*, my love – I mean people's sons who have the world before them' (DNov quotes, ID: LD159539)

With concordance line data showing *I mean* preceding a comma (15.40 per cent of occasions) or a reporting verb (7.81 per cent of occasions), it could also be said that as well as conveying clarification, elaboration and shared knowledge, the DM sometimes functioned as a marker of hesitation.

Discussion

Overall, parallels and differences in the spoken features analysed were found in the DNov–BNC Conversation comparisons. Some forms of vague language and DMs had similar frequencies and/or functions, which support the use of literature such as this as a plausible model of spoken English. With regard to vague language, common significant collocations (*hour/week/an/half or so; what/any kind of; kind of thing*), colligations (*or so* in end position; adjective + *stuff*) and functions (reducing precision, avoiding pedantry, hedging vocabulary choices and exploiting shared knowledge) were all identified in the DNov quoted text. Awareness of such features could help EFL/ESL learners become more skilful speakers who are similarly proficient at maintaining interpersonal relationships during interaction. During their linguistic development, vague language items such as *kind of* may also provide learners with successful interaction strategies (Jones et al. 2017) that they can exploit when they want to signal to listeners that their expression may not be the most accurate (Aijmer 1984). In respect of DMs, it was the analysis of *now/oh/I mean*'s functions which proved interesting. With DMs essential to turn-taking, the management of interaction, cohesion and the maintenance of flow (Carter and McCarthy 2006), DNov quote findings revealed specifically how literature can model DM use to start a turn, get a listener's attention, express speaker emotions, clarify or maintain shared knowledge and respond to new information. Similarly, unlike analysis of vague language, the selected DMs would also be able to offer learners a glimpse of how DMs work alongside prosodic features – intonation, stress, volume, pausing – via the addition of punctuation (*oh dear!*), the use of reporting verbs (*'Now' he pursued*) or a combination of the two (*he returned, 'but I mean … '*).

Despite the potential this literature has as a model of spoken language, it is equally important to acknowledge the differences found in DNov quote–BNC Conversation comparisons. Firstly, one difference is a positive in the sense that literary examples can display the true collocational flexibility of some vague language and DMs, e.g. *or so*, *stuff* and to some extent *oh*, that could otherwise go unnoticed or remain limited in other teaching materials. Nevertheless, it is apparent that the true extent of meanings and functions performed by specific lexis can be hidden behind a word frequency. For literature to act as a plausible model for learners of spoken interaction, therefore, very careful selection of the texts and items to be taught would still be required. Such text selection may also need to address the potential problems arising from learners failing to perceive the true occurrence of such lexis in real spoken interaction due to over- or underuse in the literature. As was identified in discussion of *now* and its co-occurrence with imperatives and noun phrases (e.g. *now listen, now boy*), impressions of power, authority and sometimes 'aloofness' can be conveyed in literature due to the drama added to develop characters, plots or scenes. The age of the literature used was also found to have an effect on the collocations identified in analysis with common, present-day expressions such as *loads of stuff* and *oh my God* absent from the DNov quote data.

Overall, the dialogues used in the DNov corpus could be a plausible model of spoken conversation, to some degree. With the advantages outweighing the potential drawbacks, how teachers could work with such dialogues in the EFL/ESL classroom are discussed in our conclusion.

Conclusion

In real, unplanned spoken conversation, speakers and listeners are involved in interaction which establishes and maintains the rapport between them, and which 'make[s] the discourse sound right' (Tannen 1990: 16). It should therefore be unsurprising that literature exploits such patterns for its own aims (Leech and Short 2007). While acknowledging the differences provided in Dickens' examples of literary discourse, we conclude that such literature can offer a plausible model of speech for EFL/ESL learners. The analysis shows that for vague language and discourse markers specifically, the literature examined used some of the same collocational patterns as spontaneous speech, and in doing so, it realises many of the same dominant functions and meanings. There are several implications, therefore, for both teaching and future research.

Primarily, once literary texts have been processed for meaning by learners, attention can be directed to the common features of spoken language within them and their specific meanings and uses. It is clear that teachers could then encourage learners to notice features of spoken language highlighted from novels or plays in their own conversational encounters in English. Students reporting back on such discussions in the language classroom could further increase their potential for learning. This approach could additionally help counterbalance problems arising from literary models containing archaic language. Evidently, the DNov data used in this chapter is somewhat dated, but comparisons with real, up-to-date examples of spoken conversation would act not only as a useful exercise, but also as an additional tool for extending noticing skills. Exercises involving discussion of representational language (McRae 1991) and its effects, as mentioned in the introduction, could provide a stimulating and challenging task. Teachers might, for example, discuss the representational language used in literary dialogues and compare this with the conversations students hear or have themselves.

For continuing research into the use of literature as a model for spoken interaction, there is a real need to replicate such analysis with more recent novels. Dickens' work was chosen as only one example of literature in this chapter. It allowed for greater understanding and better perceptions of dialogues' characters and contexts, but a wider range of novels would nevertheless be able to provide a more holistic view of its potential as a model of modern-day conversation.

References

Adolphs, S. and Carter, R. 2013. *Spoken Corpus Linguistics: From Monomodal to Multimodal*. New York: Routledge.

Aijmer, K. 1984. '"Sort of" and "kind of" in English conversation', *Studia Linguistica* 38: 118–128.

Amador-Moreno, C. P. 2010. 'How can corpora be used to explore literary speech representation?', in O'Keeffe, A. and McCarthy, M. (eds.), *The Routledge Handbook of Corpus Linguistics*. Abingdon: Routledge, 531–544.

Baker, P. 2010. 'Corpus methods in linguistics', in Lia Litosseliti (ed.), *Research Methods in Linguistics*. London: Continuum, 93–113.

Barnbrook, G. 1996. *Language and Computers: A Practical Introduction to the Computer Analysis of Language*. Edinburgh, Edinburgh University Press.

Biber, D., Johansson, S., Leech, G., Conrad, S. and Finegan, E. 1999. *Longman Grammar of Spoken and Written English*. Harlow: Longman

Brezina, V. 2018. Lancaster Stats Tools Online. Available at: http://corpora.lancs.ac.uk /stats/toolbox.php (Accessed 22 July 2018).

Buttery, P. and McCarthy, M. 2012. 'Lexis in spoken discourse', in Gee, J. P. and Handford, M. (eds.), *The Routledge Handbook of Discourse Analysis*. Abingdon: Routledge, 285–300.

Carter, R. 1998. 'Orders of reality: CANCODE communication, and culture', *ELT Journal* 52(1): 43–56.

Carter, R. and McCarthy, M. 1997. *Exploring Spoken English*. Cambridge: Cambridge University Press.

2006. *Cambridge Grammar of English*. Cambridge: Cambridge University Press.

2017. 'Spoken grammar: Where are we are and where are we going?', *Applied Linguistics* 38(1): 1–20.

Carter, R. and McRae, J. (eds.) 1996. *Language, Literature and the Learner: Creative Classroom Practice*. Oxford: Routledge.

CLiC. 2018. Corpus of Linguistics in Content. Available at: https://clic.bham.ac.uk/ (Accessed 1 May 2018).

Council of Europe. 2001. *Common European Framework of Reference for Languages: Language, Teaching, Assessment*. Cambridge: Cambridge University Press.

Davies, M. 2004. BYU-BNC (based on the British National Corpus from Oxford University Press). Available at: https://corpus.byu.edu/bnc/ (Accessed 2 May 2018).

Firth, J. R. 1957. *Papers in Linguistics 1934–51*. Oxford: Oxford University Press.

Greaves, C. and Warren, M. 2010. 'What can a corpus tell us about multi-word units?' in O'Keeffe, A. and McCarthy, M. (eds.), *The Routledge Handbook of Corpus Linguistics*. Abingdon: Routledge, 212–226.

Halliday, M. A. K. and Matthiessen, C. 2013. *Halliday's Introduction to Functional Grammar* (4th edn). Oxford: Routledge.

Hart, M. 2019. Project Gutenberg. Available at: www.gutenberg.org (Accessed 26 February 2019).

Hoey, M. 2005. *Lexical Priming: A New Theory of Words and Language*. London: Routledge.

Hughes, R. 1996. *English in Speech and Writing: Investigating Language and Literature*. London: Routledge.

Hunston, S. 2002. *Corpora in Applied Linguistics*. Cambridge: Cambridge University Press.

Jones, C. and Waller, D. 2015. *Corpus Linguistics for Grammar: A Guide for Research*. London: Routledge.

Jones, C., Byrne, S. and Halenko, N. 2017. *Successful Spoken English: Findings from Learner Corpora*. London: Routledge.

Leech, G., 2000. 'Grammars of spoken English: New outcomes of corpus-oriented research', *Language Learning* 50(4): 675–724.

Leech, G. and Short, M. 2007. *Style in Fiction: A Linguistic Introduction to English Fictional Prose*. Harlow: Longman.

Lewis, M. 1993. *The Lexical Approach: The State of ELT and the Way Forward*. Hove: Language Teaching.

Lin, Y. L. 2013. 'Vague language and interpersonal communication: An analysis of adolescent intercultural conversation', *International Journal of Society, Culture & Language* 1(2): 69–81.

Mahlberg, M. and Smith, C. 2012. 'Dickens, the suspended quotation and the corpus', *Language and Literature* 21(1): 51–65.

Mahlberg, M., Stockwell, P., de Joode, J., Smith, C. and O'Donnell, B. 2016. 'CLiC Dickens: Novel uses of concordances for the integration of corpus stylistics and cognitive poetics', *Corpora* 11(3): 433–463.

McCarthy, M. 2010. 'Spoken fluency revisited', *English Profile Journal* 1(1): 1–15.

McCarthy, M. and McCarten, J. 2018. 'Now you're talking! Practising conversation in second language learning', in Jones, C. (ed.), *Practice in Second Language Learning*. Cambridge: Cambridge University Press, 7–29.

McEnery, T. and Hardie, A. 2012. *Corpus Linguistics*. Cambridge: Cambridge University Press.

McEnery, T., Xiao, R. and Tono, Y. 2006. *Corpus-Based Language Studies: An Advanced Resource Book*. Abingdon: Routledge.

McRae, J. 1991. *Literature with a Small 'l'*. London: Macmillan.

O'Keeffe, A., McCarthy, M. and Carter, R. 2007. *From Corpus to Classroom*. Cambridge: Cambridge University Press.

Oakes, M. P. 1998. *Statistics for Corpus Linguistics*. Edinburgh: Edinburgh University Press.

Rayson, P. 2018. UCREL's Log-Likelihood and Effect Size Calculator. Available at: http://ucrel.lancs.ac.uk/llwizard.html (Accessed 22 July 2018).

Rühlemann, C. 2007. *Conversation in Context: A Corpus-Driven Approach*. London: Continuum.

Schmitt, N. 2010. *Researching Vocabulary: A Vocabulary Research Manual*. Basingstoke: Palgrave Macmillan.

Segundo, P. R. S. 2016. 'A corpus-stylistic approach to Dickens' use of speech verbs: Beyond mere reporting', *Language and Literature* 25(2): 113–129.

Semino, E. and Short., M. 2004. *Corpus Stylistics: Speech Writing and Thought Presentation in a Corpus of English Writing*. London: Routledge.

Short, M.1996. *Exploring the Language of Poems, Plays and Prose*. London: Longman. 2012. 'Discourse presentation and speech (and writing, but not thought) summary', *Language and Literature* 21(1): 18–32.

Stubbs, M. 2008. 'Conrad in the computer: Examples of quantitative stylistic analysis', in Carter, R. and Stockwell, P. (eds.), *The Language and Literature Reader*. London: Routledge, 230–243.

Tannen, D. 1990. 'Ordinary conversation and literary discourse: Coherence and the poetics of repetition', *Annals of the New York Academy of Science* 583(1): 15–30.

Thornbury, S. and Slade, D. 2006. *Conversation: From Description to Pedagogy*. Cambridge: Cambridge University Press.

Timmis, I. 2013. 'Spoken language research: The applied linguistic challenge', in Tomlinson, B. (ed.), *Applied Linguistics and Materials Development*. London: Bloomsbury, 79–94.

Tognini-Bonelli, E. 2001. *Corpus Linguistics at Work*. Amsterdam: John Benjamins.

Wiegland, V., Mahlberg, M. and Stockwell, P. 2017. CLiC 1.61 User Guide. Available at: www.birmingham.ac.uk/Documents/college-artslaw/elal/clic/CLiC-1-6-1-doc umentation-2017-11-08.pdf (Accessed 23 August 2018).

Wray, A. 2002. *Formulaic Language and the Lexicon*. Cambridge: Cambridge University Press.

3 Using Literature in Text-Driven Materials to Help Develop Spoken Language Awareness

Brian Tomlinson

This chapter advocates the use of contemporary literature to help second language (L2) learners to become more aware of how their target language is typically used in speech to achieve intended effect. The approach being proposed is a text-driven approach in which a written or spoken text is used initially to engage the learners affectively and cognitively and then as a source for discovery activities designed to help the learners to become aware of how a particular linguistic or discourse feature is being used to achieve intended effects. The emphasis is on spoken interaction, and the focused feature is investigated further in learner out-of-class activities. After describing, justifying and exemplifying the proposed approach, the chapter reports the results of a research project seeking to find out the responses of language teachers to the approach. Language teachers in a number of different countries were asked to rate the potential value and the contextual feasibility of such an approach by responding to units of materials driven by the approach. In the conclusion to the chapter, recommendations are made with regard to materials development, to teacher and learner adaptation of materials and to assessment of learner achievement.

Introduction

This chapter first explains, justifies and exemplifies the use of text-driven units of material. It then provides a rationale for the use of literature in a text-driven approach before reviewing the few publications on the use of text-driven approaches which have so far appeared. The chapter then focuses on a pilot study which sought to elicit responses to three units of language learning materials which make use of contemporary dialogue-based literature to facilitate spoken language awareness and which follow a text-driven approach. The study is described, the teacher responses are reported, comments are made on common characteristics of the responses and conclusions are made about what has been learned from the pilot study.

What Is a Text-Driven Unit of Materials?

A text-driven unit of material is a unit in which a core text is chosen for its potential to achieve affective and cognitive engagement for the target learners. This text (and not a predetermined language point, skill, topic or theme) then drives all the activities in the unit.

It is vital that the text is engaging and meaningful to the learners. If it is, then there is a very good chance that it will help the learners to achieve language acquisition. If it is not engaging and meaningful, then it is very unlikely to facilitate language acquisition (see Tomlinson 2013, 2016, 2018; Tomlinson and Masuhara 2017, forthcoming). See also Schutze (2017) for discussions of the importance of emotional and sensory associations in the acquisition of language and, in particular, the need for encounters with language to include information about, for example, personal responses, visual imagery and the context of use.

I have found that literature is a very rich source of affectively and cognitively engaging and meaningful texts, and when developing text-driven materials I make frequent use of extracts from literature that feature dialogues which are moving, dramatic, novel or provocative. I did this in *Openings* (Tomlinson 1994a), a text-driven literature-based activities book, and in a number of text-driven publications I have been involved in since, for example, *On Target* (1995), Tomlinson and Masuhara (1994); Tomlinson, Hill and Masuhara (2000); Tomlinson (2004). Perhaps the best example I have seen, though, of a text-driven textbook which makes rich and plentiful use of literature is Fenner and Nordal-Pedersen (1999), a coursebook for Norwegian secondary school students which uses poems, stories, songs and extracts from plays and novels on such 'sensitive' themes as colour prejudice, immigration, growing old, capital punishment, loneliness and war to stimulate affective and cognitive engagement. Other authors who advocate the use of literature which is potentially engaging and meaningful include Maley and Duff (2007), Paran and Robinson (2015) and Bland (2015, 2018). Bland (2018) is a particularly interesting book in that it advocates the use of challenging literature with young learners in order to promote cognitive engagement.

When developing text-driven materials, I use the following framework (see also Tomlinson 2013 and Tomlinson and Masuhara 2018 for further explanations of the framework), and if my main objective is to help learners to develop pragmatic awareness of speech in action, I select potentially engaging texts which feature dialogues.

1   Developing a Library of Potentially Engaging Texts

You cannot just find an appropriate and engaging text to use in material you are developing for tomorrow or even for next week. What you need to do is gradually to build up a library of potentially engaging written, spoken and audio-visual texts. You include texts which have engaged you (i.e. absorbed you by stimulating emotion and inspiring thought) and which you think might engage language learners too.

2   *Selecting a Text from My Library*

When you write a unit of materials for a target group, you go to your library and select a text which has the potential to engage that group, which is at a suitable level and which can be made locally relevant and meaningful.

3   *Experiencing the Text*

You experience the text and then you reflect on your experience of the text and ask yourself what you were doing in your mind as you experienced it? You then make use of your reflection to develop activities which could stimulate the target learners to experience rather than study the text. These could be, for example, visualisation activities (e.g. 'See pictures in your mind of your first day at school'), connection tasks (e.g. 'When you hear the words 'Not now Bernard', does it remind you of anything in your own life?'), tasks involving inner voice articulation of personal views (e.g. 'What are your views about the hunting of wild animals?') or prediction tasks (e.g. 'You're going to read a story called "Sentence of Death". What do you think it's going to be about?').

4   *Developing a Readiness Activity*

First of all you develop an activity which aims to activate the learners' minds in relation to the core text. For example, you could ask them to visualise an event in their lives similar to one described in the text they are going to experience, to think about their opinions of a topic relevant to the text or to draw and then share their images of what they think a particular city looks like. These activities are essentially mental activities involving the creation of sensory images, the use of the inner voice and the creation of emotions. Sometimes, though, I would ask learners to share their thoughts, feelings and images with fellow learners.

5   *Developing an Initial Response Activity*

An initial response activity is given to the learners before they experience the text and for them to do while they are experiencing the text. It is intended to continue their mental activation so that they will focus on responding globally to the text rather than on words they do not understand. For example, they could be asked to create pictures in their mind as they read a text and then to compare them with pictures they created in the readiness activity.

6   *Developing an Intake Response Activity*

After experiencing a text in the L1, we do not typically answer comprehension questions or fill in blanks. We respond personally by talking to ourselves (or sometimes to others) about how the text connects to our lives, or what it means to us or whether we were interested in it or not. This is what an intake response activity aims to help the learners to do. It helps them to deepen and articulate their personal response to the text by focusing initially on what they have taken in from their experience of the text.

There are two types of intake response activity.

1. A representational activity asks the learners to articulate what they have understood and remembered from the text. For example, after listening to the beginning of a novel in which the parents of a recent college graduate organise a party for him, the learners are asked to think about the following questions:
   (a) Why do you think Benjamin's parents organised the party for him?
   (b) Why do you think Benjamin didn't want to go to the party?
2. An evaluative activity asks the learners to express their opinion about a character, relationship, event or idea in the text. For example, in a unit driven by a poem called 'I'm an old, old woman', the learners were asked, 'Do you like the old woman? Why? Why not?'

7   *Developing a Development Activity*

A development activity is a written or spoken production activity which derives from the core text. For example, after reading a story called 'Sentence of Death', which is set in Liverpool, my students at Kobe University were asked to write the story 'Sentence of Death in Japan'.

8   *Developing an Input Response Activity*

An input response activity involves the learners focusing on the input they have been given (i.e. the text). They go back to the core text and analyse it in order to discover how a language feature has been used in order to try to achieve particular meanings and effects. For example, after experiencing the text 'Sentence of Death', students could be asked to focus on why and how the writer has used indirect speech to tell his story.

9   *Developing a Research Activity*

The unit could follow up the development activity by asking the students to do some out-of-class research. For example, the students could be asked to collect examples of the simple present tense in authentic use to further their investigation of the functions of the simple present tense after making discoveries about how the old lady uses the tense in the poem 'I'm an old, old woman'.

10   *Developing a Second Development Activity*

The students make use of their discoveries in the input response activity above of any findings in their research activity in order to produce an improved version of text they developed in the first development activity. Only then does the teacher respond to give feedback and, if required, a grade.

What Are the Benefits of a Text-Driven Unit of Material?

In my view the main benefit of developing text-driven units of material is that the materials are driven not only by a potentially engaging text but by coherent principles of language acquisition, such as rich exposure to meaningful language in contextualised use, opportunities to use the language for communication, opportunities for noticing and discovery, and utilisation of sensory imagery. Other benefits include
- helping to develop principled and effective units of materials in a very short time. For example, on a project in Namibia the first draft of a complete text-driven coursebook was written by 30 teachers in six days (Tomlinson 1995).
- increasing the likelihood of affective and cognitive engagement being achieved and sustained more than using a teaching point, topic or theme to drive a unit and then searching for texts to illustrate it.
- helping to achieve coherence in the sense that each activity follows from the previous activity and contributes to the next one
- helping learners to achieve:
    (i) engagement
    (ii) connections
    (iii) meaningfulness
    (iv) salience
    (v) significance
    (vi) noticing
    (vii) recycling.
All these objectives are shown by second language acquisition (SLA) research to be powerful determiners of language acquisition (Tomlinson and Masuhara, forthcoming).
- enabling learners to notice and make discoveries about how features of the target language are used in communication and thus making it more likely

that they will notice these features in subsequent input and eventually acquire them (see Chapters 4 and 7, this volume, for further discussion of noticing).

• facilitating the development of pragmatic awareness of speech in action through noticing speaker intentions and their interlocutors' reactions.

Why Use Literature in Text-Driven Materials?

One of the main points of a text-driven approach is to stimulate learner participation through the use of a core text which is accessible and meaningful and which has the potential to engage the learners cognitively and affectively. One extremely valuable source of such texts is contemporary literature, an art form which explicitly aims to achieve cognitive and affective engagement and which often has the added bonus of aiming to achieve aesthetic engagement too. It is also an art form which features contextualised use of language (both written and spoken) in ways which can stimulate visualisation, connections, reflection, noticing and retention, all mental activities which can facilitate language acquisition (Tomlinson and Masuhara 2018, forthcoming).

When using literature in text-driven materials, I do not choose texts for their literary 'worthiness' or their featuring of language items from the syllabus but for their cognitive, affective and aesthetic appeal. This is inevitably risky, as not every text actually has the effect you hoped for with every learner. This is a risk you can considerably reduce, though, by developing generic activities which can be used with a text chosen from a number of possibilities by the learner(s) (Maley 2011, 2013; Tomlinson 2013). You can also reduce the risk of non-engagement by selecting controversial (but culturally acceptable) texts with the potential to provoke disagreement and with topics or themes which are universally applicable. That is what I did in *Openings* (Tomlinson 1994a), a language through literature activities book in which a menu of activities for teachers and/or learners to choose from is presented with each of 55 literature texts chosen for their potential to engage and to provoke, and for having a theme with universal appeal (e.g. growing up, education, conflict). In one of the texts, an old lady asserts that she wants to be loved but not to love, that she wants to play and win every game and that she wants her shoes taken off her feet. In many cultures the simple intake response question 'Do you like the old lady. Why? Why not?' provoked considerable and articulate disagreement. And in Oman the intake response question in a unit of materials based on the story *Not Now, Bernard*, 'Who was responsible for Bernard's death?', provoked lengthy and animated debate about whether it was the father's or the mother's fault.

As long ago as 1994 (Tomlinson 1994a: x–xi), I summarised the value of literature in language learning under the following headings:

- enrichment of intake
- focus on content
- real use of reading skills
- stimulus for other language activities
- motivation
- experience
- self-access

For other, more recent views as to the value of using literature in language learning materials, see the other chapters in this volume and, for example, Hall (2005), Paran (2006), Paran and Robinson (2015) and Saito and Wales (2015).

I have found that using literature in text-driven materials is an engaging and efficient way of helping learners to develop language awareness, and especially spoken language awareness (see also Chapter 4, this volume). Dialogues in poems, plays, stories and novels which have engaged learners affectively and/ or cognitively can help learners in subsequent focused analysis of the text to notice and make discoveries about salient features of spoken discourse and pragmatics (Tomlinson 1994b). This makes these features more likely to be noticed in subsequent input and helps the learners gradually develop awareness of how spoken English is used to achieve intended effects.

Previous Research

Very little research has been done as yet on the impact of text-driven materials, but there have been some published indications of positive effects. Darici and Tomlinson (2016) is a case study of a text-driven lesson for 14-year-old boys in a Turkish secondary school which featured a short story about a homeless man kidnapping a lawyer and being shot in the head by a policeman, which followed the text-driven framework outlined in this chapter and which made use of open-ended questions to stimulate normally reticent students to express their responses. All 28 students enjoyed the text, 22 enjoyed the tasks, 25 found the lesson interesting and 27 found it useful. McCullagh (2010) is an evaluation of text-driven communication skills materials for overseas medical students and doctors which featured authentic interviews between patients and doctors and were found to be engaging and useful by most of the participants. St Louis (2010: 133) reports on an in-house, text-driven, eight-lesson refresher course for students at a university in Venezuela which helped students to become more 'aware of language patterns found in texts', to complete their reading programme successfully and, according to student feedback, to increase their vocabulary. Troncoso (2010) used a text-driven approach to adapt materials to help students at a university in Columbia to develop intercultural communicative competence and found that students increased both their intercultural awareness and their ability to communicate it. Al-Busaidi and Tindle (2010) led an in-house development of a writing course at Sultan Qaboos University in Oman in which students experienced texts, responded to them, wrote texts of their own, made discoveries from the original text and then revised their own texts. All the teachers and 70 per cent of the students found the course engaging, 90 per cent of the teachers and 80 per cent of the students felt the course improved writing skills and 88 per cent of the teachers and 65 per cent of the students felt that the discovery approach improved the grammatical accuracy of the students' writing.

My experience of using text-driven approaches with teachers on projects and courses (in, e.g. Belgium, Botswana, Columbia, Luxembourg, Mauritius, Turkey and the UK) has been an initial scepticism often followed by enthusiasm based on actual and positive responses from students. The main objection has often been the problem of using a text-driven approach in systems dominated by a language or skills-based curriculum. In Namibia (Tomlinson 1995), though, we found that by initially ignoring the curriculum and focusing on potentially engaging texts from a wide variety of genres and text-types, we covered over 90 per cent of the curriculum without trying (I matched the materials every night to a copy of the curriculum on my hotel wall without telling anybody). On the last day we added some of the missing language items and skills to our draft units and achieved almost complete coverage of the curriculum (Tomlinson 1995).

It would be very interesting to see the results of research projects attempting to answer the following questions:

1. Is learner engagement best achieved by following a text-driven approach or a syllabus-driven approach?
2. Can a spoken language awareness syllabus be effectively covered by a text-driven, literature-based approach?
3. Are learners more likely to develop spoken language awareness from a text-driven, literature-based approach or one driven by a spoken language awareness syllabus?

Methodology

Teachers of English as a foreign language were invited to respond to an open-ended questionnaire which asked them questions about their attitudes to three units of literature-driven materials, with a focus on developing spoken language awareness.

Objectives

The pilot study aimed to trial a questionnaire eliciting teacher responses to materials which are driven by potentially engaging, dialogue-featured extracts from modern literature to help learners to develop spoken pragmatic awareness and (ultimately) spoken pragmatic competence.

Instruments

The respondents were given the following three units to consider and then answer questions on.

Unit 1 – *Not Now, Bernard*

(Age of learners: young learners, young adults, adults
Level of learners: A2/B1
Text: McKee, D. (1980). *Not Now, Bernard*. London: Andersen Press: a short story in which a young boy is told, 'Not now, Bernard' by both his mother and his father every time he approaches them, before being eaten by a monster who is constantly told, 'Not now, Bernard' by Bernard's parents when he goes into the house. See Appendix 3A for a brief section from this extract.)

1. You are a young child. See pictures in your mind of you coming home from school. You want to talk to your mother and father but they're busy. Your mother is cooking dinner and your father is watching a football match on TV. You decide to greet them anyway and to try to get them to talk to you about your day at school.

   'Hello, Mum,' you say. What does she say?
   'Hello, Dad,' you say. What does he say?

   Form a group of four and tell each other what your mother said to you and what your father said to you.

2. Listen to your teacher reading the story 'Not Now, Bernard'. As you listen see pictures in your mind of what happens in the story.
   When the teacher has finished reading turn the story into a film in your mind.

3. Answer this question in your mind:

   Who do you think was to blame for Bernard's death?

   In your group talk to each other about your answers to the question.

4. 'Not Now. Bernard' takes place in England. In your group write a story about a girl coming home from school and trying to talk to her busy parents. Set your story in your country.

5. Read 'Not Now, Bernard' on p. x. As you read it notice how the expression 'Not now . . .' is used. What do Bernard's parents mean when they say, 'Not now, Bernard'?

6. For homework try to find as many examples as you can of the expression 'Not now ...' Write each example down and say what you think it means. Then bring your examples to the next class.
7. In your group share your examples of 'Not now ...' and then use them to complete the following table:

Meaning 1:	Examples:
Meaning 2:	Examples:
Meaning 3:	Examples:
Meaning 4:	Examples:

8. Revise your story about the girl coming home from school.
   Then practise acting out the story.
9. Act your story to another group and then watch the other group acting their story to you.
10. Act your story to the whole class if your teacher invites you.

Unit 2 – *The Birthday Party*

(Age of learners: young adults, adults
Level of learners: B1/B2
Text: An extract from Pinter, H. (1959). *The Birthday Party.*
   Tunbridge: Encore Publishing: an extract in which two complete and rather menacing strangers tell Stanley that they have been invited to a birthday party for him in the small hotel where he lives. See Appendix 3A for a brief section from this extract.)

1. It's your birthday today and you're going to celebrate.
 What do you want to do? Do you want to go out by yourself? Do you want to go out with friends? Do you want to have a party with a few friends? Do you want to have a large party? Do you want to have a party with strangers?
  Tell a partner what you want to do to celebrate your birthday.
2. You're living in a small hotel in a strange city. It's your birthday today and you've decided to go out by yourself to celebrate. As you're about to leave the hotel you meet a stranger who congratulates you on your birthday.
 How do you feel?
 The stranger says that he's been invited to your birthday party.
 What do you say to him?
 The stranger insists you stay for your birthday party and tells you about other guests.
 How do you feel now?

3. Listen to your teacher acting a scene from the play *The Birthday Party* by Harold Pinter. As you listen imagine you are Stanley.
4. You are Stanley.
   How do you feel about your conversation with McCann?
   Do you want to go to the party? Why?
   What are you going to do?
5. You are McCann.
   Why have you organised a party for Stanley?
   Who is coming to the party?
   Why are they invited?
6. In pairs write a continuation of the discussion between Stanley and McCann, with one of you writing Stanley's lines and one of you writing McCann's lines.
7. Read the extract from *The Birthday Party* on p. x.

Read the extract again and with your partner notice how the interrogative is used by the two speakers to achieve different functions.

Use the table below to list the different functions of the interrogative you find in the extract:

The functions of the interrogative		
Function	Examples	Speaker
1 Asking for information.	1 Someone out there?	Stanley
	2 Staying here long?	Stanley
2		
3		
4		
5		

8. For homework work with your partner to find other examples of the interrogative being used in conversation. Add examples to your list of functions in (7) above and add extra functions too if you find any.
9. Join with another pair and show each other your table of the Functions of the Interrogative.
10. Use what you've discovered about the interrogative to revise the conversation between Stanley and McCann which you wrote in 6 above.
11. Practise acting out your conversation between Stanley and McCann.
12. Join another pair and act out your conversations to each other. Discuss the differences between your conversations.

Unit 3 – *The Graduate*

(Age of learners: young learners, young adults, adults
Level of learners: B2/C1
Text: An extract from Webb, C. (1963). *The Graduate*. New York:
New American Library: an extract in which Benjamin's father is
trying to persuade him to come down from his room to the graduation party which he has organised for him on his return home from
college. See Appendix 3A for two brief sections from this extract.)

1. Think of a party you've been to.
   Did you want to go to the party? Why? Did you enjoy the party? Why?
   See pictures in your mind of something that happened at the party.
   Form a pair and tell each other what happened at the party you've just
   visualised.
2. Listen to your teacher reading you the beginning of a novel. As you listen
   turn the story into the beginning of a film.
3. Answer the following questions in your mind:
   Why do you think Benjamin's parents organised the party for him?
   Why do you think Benjamin didn't want to go to the party?
   Who do you feel most sympathy for, Benjamin, his father or his
   mother? Why?
4. Form a group of four and discuss your answers to the questions in (3)
   above.
5. In your group write a continuation of the story in which Benjamin's
   mother follows him to the park and then tries to persuade him to go to
   the party.
6. Read the extract from *The Graduate* on p. x and as you read it reconsider
   your answers to the questions in (3) above.
7. In your group two of you look for all the imperatives in the text and for
   each one decide what the speaker intends by using it (i.e. what its function
   is). The other two look for all the interrogatives in the text and for each one
   decide what the speaker intends by using it.
8. Share your findings in (7) with the other pair in your group. What general-
   isation can you make about how functions are achieved in English?
9. For homework find as many authentic examples as you can of the use of the
   language feature which you investigated in (7) above. For each one say
   what you think its intended function is.
10. In your group share your findings about the functions of the imperative and
    the interrogative.
11. In your group revise your story in (5) above. Then rewrite it as a script for
    a scene from a film.

If you can, video the scene with one of you as the Director, one as the camera-man, one playing Benjamin and one playing Benjamin's mother.

The questionnaire asked the participants the following questions about the three units of material.

1. Would you use this unit with language learners?
2. Why would you use it or not use it?
3. What do you think are the strengths (if any) of the unit?
4. What do you think are the weaknesses (if any) of the material?
5. Do you think using this and other similar text-driven units of material could eventually help learners to develop pragmatic competence in spoken interaction?

Participants

The aim of the project was to get a snapshot of responses from a range of EFL teachers in different circumstances with a view to gaining impressions of likely responses to the materials and the approach they are illustrating. The intention is to develop this project and increase the sample size in a future study.

The materials and questionnaires were sent to personal contacts in different parts of the world to distribute to teachers. There were eleven respondents from seven countries. Information about them is provided in Table 3.1.

Table 3.1 *Information about the respondents*

Respondent	Country	Institution	Role	Experience as a language teacher
1	Vietnam	University	Lecturer	16 years
2	China	University	Lecturer	20 years
3	China	University	Researcher	10 years
4	China	Secondary School	Teacher	12 years
5	China*	University	Lecturer	18 years
6	Japan*	University	Instructor	13 years
7	Ireland*	Foundation College	Teacher	16 years
8	Scotland*	University	EAP Tutor	26 years
9	Japan*	University	EAP Instructor	20 years
10	China	University	Teacher	15 years
11	England	University	Teaching Associate	15 years

* 5, 6, 7, 8 and 9 are native speakers.

Results and Discussion

Comments on the Responses

1. Although there seemed to be general agreement that a text-driven approach can promote pragmatic awareness of spoken language as well as an approval of the general approach taken in developing the materials in the three units, many of the participants seemed to be looking for activities which would match their beliefs, pedagogic preferences and specific teaching context. For example:

- A number of participants seemed to want the materials, regardless of their objectives, to focus on a useful language point. For example, respondent 3 said that she would not use Unit 1 because 'The major reason is: the language point is not of prominent value to the students and it can hardly be fit into any existing syllabus' and respondent 9 said, 'The phrase "Not now" seems to have very limited usage in the text'). Respondent 10 focused entirely on the language points in her feedback and thought that Units 2 and 3 would only be useful to learners who were already familiar with the functions of the grammar points which are focused on. Interestingly though, respondent 3 did appreciate that 'Students ... are encouraged to explore materials bearing the same language feature from outside the classroom.'
- Over the years I have found that a fairly common response of teachers to 'innovative' materials is appreciating the potential value of the materials while pointing out their inappropriacy for the local teaching context. This is evident too in the feedback to this pilot study with, for example, respondent 3 being reluctant to use Unit 1 because 'The life of the little boy is too far away from that of a child living in a Chinese town or city nowadays', respondent 4 saying about Unit 1 that 'The target expression is too easy for secondary school students in Shanghai while the central idea of the text is somehow a little difficult for them to understand' and respondent 10 dismissing the text in Unit 2 as being inappropriate for her students and only being willing to use the first few activities in Unit 3 because 'the remaining part is not applicable for my students'.
- None of the respondents seemed aware that discovery activities aim to help learners to develop the very useful, life-long attribute of making discoveries about language use for themselves, and many of them seemed to want learners to discover something of immediate usefulness (for example, common structures and lexis which feature in the syllabus and would help learners to perform well on tests and in examinations).
- Some respondents felt that not enough help had been given to the students in the discovery activities (e.g. 11 'In activity 7, many of my students would probably struggle in terms of identifying different meanings of the phrase "not now"; perhaps more scaffolding should be provided'). I have found this to be a common response from teachers to open-ended discovery activities.

What I have found when using discovery activities, though, is that scaffolded activities tend to lead to a focus on the language, whereas open-ended activities tend to encourage a focus on the users of the language and their intended effects.

- Some of the respondents seemed to want more input to be given to the learners (e.g. respondent 7 criticised Unit 1 by saying, 'I feel that it is asking a lot of the students – they seem to be doing most of the heavy lifting in the class with very little input from the teacher who only reads out a story.').

Responses to Each Unit

The respondents were generally positive about the approach and the manifestations of it in the three units of material. However, there were some interesting differences of opinion, as demonstrated in the summary below.

SECTION A

Unit 1 (*Not Now, Bernard*)

1. Would you use this unit with language learners?
   Yes (1, 2)
   Yes (7 'with young learners')
   Yes (8 'but not with current groups')
   'I think so (depending on the level of my students and pedagogical goals)' (11)
   'Perhaps'(6)
   'Probably not'(3)
   'Sorry, maybe I wouldn't' (4)
   No (9)
2. Why would you use it or not use it?
   Positive
   1 'To help learners know how to use the expression "Not now …" in some different contexts.'
   6 'It is interesting to talk about the roles of parents and children and distraction.'
   7 'I like the first part which starts with imagining. I also like the quirky, morbid tone of the story.'
   11 'I like the story and I think it has a lot of pedagogical potential.'
   Negative
   3 'The text is too simple, both linguistically and cognitively, for my students (young adults).'

'The major reason is: the language point is not of prominent value to the students

and it can hardly be fit into any existing syllabus.'

4 'I wouldn't use it because the conversation would be too short and simple for my students while the idea that the author of the text wanted to convey would be too difficult for them to understand.'

7 '... I don't have a lot of confidence in instructions like "turn it into a film in your mind" – I've never done something like that in class, and I don't know how I would react to this as a student ... I feel that it is asking a lot of the students – they seem to be doing most of the heavy lifting in the class with very little input from the teacher who only reads out a story.'

8 'I wouldn't use it with groups with specific ESP needs unless they had literature related needs. With other groups without specific needs, I would if I felt they would engage with it, and if it fitted thematically with preceding/following classes.'

9 'The phrase "Not now" seems to have very limited usage in the text. It only appears to be used with the phrase "Not now (name of person)" rather than demonstrating other uses, such as "Not now, I'm busy / cooking dinner at the moment".'

3. What do you think are the strengths (if any) of the unit?

2 'Contribute to pragmatic awareness (esp. 5 and 7).'

3 'Students are given chances to experience the text, share their opinions and create another text. Most importantly, they are encouraged to explore materials bearing the same language feature from outside the classroom.'

4 'I'm quite impressed by the after-reading activities, especially the tasks of imitative writing and acting out, which help putting what has been learnt into practice, with the reading text serving as a very good example.'

6 'Connected to the theme of distraction and ignoring children/family members which a lot of people have strong feelings about and may find it interesting.'

7 'As I mentioned, I like the story and the morbid tone. I do like many of the practice exercises. My objection, I suppose, is to their frequency.'

8 'It is task-based with a primary focus on meaningful use. I find it interesting and engaging on a personal level. I think students will be engaged with the text and in any following discussion.'

9 'It seems like an amusing story which younger learners would enjoy.'

11 'A variety of activities and different forms of interactions; also, inter-cultural elements (write a story about a girl and set it in your country).'

4. What do you think are the weaknesses (if any) of the material?

2 'S might have problems finding examples of their own and turning the poem into a film in their minds after listening to it. (Need suggestions; no probs with visualisation once introduced).'

3 'The life of the little boy is too far away from that of a child living in a Chinese town or city nowadays.'

4 'The target expression is too easy for secondary school students in Shanghai, while the central idea of the text is somehow a little difficult for them to understand. Last but not least, the text has some violent elements, for example, "the monster ate Bernard up, every bit". It's really scary!'

6 'Lacks the pictures of the original picture book which I am familiar with.'

7 'I'm not sure how useful or ubiquitous the "not now" phrase is . . . I'm just wondering how useful or achievable it would be for students to go off and find lots of examples of this phrase.'

8 'The form focus may not be a priority for learners. Do they need to produce it? Do they need to spend so much time on just one exponent, albeit serving different functions? . . . I suppose my criticisms are task-based ones regarding externally-selected focuses on forms.'

9 'It would be better if there were some different examples of the phrase "Not now . . . " to expose learners to a wider range of usage.'

5. Do you think using this and other similar text-driven units of material could eventually help learners to develop pragmatic competence in spoken interaction?

1 'Yes – engagement, connection with own lives, sharing of understanding, opportunities for meaningful production.'

2 'Help develop pragmatic awareness but this might not convert to pragmatic competence.'

3 'Yes only if such kind of lessons were given on a regular basis and the texts chosen are to the students' interest.'

4 'I do believe so, because text-driven units of material help create a real-life context or a semi-real context, which is certainly bound to promote the learners' understanding of the target language as well as the development of the learners' pragmatic competence in spoken interaction.'

6 'It would need a considerable amount more exposure I suspect.'

7 'Yes. I like using text-driven units like this.'

8 'Yes. I am sure it can help raise awareness and that this can be useful for receptive purposes.'

9 'Yes, I strongly believe in trying to expose learners to natural use of vocabulary or grammar to provide natural models which they can learn from and which can help them to develop more natural use of language.'

6. What changes (if any) would you recommend me making to the unit?

7 'I think perhaps a bit more input – perhaps another short text related to the first.'

8 'I would downplay the form focus and prioritise the authentic reading and discussion.'

9 'Include some different examples. For example: "Not now, Bernard, I'm cooking' or 'Not now, Bernard, it's late / time for bed".'

'Yes, but I think they would need some support from the teacher. Many international students struggle with pragmatic functions/information and may not understand the implied meaning.'

11 'In activity 7, many of my students would probably struggle in terms of identifying different meanings of the phrase "not now"; perhaps more scaffolding should be provided.'

Unit 2 (*The Birthday Party*)

1. Would you use this unit with language learners?

   Yes (1, 4, 5)

   No (3, 7, 10)

   No ('or only with the reference to the Mountains of Morne excised. It might be better with a video.' (6))

2. Why would you use it or not use it?

   Positive

   1 'support learners to be aware of some aspects of spoken discourse in context; develop conversational strategies for learners, e.g. Keeping on the conversation by asking questions.'

   4 'I would use it because the topic is very familiar to the learners and the story is quite intriguing, which would help arouse the learners' interest. Moreover, the language level of the text is compatible to the learners' English abilities.'

   5 'I think it is quite a good way to get language learners to appreciate a range of functions associated with questions.'

   'Students in China often seem to take language at face value, and this activity is engaging and achievable.'

   Negative

   3 'I found the text kind of dark and weird. I don't like it personally.'

   6 'The dialogue rings a bit too theatrical and it's possibly not so interesting for my students.'

   7 'I find it very difficult to read scripts. I quickly lose track of who is who. It might just be me, but I find them confusing, especially when they are quick fire like this one – I get lost.'

   10 'Because it is not very applicable since my students are not familiar with the functions of the interrogative, and it is a little boring as well as hard to understand.'

3. What do you think are the strengths (if any) of the unit?

   1 'The topic of "Birthday Party" has become popular now, particularly among young people. Therefore, it would be a good start for the lesson.'

   2 'Personalised. Could work with any age, any culture.'

3 'It's very useful to get the students to analyse the functions of the interrogatives. I like the activities that ask the students to switch perspectives.'

4 'It begins with a free talk, of which the topic is quite familiar to the learners. The following prediction part is easy to catch the learners' attention. What interests me most is the pair writing, which asks the learners to write a continuation of the discussion between the two main characters in the text.'

5 'I like the appeal to imagination and reflection. The text has a certain mystery about it which interests the learners.'

6 'Short conversational turns that are easily understood.'

7 'I like the table of functions.'

10 'It tries integrating analysis of the functions of the interrogative into the unit.'

4. What do you think are the weaknesses (if any) of the material?

1 'It would be strange for Vietnamese learners if some stranger hold a party for them, it could be a bit challenging for teachers to get students involved in this at the first time.'

2 'Noticing different functions of the interrogative too difficult for A2/B1?' 'Assumption that have to use interrogatives in their dialogue to make it better.'

3 'If there were clips of a longer video available and students were given a complete picture of what's going on, the story would sound less odd to them and perhaps it would be more accessible.'

4 'The table which is used to help explore "how the interrogative is used by the two speakers to achieve different functions" is a little boring and difficult for the learners. I suggest the learners discuss the functions of the interrogatives one after another in the text with the help of some questions as scaffolds.'

6 'It's a bit odd for odd's sake. Nobody would ever be in that situation, so it's difficult for language learners who want utility in their language learning to see as much benefit as in "straight" material.'

10 'Not applicable if students are not familiar with the functions of the interrogative, and it is hard to understand (for example, readers will feel puzzled at the possibility of stranger's holding a birthday party for another stranger).'

5. Do you think using this and other similar text-driven units of material could eventually help learners to develop pragmatic competence in spoken interaction?

1 'Yes – personal experience, personal engagement, relates to personal knowledge, think deeply about the text and discover themselves about the purpose and language of the text, purposeful communication is involved between learners and rehearsal is allowed for real-life conversation when learners can make it in their context.'

2 'Pragmatic awareness but not nec pragmatic competence.'

3 'Yes. And it's very necessary to integrate pragmatic competence into the desirable learning outcomes of the English Curriculum Standards or even College English Curriculum Requirements in China.'

4 'I do believe so, because text-driven units of material help create a real-life context or a semi-real context, which is certainly bound to promote the learners' understanding of the target language as well as the development of the learners' pragmatic competence in spoken interaction.'

5 'Yes. I think it is a really interesting way to present the multiple functions of different forms. In many cases I think they would probably interpret the functions intuitively, but being made aware of the disconnect between form and function is an important part of higher intermediate work in my context.' 'I also think that learners find the links between literature and "imaging a movie" and real life engaging.'

6 'It could do with interrogatives. They're particularly salient, though maybe they need to be contrasted more fully with actual questions.'

7 'Yes.'

10 'Maybe.'

6. What changes (if any) would you recommend me making to the unit?

6 'Use video of *The Birthday Party* if possible, or use another birthday party scene in another play.'

Unit 3 (*The Graduate*)

1. Would you use this unit with language learners?

'Yes'(1, 2, 3, 4, 5, 6, 7)

'I will just use the first several questions.' (10)

2. Why would you use it or not use it?

Positive

1 'support learners to be aware of some aspects of spoken discourse in context'.

3 '... the film is quite popular among my students. The text at least appeals to them. The state of the mind of the protagonist also echoes among some of the students.'

4 'I would use it because the topic is very familiar to the learners and the story is quite intriguing, which would help arouse the learners' interest. What's more, the text is a more complete dialogue which will help the learners learn the target language in a more authentic and vivid context. However, I will not use the unit as an intensive reading text due to the length of the text. Instead, I will ask them to read after class and finish all the exercises, except the free talk, as homework.'

5 '... the topic and activities are good for young adults and adults.'

'The passage is relevant and includes interesting aspects of parent–child relationships and social expectations. As well as that, I liked the way the activities required learners to look at the situation from different viewpoints.'

6 'It's interesting, brief and relates to a situation that my learners may find themselves in although they would likely respond differently.'

7 'I love the film. I think the scene is relatable. And I think the flow of conversation is natural and well written. There is also a sense of why.'

10 'Because the first several questions can be used in their speaking activities, but the remaining part 'is not applicable for my students.'

Negative

There were no negative comments.

3. What do you think are the strengths (if any) of the unit?

1 'The content of the materials is quite close to Vietnamese context where parents also have parties to celebrate their children's graduation.'

'The unit includes the imperative and interrogative which is useful to prepare for learners in daily conversation: persuading to have someone to do something.'

3 'I like the continuation activity where students can develop their creativity. I also like the discovery activities, which focus on the prominent language features in the text. And the students are given chances to act the story out.'

4 'The story is really intriguing and the situation Benjamin faces may be quite familiar to the learners. Therefore, it will be quite easy for the learners to be attracted by the story and then feel connected with the characters in the story, which will eventually help them understand the text. Moreover, the exercises are arranged in a logical and reasonable way.'

5 'Again, like Unit 2, this highlights many differences between form and function. This is really useful for students in China, who often expect one form to have one meaning, and one meaning to be expressed by a specific structure.'

'It is interesting to see the power relationship and the use of questions and commands.'

6 'The text is dialogue heavy.'

7 'The text ... The interrogative focus is an interesting point and emerges naturally from the text. I like the question asking who they sympathise with. I also like how the language is guided discovery – they come up with the rules.'

10 'It is beneficial to students who are familiar with the functions of the imperative and the interrogative.'

4. What do you think are the weaknesses (if any) of the material?

1 'The parents–children relationship in Vietnam is quite different with the one in Western countries. Children in Vietnam have less freedom to raise

their voice. This could cause some difficulties for the teacher to engage learners' involvement at the beginning.'

3 'I'm thinking of asking the students to consider the cultural differences and similarities on the relationship between the grown-up child and his/her parents. Perhaps they can discuss the language they would use while talking with their parents in a similar situation: what kind of tone they would take and whether they would choose to use imperatives or interrogatives in a similar manner.'

4 'There are 11 tasks in all, which will certain take a large amount of time to finish all of them. However, in China, it's nearly impossible for teachers to spend so much time on only one unit.'

6 'A lot is made of the imperatives and interrogatives, but I would assume that most of my learners would already be fairly adept with these receptively. I would personally forego this until after the filming of the scene with Ben and his mother and use it as a focus on form if necessary or just use the dialogue to compare and contrast in order to see if the characters maintain their voice then examine how and why.'

7 'Nothing springs to mind. I liked this a lot. I mean, you might say that the graduate is a bit old now, but surly, disaffected teens are a constant.'

10 'It is not beneficial to students who are not familiar with the functions of the imperative and the interrogative.'

5. Do you think using this and other similar text-driven units of material could eventually help learners to develop pragmatic competence in spoken interaction?

1 'The text-driven approach first helps learners to achieve the mental readiness by activating connections to learners' live, personal engagement, which get learners invest cognitive energy and attention in the learning process, help to activate the learners' existing knowledge of target knowledge and culture as well as awareness of the influence of their native culture, help learners to make discoveries themselves about the language of the text, opportunities for further understanding and meaningful language production later based on what they have already understood from the text.'

3 'Yes (if developing learners' pragmatic competence were included as one of the learning outcomes in the syllabus and the textbook).'

4 'I do believe so, because text-driven units of material help create a real-life context or a semi-real context, which is certainly bound to promote the learners' understanding of the target language as well as the development of the learners' pragmatic competence in spoken interaction.'

6 'Yes. Examining how the disagreement escalates could be particularly useful.'

7 'Yes, very much.
10 'Maybe.'
6. What changes (if any) would you recommend me making to the unit?
  6 'None other than re-ordering activities, but that could be done with a suggested adaptation addendum.'
  7 '"Maybe you could include a debate as an extension of the 'who do you sympathise" with question.'
One of the native speaker respondents from China (respondent 5) trialled Units 2 and 3 of the materials with a small group of C1 level young adults. Here are extracts from his responses.

Unit 2 (*The Birthday Party*)

3. Do you think the unit engaged most of the students?
  'It was a small group (6), so we were able to discuss the text together; they found it engaging because the text seemed strange.'
4. Were the students able to accomplish the activities?
  'The group included some students who had studied linguistic modules including SFL and mood, and so they were able to pick up on the task more quickly. However, the others found looking at the functions very interesting, although they didn't use linguistic terminology ...'
5. What do you think the students are likely to gain (if anything) from their experience of this unit?
  'Yes, it was valuable to them to see the different uses (functions) of questions.'
6. What changes (if any) would you recommend me making to the unit?
  'One of the things they noticed was the lack of response in some cases – and so an additional column in the table for the outcome (did the speaker accomplish their intended goal for each question).'

Unit 3 (*The Graduate*)

3. Do you think the unit engaged most of the students?
  'Yes, as they are nearing graduation themselves, the text and unit was engaging.'
4. Were the students able to accomplish the activities?
  'As with the birthday party topic, there was a bit of a problem getting students to talk about parties, because of cultural differences; many of the students said they hadn't really attended a "party", although (fortunately) one had had a birthday party in the summer after the college entrance examinations ... this gap in their own experience made the beginning a bit hard going. The first few text activities were fine, though.'

5. What do you think the students are likely to gain (if anything) from their experience of this unit?

'Again, this led on nicely from Unit 2, opening up the functions of questions and orders; they found it quite interesting to see how the son "orders" the father to do things, while at the beginning the father uses statements to imply what the son should do.'

6. What changes (if any) would you recommend me making to the unit?

'We found it interesting to see how statements can be used to imply commands, while questions and commands may not necessarily be real commands or real questions. If I were teaching this with a group again ... I would probably get students to make a similar table to Unit 1 – and possibly add a column again for "outcome".The other thing I would do as a teacher using this again would be to add a comment like – "or think about a party you've seen in a movie or TV show". I might even play a few seconds of surprise parties from *Friends* or something. It would be possible to add something along these lines to the instructions "You may talk about a party from a film or TV show if you prefer".'

Comments on the Responses

What really struck me about the responses was that I was being naive in expecting respondents to appreciate the principles driving my materials without me drawing explicit attention to them. For example, discovery activities are an investment in the future in that a discovery in one unit does not magically lead to acquisition, but it can help learners to notice a feature in subsequent exposure and eventually to acquire it.

When finalising my questionnaires, I need to find a way of drawing attention to underlying principles without making the questionnaire too dense with information or too demanding of time and mental energy. Certainly getting respondents to actually use the materials with learners would help them to appreciate principles and objectives and would also provide very useful information about actual learner responses (for example respondent 3 from China thought that the text in Unit 2 was too dark and weird to be engaging, whereas respondent 5 found that when using the materials Chinese students were engaged by the text because it was dark and weird).

What also struck me was that you cannot really expect respondents to evaluate an approach and exponents of it at the same time. As a number of respondents demonstrated (e.g. respondent 3), you can be critical of a particular unit while appreciating the approach which drives it. In the revised questionnaire, I will therefore separate questions on a specific unit from general questions relating to the approach which drives all three units.

Only one respondent mentioned the value of using literature in language learning materials. I was hoping that more of the respondents would notice that all three units were driven by literature texts and would express their views. It would seem that I need to ask a question directly on their view as to the value of literature, even though this could turn out to be a leading question.

Conclusion

This study has confirmed my experience and belief that teachers (and hopefully materials developers) could develop literature-based, text-driven materials to help learners to become more aware of how the target language is used in speech to achieve intended effects and ultimately to become more communicatively competent users themselves. As mentioned in the chapter introduction, to achieve this teachers need to

- collect a library of potentially engaging literature texts featuring the use of spoken language;
- select texts from this library likely to be engaging, meaningful and accessible for their target learners;
- develop readiness activities, initial response activities, personal response activities, input response activities and development activities for each of the selected texts.

I think that the responses in my study justify continuing with the project, as they indicate a general approval of the text-driven approach and of its value in fostering pragmatic spoken awareness (and maybe eventually pragmatic spoken competence). However, I think I need to

- solicit a more diverse (and obviously larger) group of respondents;
- encourage the respondents to both predict and evaluate the value of the materials in use;
- draw attention to some of the underlying principles of the materials (e.g. facilitating the transfer of input to intake through engagement, connections, coherence, contextualisation, personalisation, noticing and recycling (see Tomlinson and Masuhara forthcoming); helping learners to increase their awareness of how the language is used to achieve intended effects; increasing the likelihood of eventual acquisition from noticing in subsequent input).

This study has helped me to reflect on my research - and experience-informed beliefs about the value of literature in language learning, of experiential and discovery approaches to the development of pragmatic awareness and of the text-driven approach. It might modify some of my actual approaches to the development of materials in the light of the reality of the pervasive strength of teacher beliefs and resistance, but it certainly reinforces my conviction of the potential value to learners of the approach.

Appendix 3A Extracts from the Texts Used in the Research

Not Now, Bernard (McKee 1980)

A brief extract from the story which illustrates one of the functions of Not now X and raises the issue of responsibility.

> 'There's a monster in the garden and it's going to eat me,' said Bernard.
> 'Not now Bernard,' said his mother.
> He went into the garden.
> 'Hello monster,' he said to the monster.
> The monster ate Bernard up.
>
> Then the monster went indoors.
> 'ROAR!' went the monster behind Bernard's mother.
> 'Not now Bernard,' said Bernard's mother.

The Birthday Party (Pinter 1959)

A brief section from the extract which illustrates communicative uses of the interrogative in social interaction and raises questions about McCann's intentions.

MCCANN: I don't think we've met.
STANLEY: No, we haven't.
MCCANN: My name's McCann.
STANLEY: Staying here long?
MCCANN: Not long. What's your name?
STANLEY: Webber.
MCCANN: I'm glad to meet you sir. (He offers his hand. Stanley takes it, and McCann holds the grip.) Many happy returns of the day. (Stanley withdraws his hand. They face each other.) Were you going out?
STANLEY: Yes.
MCCANN: On your birthday?
STANLEY: Yes, why not?

The Graduate (Webb 1963)

Two brief sections from the extract which illustrate the tension between father and son and the way they try to manipulate each other through the use of the imperative and the interrogative.

1   'What is it Ben?'
      'Nothing.'
      'Then why don't you come on down and see your guests?'
      Benjamin didn't answer.
      'Ben?'
      'Dad, he said, turning around. 'I have some things on my mind
          right now,'
      'What things?'
      'Just some things.'
      'Well, can't you tell me what they are?'
2   'Tell them I have to be alone right now.'
      'Mr Robinson's out in the garage looking at your new sports car. Now
          go on down and give him a ride in it.'
      Benjamin reached into his pocket for a pair of shiny keys on a small
          chain.
      'Here', he said.
      'What?'
      'Give him the keys. Let him drive it.'

References

Al-Busaidi, S. and Tindle, K. 2010. 'Evaluating the results of in-house materials on
      language learning', in Tomlinson, B. and Masuhara, H. (eds.), *Research for
      Materials Development in Language Learning*. London: Continuum, 137–149.
Bland, J. (ed.) 2015. Teaching English to Young Learners: Critical Issues in Language
      Teaching with 3 to 12 Year Olds. London: Bloomsbury.
      (ed.) 2018. *Using Literature in Language Education: Challenging Reading for
      8–18 Year Olds*. London: Bloomsbury.
Darici, A. and Tomlinson, B. 2016. 'A case study of principled materials in action', in
      Tomlinson, B. (ed.), *SLA Research and Materials Development for Language
      Learning* . New York: Routledge, 71–86.
Fenner, A. N. and Nordal-Pedersen, G. 1999. *Search 10*. Oslo: Gyldendal.
Hall, G. 2005. *Literature in Language Education*. Oxford: Palgrave Macmillan.
Maley, A. 2011. 'Squaring the circle: Reconciling materials as constraint with materials
      as empowerment', in Tomlinson, B. (ed.), *Materials Development in Language
      Teaching*. Cambridge: Cambridge University Press, 379–402.
      2013. 'Creative approaches to writing materials', in Tomlinson, B. (ed.), *Developing
      Materials for Language Teaching*. London: Bloomsbury, 167–188.
Maley, A. and Duff, A. 2007. *Literature*. Oxford: Oxford University Press.
McKee, D. 1980. *Not Now, Bernard*. London: Andersen Press.
McCullagh, M. 2010. 'An initial evaluation of the effectiveness of a set of published
      materials for medical English', in Tomlinson, B. and Masuhara, H. (eds.), *Research
      for Materials Development in Language Learning*. London: Continuum, 381–393.
On Target. 1995. Written by a team of writers. Windhoek: Gamsburg Macmillan.

Paran, A. (ed.) 2006. *Literature in Language Teaching and Learning.* Alexandria, VA: TESOL.

Paran, A. and Robinson, P. 2015. *Literature.* Oxford: Oxford University Press.

Pinter, H. 1959. *The Birthday Party.* Tunbridge: Encore Publishing.

Saito, Y. and Wales, K. (eds.). 2015. *Literature and Language Learning in the EFL Classroom.* Oxford: Palgrave Macmillan.

Schutze, U. 2017. *Language Learning and the Brain.* Cambridge: Cambridge University Press.

St Louis, R. 2010. 'Can a 48-hour refresher course help first year English for Science and Technology reading students? A case study of English CIU at Universidad Simon Bolivar, Venezuela?', in Tomlinson, B. and Masuhara, H. (eds.), *Research for Materials Development in Language Learning.* London: Continuum, 121–136.

Tomlinson, B. 1994a. *Openings: Language through Literature.* London: Penguin.

1994b. Pragmatic awareness activities. *Language Awareness* 3(3/4): 119–129.

1995. 'Work in progress'. *Folio* 2(2): 26–30.

2004. *Improve your English: A Course for Ethiopian Teachers.* Addis Ababa: Ministry of Education, Ethiopia.

2013. 'Developing principled frameworks for materials development', in Tomlinson, B. (ed.), *Developing Materials for Language Teaching.* London: Bloomsbury, 95–118.

2016. 'Achieving a match between SLA theory and materials development', in Tomlinson, B. (ed.), *SLA Research and Materials Development for Language Learning.* New York: Routledge, 3–22.

2019. *Evaluating, Adapting and Developing Materials for Learners of English as an International Language.* Malang: TEFLIN.

Tomlinson, B. and Masuhara, H. 1994. *Use Your English.* Tokyo: Asahi Press.

2018. *The Complete Guide to the Theory and Practice of Materials Development for Language Learning.* Hoboken: Wiley-Blackwell.

Forthcoming. *SLA Applied: The Application of Second Language Acquisition Research to the Learning of Languages.* Cambridge: Cambridge University Press.

Tomlinson, B., Hill, D. A. and Masuhara, H. 2000. *English for Life 1.* Singapore: Marshall Cavendish.

Troncoso, C. R. 2010. 'The effects of language materials on the development of intercultural competence', in Tomlinson, B. and Masuhara, H. (eds.), *Research for Materials Development in Language Learning.* London: Continuum, 83–102.

Webb, C. 1963. *The Graduate.* New York: New American Library.

4   Literature, TV Drama and Spoken Language Awareness

Christian Jones and Jane Cleary

This chapter reports on research in a study abroad context at a UK university. It centres on the use of literature which has been dramatised on television (the popular TV series *Sherlock*) and how this can be harnessed to develop a greater awareness of typical features of spoken language – in this case the use of ellipsis. An experimental study was undertaken which compared the results of three groups: one receiving explicit instruction plus input enhancement (experimental group 1), one receiving explicit instruction only (experimental group 2) and a control group who received no instruction. Both treatment groups worked with three short extracts from *Sherlock* over three lessons and were given explicit instruction, comprehension tasks and exercises to raise awareness of several features of spoken language, including ellipsis, requesting and modality. The experimental groups received the same explicit teaching (here understood as the teacher making it clear to the students what the lesson focus was), but experimental group 1 also had their transcripts enhanced via textual enhancement to highlight the aforementioned features of spoken language. Results were measured using a comprehension test and a test which measured receptive knowledge of ellipsis in spoken language administered at a pre-, post- and delayed test stage, which was 3 weeks after the classes. In addition, six members of each experimental group took part in a focus group to discuss the extent to which participants found the classes helped to develop awareness of ellipsis and how useful and motivating they found the literature materials to be. Results show clear effects for instruction, with significant gains made over time on the receptive tests for experimental group 1 when compared to the control group. However, no significant difference between treatment types was shown in the post- and delayed tests. Focus groups indicated that participants found the dramatised literature materials to be motivating and useful, and they also reported some noticing of ellipsis in their contact with English outside class time.

Introduction

Research in corpus linguistics has done much to provide a clearer picture of how spoken grammar (particularly as used in conversation) and written grammar differ. Key findings of Biber et al. (1999) and Carter and McCarthy (2006, 2017), for instance, suggest that it is more fruitful to think of spoken language in terms of 'utterances' and turns rather than sentences and to see that dialogic speech is something speakers co-construct (McCarthy 2010). This research has also shown that some frequent elements of spoken language features such as ellipsis, stance markers (e.g. 'to be honest') and discourse markers (e.g. 'I mean') occur with greater frequency than we might guess and are an important part of how we use spoken language to fulfil textual, interpersonal and ideational functions (Halliday and Mathieson 2013). To take a simple example, a discourse marker such as 'I mean' allows a speaker to hold their turn by marking the fact that they are reformulating (textual), it can also help speakers to orientate to the listener who signals misunderstanding (interpersonal) and it can simply help us to express our ideas more precisely (ideational).

Research has also shown that just as we find with written language, these features are context dependent, that is, they often occur more, or less, depending on particular genres of speech, and there is always an element of speaker choice in the language used. Although much of this research has been based on corpora of native speaker talk (e.g. Carter and McCarthy 2017), increasingly, research is showing that these features also occur in the speech of learners (e.g. Jones, Byrne and Halenko 2017). Despite this, there are still relatively few studies which have sought to investigate how these features could be learned, as part of either receptive or productive knowledge (Timmis 2012). It is clear that for learners in some contexts, it may not be important to develop such knowledge, and we would not argue that simply because features such as discourse markers are frequent, we should automatically wish to teach them. However, we would suggest that for learners in contexts where English is the predominant L1, a focus on common features of speech can help learners to both understand and interact more easily.

While it is perfectly possible to take unscripted naturally occurring dialogues from corpora and use these with learners, such material can often be uninteresting and demotivating (Timmis 2005; Jones 2017). The conversations in corpora are real examples of spoken interaction, but as they are often far removed from learners' own interests and experience, they often need a lot of

From 'A Sudy in Pink' (Sherlock) (transcript from Devere 2012)

MIKE: It's an old friend of mine, John Watson.
                        (Sherlock reaches John and takes his phone from him. Turning par-
                        tially away from him, he flips open the keypad and starts to type on it.)
SHERLOCK: Afghanistan or Iraq?
                        (John frowns. Nearby, Mike smiles knowingly. John looks at Sherlock
                        as he continues to type.)
JOHN: Sorry?
SHERLOCK: Which was it – Afghanistan or Iraq?
                        (He briefly raises his eyes to John's before looking back to the phone.
                        John hesitates, then looks across to Mike, confused. Mike just smiles
                        smugly.)
JOHN: Afghanistan. Sorry, how did you know…?

From *A Study in Scarlet* by Arthur Conan Doyle

> 'Dr. Watson, Mr. Sherlock Holmes,' said Stamford, introducing us.
> 'How are you?' he said cordially, gripping my hand with a strength for which I
>   should hardly have given him credit. 'You have been in Afghanistan, I
>   perceive.'
> 'How on earth did you know that?' I asked in astonishment.
> 'Never mind,' said he, chuckling to himself. 'The question now is about
>   hoemoglobin. No doubt you see the significance of this discovery of
>   mine?' (Conan Doyle 2008)

Figure 4.1 Comparison of dialogue from *Sherlock* and *Sherlock Holmes*

supporting material and guidance (see Carter, Hughes and McCarthy 2000 for a good example), For these reasons, the scripted spoken English of TV dramas may be a useful 'halfway house' between dialogues from corpora and the heavily contrived dialogues which we can find in textbooks (Jones 2017). Such dialogues contain many of the features of speech and may be more interesting and motivating when viewed from a pedagogical perspective (McRae 1991; Carter and McRae 1996).

Based on this rationale, the study in this chapter employs materials from *Sherlock* (BBC 2016), a dramatised version of the well-known Sherlock Holmes stories. This series takes the original Arthur Conan Doyle publications, adapts them and places them in the modern world. The dialogue is also updated to fit this context, as the example in Figure 4.1 shows.

The extracts in Figure 4.1 show that the core of the popular original detective stories remain, which means they are likely to be of interest for many learners given that *The Adventures of Sherlock Holmes* collection is said to have sold 60 million copies (Chirravoori 2018) and the Sherlock Holmes museum in London attracts an average of 70, 000 visitors a year (Pawloski and Han 2010). However, these extracts also show that the dialogues in *Sherlock* are closer to the kind of spoken English learners may hear in an English-speaking context than the original stories. We also felt that the popularity of *Sherlock* (a recent episode attracted more than 11 million viewers in the UK alone (BBC 2017)) meant it was a programme that many learners would have at least a passing interest in and knowledge of and that this would enhance the chances they would engage with the materials.

This study takes a text-based approach (Timmis 2018) to the use of extracts from *Sherlock* (see Chapter 3, this volume, for a study using a text-*driven* approach). Three sections from different episodes were chosen firstly because we felt students would find them engaging and interesting. Following this, we examined them for features of spoken English. Across the course of three lessons, learners worked on global understanding, and then noticing and discussion tasks focused on several features of spoken language including ellipsis, requesting and modality, which were recycled across all lessons. We then sought to understand whether receptive knowledge of ellipsis developed following instruction and how this differed between two experimental groups and a control group, one working with enhanced transcripts and one without, and one group not receiving any instruction. We also sought to understand to what extent students themselves felt the material was useful and whether they noticed the use of ellipsis in English they heard outside of classes.

Previous Research

Before we turn to a review of previous studies in this area, it is important to define the term 'language awareness' as a process which involves 'developing an enhanced consciousness of forms and functions of language' (Carter 2003: 64). It is therefore a form of receptive knowledge: a developed understanding of why, when and how forms are used. In the classroom, commonly this means undertaking activities which can be broadly defined as 'receptive practice' (Jones 2018), whereby the teacher will engage in activities helping to process 'form-meaning links in the input' (Jones 2018: 1). This may be achieved via such activities as comprehension tasks, discovery activities relating to how forms are 'made', discussing why certain forms may have been chosen in particular contexts or via comparison to L1. It is explicit in the sense that learners know what it is they are being asked to focus upon. Crucially, however, as we define it here, it excludes activities where learners have to actually produce the form(s). Language awareness activities are undertaken to help foster habits of 'noticing' (Schmidt 1990) in the belief that conscious registration of forms in the input may enable learners to more quickly convert these forms into intake when they encounter them and also to become more aware of choices they themselves can make when producing language. Language awareness may be particularly appropriate when focusing on common features of spoken language such as discourse markers, ellipsis or vague language (see Carter and McCarthy 2006 for a detailed description of these features and others in spoken language) because learners may not always want or need to produce such forms. A pedagogy which raises learners' awareness of these forms as a choice can be particularly beneficial (Timmis 2005, 2012; Jones 2007; Carter and McCarthy 2017) in English-speaking contexts, as it enables learners to better understand language they encounter in different situations and to make more informed choices in their own language production.

Previous research into ellipsis (the feature of spoken language focused upon in this chapter) is one such feature of spoken grammar. It is not something which learners necessarily need to produce (aside from its presence in lexical chunks), but it is something they will encounter in the spoken language they need to comprehend, and which research into spoken corpora has demonstrated is a very frequent aspect of spoken language (e.g. McCarthy and Carter 1995; Carter and McCarthy 2006, 2017). In speech, ellipsis is mainly situational, that is, what speakers omit is mutually understood by speakers in the situation in which it occurs (Carter and McCarthy 2017). This is in contrast with ellipsis in writing, which is predominantly textual (Halliday and Hassan 1976; Carter and McCarthy 1997) meaning it is understood within the discourse of a particular text.

Figure 4.2 shows an example of each type of ellipsis, with the mutually understood 'missing' language in brackets. The first is taken from a corpus–informed grammar and the second from the BYU-BNC (Brigham Young University–British National Corpus) newspaper corpus (Davies 2004)

Ellipsis in spoken language has been studied extensively within the field of corpus linguistics. Such research has demonstrated that alongside being highly frequent, ellipsis has common identifiable patterns of usage. Some frequent

Situational ellipsis (from Carter et al. 2011: 191–192)

A.   (Do you) want some coffee?
B.   Is there any (coffee)?
A.   Yeah. (I've) just made some.
B.   No (I don't)

Textual ellipsis (from Davies 2004)
We met with senior NIO officials and (we) expressed the opinion that unless something was done

Figure 4.2 Examples of situational and textual ellipsis

Table 4.1 *Common patterns of ellipsis in spoken English*

Ellipsis at the start of the turn		Ellipsis at the end of the turn	
	Subject pronouns (especially 'I') e.g. Bye! (I) hope you have a nice holiday		Complements after the verb 'be' Are you hungry Yes I am (hungry)
	Subject and auxiliary verbs (especially in questions) e.g. (Do you) want some coffee?		Quantifying expressions after repeated noun phrases Do you want some of that stuff? No I've got loads (of that stuff)
	Auxiliary verbs (especially in questions when the subject is 'you') e.g. (Have) you finished your essay yet?		Emphatic 'do' Do you have ambitions? Yes I do (have ambitions)
	Subject pronouns in question tags e.g. (He) didn't like it, did he?		Verbs of loving, hating, wanting and asking after 'to' Would you like to come? Yes, I'd love to (come)
	Articles e.g. What are you looking for? (A) pen		After possessive forms Is that your pen? No, it's Robert's (pen).
	Fixed expressions (I'll) see you later		Fixed expressions It's a good job (I haven't forgotten)

(but not exhaustive) patterns of ellipsis at the start and end of the turn are summarised in Table 4.1 and are based on the work of Biber et al. (1999), McCarthy and Carter (1995), Carter et al. (2000), Carter and McCarthy (2006) and Carter et al. (2011). See also Wilson (2014) for a recent detailed description of ellipsis. Examples are taken from Carter et al. (2000, 2011) and the omitted words are included in brackets for reference.

It is important to note that there is no rule which requires speakers to use ellipsis; rather, these are patterns of common use. It is perfectly possible, therefore, that an individual speaker may choose not to omit a subject pronoun, for example. It is also important to re-emphasise that ellipsis relates to the situation in which speakers interact and there will therefore be genres of speech where we are far more or less likely to see speakers using ellipsis. Carter et al.

(2000), give the example of a service encounter as one where we are likely to see ellipsis because of the need to be quick and to the point, while relating a story or anecdote to a friend as situations where the use of ellipsis is less likely as the details of the story will be important.

Research has shown that while ellipsis is frequent in unscripted speech (such as conversation), there is also some evidence it is a frequent feature of scripted dialogues in fiction and dramas (see also Chapter 2, this volume, for a discussion of spoken language in fictional dialogues). Short (1996) argues that ellipsis is one feature of unscripted conversation which can be found in dramatic dialogues, whereas certain other features such as hesitation devices may be absent. Carter (1998) makes a similar argument, suggesting that dialogues from plays often contain many features of spoken English found in spoken corpora, including false starts and ellipsis, and gives an example of a dialogue from Pinter to illustrate this point. Greenbaum and Nelson (1999) found a number of examples of what they term independent ellipsis (broadly equivalent to the notion of situational ellipsis described above) in fictional texts from the International Corpus of English. Mackenzie (2000), although not specifically examining ellipsis, argues that many fixed expressions (which will contain ellipsis, as mentioned in Table 4.1) can be found in literature. More recently, Wilson (2014) shows that ellipsis occurs with regularity in literary dialogues, and Jones (2017) has explored a corpus of the UK soap opera *EastEnders* and found that ellipsis occurs with some frequency in scripted soap opera dialogues.

The term 'input enhancement' is credited to Sharwood Smith (1991, 1993), who suggested that some form of enhancement may be helpful to make input more salient to learners. Without such salience, learners may fail to notice forms within the input they receive because much input is likely to be processed for meaning. Noticing, as described by Schmidt (1990, 1993, 2010), can be defined broadly as 'conscious registration of attended specific instances of language' (Schmidt 2010: 725). It is this conscious registration which is considered to be the first step needed to help convert input into intake and which a number of studies have demonstrated the positive effect of (see Bergsleithner, Frota and Yoshioka 2013 for a recent collection). Input enhancement may be viewed as one type of 'consciousness raising' (Sharwood Smith 1981) activity, which teachers and researchers can use to help learners notice forms within input they comprehend. It is undertaken in order to manipulate the input learners receive in the hope this enhancement will make it more salient. Sharwood Smith (1993) suggests a number of methods which might be used to enhance input, including the bolding of texts for visual input and repeating targeted items with greater stress for aural input.

Studies which have investigated the effects of input enhancement have often focused upon textual enhancement (TE) and its effect upon receptive and productive knowledge (broadly the ability to understand/produce the forms in the short or longer term following treatment). Results indicating the positive effects of TE have been mixed in terms of its impact. Doughty (1991), Alanen (1995) and Jones and Waller (2017), for example, all report that TE had some positive effects on productive knowledge of the targeted forms, while Izumi (2002) and Wong (2003) report that there were no positive effects for TE. Choi (2017) reports positive effects upon receptive knowledge and yet in several studies there were no discernible effects (e.g. Petchko 2011). In a review of a number of studies focusing on the effect of input enhancement on learning grammar, Lee and Huang (2008) found that, overall, there was a small effect. This suggests that while TE *can* help to focus attention and help learners to notice and learn items, it does not always do so. This may be, in part, due to different study designs (see Han, Park and Combs 2008 for a discussion of these issues), with some studies not including delayed post-tests and many including varied amounts of input. Results from studies reviewing the effects of explicit teaching have, however, shown more consistently positive results (e.g. Norris and Ortega 2000; Spada and Tomita 2010), and studies which have combined explicit teaching with TE have also demonstrated strong effects. Indrarathne and Kormos (2017), for example, focused on causative 'have' forms and found that explicit teaching (metalinguistic explanation and rule explanation in this case) together with TE was significantly better when compared with input flood, TE alone and a control group. Results were also positive when learners in another group were instructed to simply pay attention to the highlighted forms. Groups were measured on a receptive and productive test and by the use of eye tracking. Findings show that the explicit teaching and TE group paid more attention to the targeted forms as they read them and had the highest correlation between attention and learning gains, according to the eye-tracking results.

Studies analysing the use of ellipsis in spoken or written modes are common and have tended to focus on its use or non-use in the language of native or non-native speakers with many drawing upon corpus data (e.g. Carter and McCarthy 2006, 2017). A number of studies have also focused on its use in L1 (e.g. Ricento 1987), but those focused upon its acquisition in instructed second language acquisition (SLA) are noticeably absent from the literature. Some studies, however, have tested materials which feature aspects such as ellipsis, as one of several features of spoken language. Timmis (2005), for example, developed materials based on videos employing a framework of cultural access tasks, global understanding tasks, noticing tasks and language discussion tasks. Timmis deliberately avoided tasks where students were asked to produce the forms because learners may not need to produce them and giving precise rules about when to use features such as ellipsis is impossible. Rather, when we focus on features such as ellipsis, we are describing common patterns of usage and speaker choice (see McCarthy and McCarten 2018 for a discussion of speaker choice in conversation). Timmis piloted these materials with six teachers based in the UK and Austria and approximately sixty learners and then surveyed them for their responses. Data from learners and teachers show that responses to the materials were generally very positive with comments clearly indicating that materials had helped learners to notice features such as ellipsis, which they may previously have missed. Such results may of course be in part due to the context in which classes take place. In a different context, Goh (2009) reports on a discussion between English language teachers from China and Singapore in relation to the teaching of spoken grammar and features such as ellipsis and suggests that there can also be differences in the views of teacher on the usefulness of such a language focus. While there was general agreement that a focus on these features could improve learners' language awareness, there was some divergence of views regarding how useful these features may be and how positively they may affect learners' language performance. Teachers from China were generally more positive about the last two aspects, while teachers from Singapore expressed notably more reservations about them. Such differences are, we feel, to be expected and respected. We should note that in focusing on features such as ellipsis, which are common in spoken language (Carter and McCarthy 2017), we would always argue that it is important to consider the context in which teaching takes place and evaluate the usefulness in relation to student needs and level. It is also possible to reframe such a focus in regard to specific teaching contexts. Rebuck (2011) focused upon common features such as overuse of vague language as what he termed native speaker 'errors'. He played a number of such features in clips from radio programmes to adult Japanese learners of English at two universities. After each listening, learners identified and discussed the 'errors'. Feedback from over a hundred students indicated a positive response to these activities and a number of students reported that their awareness had made them more confident and feel they should be much less worried about their own mistakes.

No studies, to our knowledge, have attempted to use dramatised dialogues from literature as a form of material to develop awareness of feature such as ellipsis, although this has been argued for previously. There are, however, studies which demonstrate that literature can be used to successfully enhance language awareness in general. As mentioned in Chapter 1 (this volume), Lin (2010) demonstrates how the use of Shakespeare's texts can develop language awareness in Taiwanese EFL learners, when measured using quantitative pre- and post-test measures in addition to qualitative data in the form of learner diaries. Warner (2012) found that a stylistic approach to literature can help learners of German as a foreign language to read texts more critically and creatively and this awareness can be applied to non-literary texts. More recently, Bloemert et al. (2019) surveyed 635 students in the Dutch secondary school system and asked them for their perceptions of the benefits of reading literature in a second language. Although answers varied, 74 per cent of the learners suggested that learning language of various kinds was a benefit of reading literature.

The research relating to ellipsis reviewed shows that this feature is highly frequent in many forms of speech and therefore it is a feature of language which deserves some attention, especially if learners are situated in an English-speaking context and likely to be exposed to it in the speech they hear. The studies which have examined the acquisition of spoken ellipsis are rare and those employing dialogues as a form of teaching or testing materials are even rarer. The studies that do exist have not focused upon the use of input enhancement for features of spoken language or literature as source materials.

This chapter is therefore an attempt to address this gap and explore whether we can use a televised version of literature and input enhancement as an effective way to focus on ellipsis in spoken language. Textual enhancement was used alongside explicit teaching in order to try and determine the effect upon what Sharwood Smith and Truscott (2014) have termed perceptual, conceptual and affective processing. We wished to determine the extent to which the treatment could make learners more aware that ellipsis is common in spoken English (perceptual), to notice when and why it is used (conceptual) and to understand that it could be important (affective) as it is a common feature of such dramatised dialogues and the speech learners will hear. We were interested in developing only particpants' language awareness in relation to ellipsis and not their ability to actually use it, as we felt this was appropriate for this aspect of spoken language. As Timmis (2005) suggests, ellipsis is not a feature of language students always have to use unless part of a lexical chunk (most situational ellipsis is a choice made by speakers), and the patterns we describe are just that, they are not hard-and-fast rules. However, we would argue that an awareness of these features can help learners, particularly in an English-speaking context, to understand the language they hear and, in time, they may also choose to use this feature themselves. We would also argue that if learners can encounter such features of spoken language in engaging literary texts in a dramatised form, this in itself can encourage them to further engage with and notice such language outside of class. Finally, as we will show in the next section, we agree with Timmis (2005) that it is not appropriate to isolate one feature of spoken language in instruction materials, so although the focus of our tests was upon understanding of ellipsis, this was taught alongside several other features of spoken language in *Sherlock*. The study therefore seeks to address the following research questions:

RQ1: To what extent does explicit instruction using dramatised literature improve participants' receptive knowledge of ellipsis?

RQ2: Is either of the treatments (with input enhancement and with no input enhancement) more effective than the other in developing participants' receptive knowledge of ellipsis?

RQ3: To what extent do participants themselves feel that the materials used and the focus on ellipsis is useful to them?

Methodology

This study used an experimental design. Three groups were formed: two experimental groups and a control group. We employed pre-, post- and delayed tests to measure the receptive knowledge of ellipsis and also two focus groups to measure learner perceptions of the materials in terms of usefulness and the extent to which the materials developed their language awareness in relation to conversational features.

Participants

The study was conducted at a UK university and participants consisted of study abroad students who volunteered to take part in the study and were randomly assigned to different groups. At the time of the study, the participants had been in the UK for one month on average and had previously learned English for an average of ten years. Based on placement tests scores, all students were broadly at the B2 level, as defined by the Common European Framework of Reference for Languages (CEFR, Council of Europe 2001). Learners at this level can be described as being able to 'interact with a degree of fluency and spontaneity that makes regular interaction with native speakers quite possible without strain for either party' (Council of Europe 2001: 24). Students were divided into three groups: experimental group 1 (explicit teaching + input enhancement, $n = 17$), experimental group 2 (explicit teaching only, $n = 17$) and a control group (no teaching, $n = 17$).The participants ranged in age from 19 to 22 years (mean = 20 years) with a gender distribution of 38 female and 13 male and were either of Chinese (41), Japanese (7) or Korean nationality (3).

Procedure

Participants in the two experimental groups received three hours of instruction over three weeks, based on three clips from the *Sherlock* series. Each type of instruction was explicit, based on the definition from Richards and Schmidt (2002) meaning that students were clearly told what the lesson focus was and so were fully aware what they were studying. Lessons consisted of four main stages, based on Timmis' (2005) framework for teaching spoken grammar:

1. Lead-in and engagement
2. Global understanding tasks
3. Noticing tasks
4. Discussion tasks

This procedure emphasises the development of language awareness and, as a result, there is no requirement for learners to produce the forms being focused upon. As mentioned, clips were chosen based on a text-based approach (Timmis 2018), meaning that our first priority was that we felt the clip could be interesting and engaging for learners. Following this, we then examined it for the features of spoken language which appeared in and then made material following the framework outlined previously (see Appendix 4A for a sample procedure). This meant that over the three classes, learners looked at the use of ellipsis, modality and spoken request forms, with different forms also being recycled across the lessons. Each group was taught in the same way, but experimental group 1 were given transcripts of the conversations they had listened to, which were enhanced to highlight the features of spoken language focused upon. Experimental group 2 received the same transcripts, but no features were enhanced. Figure 4.3 gives a sample of an enhanced text, in this case highlighting the ellipsis.

SHERLOCK:
Okay, you've got questions! ^^^

JOHN:
Yeah.^^^ Where are we going?

SHERLOCK:
^^^**Crime scene.** ^^^**Next?**

JOHN:
Who are you? What do you do?

SHERLOCK:
What do you think? ^^^

JOHN:
I'd say ^^^ private detective

SHERLOCK:
But ^^^?

Figure 4.3 Sample of enhanced text

Tests measuring general comprehension and receptive knowledge of ellipsis were given as pre-tests, immediate post-tests and as a three-week delayed post-test. Tests were based on dialogues from BBC Learning English (BBC 2016) featuring conversations between students in a UK academic study abroad context. Participants were first asked to complete a comprehension task consisting of true or false statements about the content of the dialogue. Following this, they were given an expanded text version of the dialogue which had to be compared to the version they heard. They were then required to listen to the dialogue again and write which words in each line of the expanded dialogue were not spoken in the conversation they heard (see Appendix 4B for a sample).

Following the tests, two focus groups were conducted with six volunteers from each experimental group. These groups allowed us to discuss the extent to which learners perceived the materials to be useful and also allowed us to assess whether learners seemed to report noticing any of the features of spoken language from the instruction outside of class time. Prompts and transcripts can be found in Appendix 4C.

Data Analysis

In order to analyse and compare the effects of instruction, the data were analysed with a 3 x 3 repeated-measures analysis of variance (ANOVA) with group as the between-subjects factor and time as the within-subjects factor. Focus group data were transcribed and analysed to find common themes in relation to the research questions set and establish the extent to which student perceptions matched the test results. Effect sizes were measured using partial eta-squared with 0.1 taken as a small effect, 0.6 as a medium effect and 0.14 taken as a large effect, based upon suggestions made in Cohen (1969, 1988).

Results and Discussion

RQ1: To what extent does explicit instruction using dramatised literature improve participants' receptive knowledge of ellipsis?

The first set of data explored was a simple check whether comprehension improved and whether this was significantly impacted upon by the instruction. Table 4.2 gives the means (M) and standard deviations (SD) for the comprehension tests used at each stage for the comprehension tests. These results revealed no significant effect for time ($p = 0.189$), group ($p = 0.407$) or interaction between time and group ($p = 0.359$). This shows no group performed significantly better than the other on the comprehension tests at any

Table 4.2 *Descriptive statistics: comprehension tests*

Group	Pre M (SD)	Post M (SD)	Delayed M (SD)
Experimental 1 (N= 17)	5.00 (1.061)	5.41 (1.228)	6.00 (1.658)
Experimental 2 (N = 17)	5.06 (1.478)	5.12 (1.576)	5.18 (2.243)
Control (N =17)	5.00 (1.275)	4.82 (.883)	5.24 (1.393)
Total (N = 51)	5.02 (1.257)	5.12 (1.259)	5.47 (1.804)

Note: Maximum score = 8.

Table 4.3 *Descriptive statistics: receptive test*

Group	Pre M (SD)	Post M (SD)	Delayed M (SD)
Experimental 1 (N = 17)	16.18 (5.423)	23.59 (1.064)	18.53 (2.809)
Experimental 2 (N = 17)	16.41 (4. 431)	22.71 (2.392)	17.82 (3.795)
Control (N = 17)	18.53 (2.154)	21.12 (3.039)	14.71 (4.620)
Total (N = 51)	17.04 (4.280)	22.47 (2.671)	18.18 (3.307)

Note: Maximum score = 24.

stage, and the gains within each group did not show significance. Although the results for the comprehension tests improved to a small degree for both experimental groups, this may simply have been due to a practice effect. We would not have expected a large improvement in general comprehension because of increased language awareness, so the result is largely as expected. Table 4.3 gives the descriptive statistics for the test designed to measure receptive knowledge of ellipsis. These results show a significant effect for time with a large effect size F (1.709, 82.043) = 44.450, p <0.001, partial η2.48, a significant time and group interaction with a large effect size: F (3.418, 82.043) = 4.541, p = 0.004, partial η2.15 but no significant effect for group (p = 0.254). Further analysis of results shows no significant differences between the groups at the pre-test stage (p=0.213). When looking at gain scores for pre-post, pre-delayed and post-delayed tests stages, there was a significant effect for time with a large effect size F (1.426, 68.472) = 113.135, p = <0.001 partial η2 .70, a significant effect for group with a large effect size F (2, 46.221) = 4.741, p = 0.013 partial η2.16 but no significant effect for time and group interaction (p = 0.510). Pairwise comparisons confirm that experimental group 1 significantly outperformed the control group (p = 0.018), and we can see evidence for this when we examine the pre-post and pre-delayed test gains (M = 7.4118, M = 2.3259), which were much larger in comparison to the control group. The gains for experimental group 2 also approached significance (p = 0.061) in comparison to the control group, and we can see that their gains at each stage were also much larger than the control group at the pre-post and pre-delayed test stages (M = 6.2941, M =1.4118). These results show clear effects of the treatment with stronger gains being made over time by experimental group 1.

RQ2: Is either of the treatments (with input enhancement and with no input enhancement) more effective than the other in developing participants' receptive knowledge of ellipsis?

Pairwise comparisons show that for each test, there were no significant differences evident between the experimental groups at any of the test stages (comprehension test $p = 1.000. p = 1.000, p = 0.541$; receptive test $p = 1.000, p = 0.934, p = 1.000$). This underlines the results given for research question 1 – although it is clear that both experimental groups outperformed the control group on the receptive test, results only show a slight additional benefit for input enhancement in this study because the gain scores for experimental group 1 did reach significance when compared to the control group.

RQ3: To what extent do participants themselves feel that the materials used and the focus on ellipsis is useful to them?

Focus groups revealed that, in general, learners from both groups found the *Sherlock* material engaging and useful. The most common reasons given were that the listening was fast and challenging and in some sense prepared students for the speed of English heard outside class. Typical comments which reflected this are displayed below (note: experimental group 1 = explicit teaching + textual enhancement, experimental group 2 = explicit teaching only).

<S03>: First I think, I feel same feeling (<S00>: mmm) as S 04, (<S00>: mmm) ahh so quickly, (<S02>: Yeah) so I can't, I can't catch (<S00>: mmm) him (<S00>: mmm) so first I was disappointed, ahh but, but thanks for the experience (<S00>: mmm) I decided to, umm, I decided to watch more of English movie, (<S05>: Ah yeah) so after that I, I watched a lot of English movie (<S00>: mmm) so I think it's good opportunity. (Experimental group 2)

<S01>: I think I, I love it I think that way to use the Sherlock is really good to learn the British English and especially listening (<S00>: mmm) because it was so fast to speak. (Experimental group 1)

<S04>: Uh the class uh there was kind of test of listening what Sherlock said and that time I could listen what he said just one time and uh it was almost correct so I was really glad. (Experimental group 2)

<S02>: Yes. I think it was good because like, like as she said it, he speaks= he spoke very fast and like, usually in our class like teachers speak more slowly because we're studying English. (Experimental group 1)

Despite this, students were in general less sure of the extent to which they would hear the same kind of language used in the drama in their life outside of classes. There seemed to be an agreed feeling that *Sherlock* is a scripted and stylised drama, which is quite different in some ways from everyday conversation. Some comments which typify this view were:

<S05>: I think is helpful was used but the English which used in Sherlock is like not ordinary, (<S00>: mmm) daily so it's really hard to listen but it's very useful to practice listening skills. (Experimental group 1)
<S01>: Oh yeah Friends. oh yeah something is better I think.
<S00>: Right, because?
<S01>: Because mmm, such a drama or a movie includes a phrase which we can use in daily life so, maybe we can understand more easily (<S04>: Ahh yeah). (Experimental group 2)
<S04>: Sherlock is more s=special like specialised word (<S00>: yes yes) so we rarely heard outside the class. (Experimental group 1)

Despite this opinion, there was evidence from both groups that they had reported noticing the types of ellipsis used in the drama outside of class. This suggests that although they felt the topics of conversation may be different, the instruction seemed to have developed this awareness. Typical comments in this regard were as follows:

<S04>   + me too but in daily life umm British people they they use short= word (<S00> Yes) not long sentence (<S00> Yes) I just remember that. [Laughter] (Experimental group 2)
<S02>: Uh Sherlock usually like make his sentence shorter like not and you example not and you he usually say you or something, so it is really useful for me because like usually they in conversation with my flatmate we= I usually don't use like are you or like you like you so it was pretty useful for me. (Experimental group 1)

These data, although limited, give clear indications that the learners in this study did engage with this kind of material and did find it challenging and useful. This suggests that the speed of such authentic material can, in this context, be perceived as useful preparation for what the language student may encounter in conversations outside of class. At the same time, there was clearly a perceived mismatch between the conversations in *Sherlock* and those that students would encounter outside of class. Participants felt that they were unlikely to hear these conversations outside of class time due to their specialised, dramatised nature and therefore found the material less useful in that respect. They did, however, clearly notice the use of ellipsis, which had been given a focus, and could see how this was used in the language they heard outside of class. This gives some evidence that the instruction did enhance the language awareness of both experimental groups, and examining the transcript (see Appendix 4C) shows that there was marginally more reported noticing by members of experimental group 1. This is only a suggestive and tentative result, but one which is positive given that noticing is an initial step towards longer-term intake of a form or forms.

Conclusion

Overall, these results show that explicit instruction with TE and explicit instruction alone can both benefit receptive knowledge of a common feature of spoken language such as ellipsis. This is shown in the clear gains made when we compare pre-test to delayed test stages for both experimental groups compared with the control group. The fact that the TE group significantly outperformed the control group when we look at their gains suggests that TE did boost results in comparison to a control group when used alongside explicit teaching, as has been found in other studies (e.g. Indrarathne and Kormos 2017), but in comparison to explicit teaching alone, it was not significantly superior. Qualitative focus group data show that dramatised literature can be used as a potentially motivating model of spoken language, albeit with some caveats. Participants in this study found both the speed of delivery and the stories themselves to be useful and interesting. They also gave some evidence that instruction helped to develop their language awareness, which we defined broadly as 'developing an enhanced consciousness of forms and functions of language' (Carter 2003: 64). This was evident in reported noticing of features such as ellipsis when used outside the class, which suggests that the instruction could potentially have a much longer-term effect: as learners encounter more spoken language, their exposure to a feature they have noticed means their receptive knowledge could increase. However, there were also some doubts expressed in the focus group about the stylised nature of dialogues in a programme such as *Sherlock*. Students felt that because it belongs to a particular genre and characters behave in a certain manner, they are not likely to hear similar conversations outside of class. This led to some students questioning how useful such materials may be.

Implications for Teaching

These results suggest that using dramatised literature has clear potential for classroom use. In this case, results show that using such material can develop awareness about features such as ellipsis and that significant gains to receptive knowledge can be made. This shows that the instruction in this area can have an impact upon what Sharwood Smith and Truscott (2014) have termed perceptual, conceptual and affective processing. Participants were generally more aware that ellipsis is common in spoken English (perceptual) and could recognise this in the tests; some reported noticing when and why it is used (conceptual) and there were also reports showing that it could be important (affective). Combined with the generally positive reaction from students to this material, this suggests that for teachers, making use of such materials is a plausible option in the classroom in order to develop spoken language awareness. As mentioned earlier in the chapter, such material is likely to be more motivating and engaging than simply working with 'raw' transcripts of spoken language from corpora, although such data can certainly be used to inform classroom materials if adapted (see McCarthy and McCarten 2018 for helpful examples). Decisions regarding which dramatised literature to use will depend on the context of teaching and student interests, but we would encourage teachers to choose materials following a text-based approach (Timmis 2018), whereby the choice of material is first based on the fact it is likely to engage and motivate learners and then examined for its language features, rather than choosing a clip because it seems to illustrate a particular language feature. This does not preclude the kind of older texts which may also exist in a dramatised form and have potential to be a useful and engaging model of spoken language (see Chapter 2, this volume). Once a suitable clip or set of clips has been found, we would then suggest that teachers could follow the type of plan used in this study (see Appendix 4A) and make use of the basic framework developed by Timmis (2005):

1. Lead-in and engagement
2. Global understanding tasks
3. Noticing tasks
4. Discussion tasks

While TE was not found to be superior to explicit teaching alone in this study, it is clear from the greater and more significant gains made by experimental group 1 in comparison to the control group and the other studies reviewed that it *can* have a positive effect when combined with explicit teaching, and so it could certainly be used to highlights forms in materials.

Focus group data also show that there is a need for teachers to make explicit how literary dialogues (in this case from *Sherlock*) do have features which relate to the kinds of conversations learners will encounter outside class, despite being stylised in a particular way. Such explanation could motivate learners to further re-listen to such dialogues outside of class time, as they can become useful sources of input.

Implications for Research

The inclusion of a delayed post-test in this study was intended to introduce a longitudinal element to the study. Ideally, future studies would extend this and introduce a delayed test after (for example) two or three months. Such tests are often difficult to administer as participants will not be available, but they would allow us

to measure longer-term effects. Related to this, other measures of language awareness could also be used, such as the type of test developed by Lin (2010). This
involved asking learners to analyse a literary text, identifying stylistic features and
explaining how they contribute to the way a text makes meaning. Quality of student
responses was then evaluated by raters. Such a test could be adapted for spoken
language and learners could be asked to listen to a dramatised dialogue and identify
features of spoken language and discuss why these are used, for example.

Other measures which can be used to analyse which aspects of spoken
language participants report noticing could also be used with a study of this
nature. One example might be to ask learners to keep diaries that describe
common situations where they interact in or listen to spoken English outside of
classes. They could then report what (if anything) they notice. This data could
be analysed in order to understand how it relates to the instruction.

Finally, eye tracking could be used to check what participants are focusing upon
in materials with TE such as the ones used in this study. As Indrarathne and Kormos
(2017) show, it is then possible to measure how learners' attention correlates with
their test scores.. Such studies could be undertaken with a focus on different aspects
of spoken language and employing different dramatised literary materials.

Appendix 4A Sample Lesson Procedure

Teaching plan
1. Warmer – start with a Sherlock Holmes quiz.
2. Students can discuss what they know about the BBC TV series (if anything)
   and how it is different from the book.
3. Set up the context – Sherlock and Watson have only recently met. They are
   now taking a taxi together to investigate something. Watson does not really
   know or understand Sherlock at this point. They may need to know
   Afghanistan/Iraq/Barts Hospital.
4. First watch:
What is the main purpose of the conversation?
   a) To pass the time by having a chat
   b) To allow Watson to find out something about Holmes
   c) To allow Watson to find out something about a new crime
5. Second watch:
True or false:
   a) They are travelling to a crime scene.
   b) Sherlock is a private detective.

c) The police ask Sherlock for his views on certain crimes.

d) Sherlock and Watson first met two days ago.

e) Watson was in the army.

f) Watson had told Holmes he had been to Afghanistan.

6. Third watch:

Read and listen and then discuss:

How is this conversation different from a normal conversation between friends? Why?

(It is set up to be in the style of a police interrogation, to fit the theme of the programme.)

How do they feel about Sherlock, based on this scene? And Watson?

7. Ask students to look at the transcript and find words which are 'missing' or have been left out in the conversation but which are understood by both in the context:

Give them an example and ask them to tell you what is missing:

SHERLOCK: Ok, you've got questions = Ok, I understand you've got some questions you want to ask me.

8. Get feedback on the examples.

Ask them to tell you why speakers can do this (they do not need to over elaborate). Ask students: do speakers do this in their first language? (they will of course do so).

Make it clear that ellipsis is common in spoken English and discuss why it is common.

9. Can students find any of the following patterns?

Leaving out a pronoun as a subject (e.g. *crime scene, means when the police* ...)

Leaving out main or helping verbs (e.g. *we're going to* ...)

Leaving out articles (e.g. *police don't go, I'd say private detective*)

Allow students to discuss and find any other patterns they can.

10. What types of words are not left out? (Nouns). They should notice how these are repeated throughout to give the conversation cohesion.

11. Give the experimental group the dialogue with the ellipsis marked heavily and ask them to pay attention to this as they listen to conversations. The other group just get the 'standard' tapescript.

12. Give students a short dialogue from the book *A Study in Scarlet*. How is this different from the TV show? It is clearly less 'up to date' and seems more 'writerly', as befitting a book, where there is less context for us to 'fill in the gaps' and thus less ellipsis.

Appendix 4B Sample Test Items

(Please note: this is not the complete test.)

Listening Test: In the University Library

(from www.bbc.co.uk/learningenglish/english/features/english-at-university/)

Task 1

Listen and answer the questions below either true (T) or false (F).
   Example:

I live in the USA *F*
1.   Mary has met Sharon before._____
2.   Mary is looking for books for her Biology degree. _____
3.   Mary was able to find just one of the books she was looking for. _____

Task 2

Listen again. In the tapescript below, extra words have been placed in some sentences which the speakers on the video do not actually say. In each, the number of **extra** (unsaid) **words** is given at the end of some sentences. Listen and **underline** which words are **not said.**
   Example:

   I would <u>really</u> like to live in the USA one day <u>perhaps</u> (2 extra words)
   [Speaker actually says on the recording: *I would like to live in the USA one day].*

Transcript:

SHARON: NEXT!
MARY: Hello Sharon! Do you work here as well? (1 **extra word**)
SHARON: **Yes, we tend to double up round here. It's the funding cuts – the university's not got that much money – anyway dear, I suppose you're looking for some books?**
MARY: Yes, that's right, I am. Where can I find books about business, please? (2 **extra words**)
SHARON: **Go down there, then turn left, then turn right, then to the end ... under 'B' ... 'B' for biology ... (3 extra words)**
MARY: And Business, thanks ... . On no! oh dear ... none of the books are here ...

Appendix 4C Focus Group Transcriptions and Prompts

Note: <S00> = the researcher. All other speakers are the participants. Language errors have not been corrected.

Transcription code

+ – overlap

= – correction within the same turn

Focus group 1 (Experimental group 1- explicit teaching + textual enhancement)

<S00>: Okay so we're just gonna have a general discussion about the classes, about the Sherlock classes if you can remember. Hopefully (<S01>: yes [Laughter]) you can remember that a few weeks ago. Okay and you're not being asked to make a big judgement about them or make any comments about the teacher or anything like that um, it's just your general views about the class content and what, whether it was useful to you or not, so you can be as honest as you like, it doesn't matter and um as I said before when we transcribe it it'll all be anonymous so don't worry about it. Okay so you finished the classes where you used Sherlock a few weeks ago? (<S01>: yeah) I guess? Um and, I just wondered first of all if you could tell me any general thoughts you had about the classes? Anybody?

<S01>: I think I, I love it I think that way to use the Sherlock is really good to learn the British English and especially listening (<S00>: mmm) because it was so fast to speak so I think that was good. But sometimes I'm= I want to study with more native British people because it was just us so uhh, we sometimes our English is not so correct so I ne= I thought I need more other student.

<S00>: Okay, mmm, okay. What about the rest of you do you have the same feeling or a different feeling?

<S02>: Yes. I think it was good because like, like as she said it, he speaks= he spoke very fast and like, usually in our class like teachers speak more slowly because we're studying English, (<S00>: Yeah) so they make us like understand? (<S00>: mmm) Understand all and it was like rush for me (<S00>: mmm) because like we can like listen more like native= native English. It was nice I think.

<S00>: Okay, okay. Other people?

<S03>: Yeah, I was satisfied with the Sherlock class because I prefer to watch the videos and reading literature, to be honest, [laughing] yeah and uh so the guys says that uh so we can listen to the native, um native speakers umm, so too fast so yeah and my teacher often yeah speak clearly and (<S02>: yeah <S00>: mmm) slowly yeah than other native speakers. (<S00>: yes) yeah it was good way to learn and get used to listening to the speed of native speaker yeah. (<S01>: mmm).

<S04>:   It really helped me to understand what flatmate talking. (<S00>: Oh okay <S01 S 02>: mmm) Because they are native British so a little bit difficult to understand (<S00>: mmm yeah). But I think Sherlock= errr the studying with Sherlock is helped me to understand their talk= what talking. Yeah.

<S00>   Okay, okay, and you guys

<S05>:   I think is helpful was used but the English which used in Sherlock is like not ordinary, (<S00>: mmm) daily so it's really hard to listen but it's very useful to practice listening skills, I think it's a good class.

<S00>:   Okay, okay. What do you think?

<S06>:   The class was beautiful but it was hard to understand what Sherlock in this video said.

<S00>:   Mmm, mmm, okay yeah okay because of the same reason the speed?

<S06>:   Mmm

<S00>:   Right okay. Okay um, and can you remember anything about the conversations in Sherlock that you studied? (<S04>: Ohh uh) Can you remember anything about them at all?

<S04>:   Yeah, uh, what Sherlock said?

<S00>:   Yeah anything, anything (<S02>: anything) at all, (<S04>: Uhh) what he said or what you learnt from it or yeah anything really.

<S04>:   Uhh Sherlock was really unlikable person [laughter] that met uh, I don't= I can't remember, uh Joe, John, Jack? The (<S02>: John?) John, John yeah. He met John he's more likeable normal person and at the first time they met to Sherlock just say about J=, J= Joe, just obvious ending no just they uh Sherlock knows almost everything of Joe so yeah and I remember that, yeah that's it.

<S00>   Okay okay, anybody else? Anybody else remember anything from the conversations?

<S02>   Like, it's the first time like he met John. Like, John was confused about= confused by Sherlock because he knew everything about John and he like uh after, after that they went to cri= not criminal scene but, how can I say, that= that place that like that body are. (<S00>: Ahh Crime scene>) Yes yes, crime scene (<S00>: That's okay) Crime scene and like John also= John helped him because he was doctor in Army in Iraq (<S00>: Yes). Yes, so. Yes.

<S00>:   Okay (<S02>: [Laughter]) It's okay alright it's not a test. Yeah alright yeah. Anybody else or?

<S03>:   I don't remember what Sherlock and John said (<S00>: mmm) in the um yeah but I thought uh Sherlock is more like talkative and more faster than other ordinary people. (<S00>: yes) um so it's makes me feel awkward (<S00>: mmm) yes.

<S00>:   Okay so is there anything from the conversations or lessons that you heard outside the classes? Or you used outside the classes that you can remember, so you did it in the lesson you heard it and then you also thought ah that's the same thing outside the class or maybe (<S02>: like same conversation). Not the same conversation maybe something or some as= some some part of it you heard that you thought oh yeah that= oh yeah that's that again (<S02>: oh) yeah okay people say that liking that or maybe you took something and you used it I don't know.

<S02>:   I have never but [inaudible]but like some phrase outside the class just inside the class.

<S00>:   Just inside the class, (<S04>: Yeah) right, okay

<S04>:   Sherlock is more s=special like specialised word (<S00>: yes yes) so we rarely heard outside the class.

<S00>:   What do you think? What about you?

<S06>:   I haven't used it.

<S00>:   Okay that's fine.

<S04>:   But [inaudible] (<S00>: Yeah) the way to response is I think I can use and learn from the Sherlock.

<S00>:   Okay c= can you give me an example of what you mean, you know anything at all you don't have to remember exactly but just roughly

<S04>:   Like the way too if somebody ask me in the= uh how to response to [Inaudible] the way and uh pronunciation I learned from Sherlock I think.

<S00>:   Okay okay you're agreeing? (<S02>: Yeah) Can you say a little bit more?

<S02>:   Uh Sherlock usually like make his sentence shorter like not and you example not and you he usually say you or something, so it is really useful for me because like usually they in conversation with my flatmate we= I usually don't use like are you or like you like you so it was pretty useful for me.

<S00>:   So have you noticed people doing that outside the class (<S02>: Yes) not= not speaking in the same conversation as sherlock but that same style. (S 04>: Yeah yeah yeah) Have you noticed it?

<S0?>:   Yeah. Specially British people.

<S00>:   [Laughing] Okay, especially British people. Right, okay. Interesting, okay. Umm right my final thing was just if you have any uh final thoughts about the class maybe something you forgot to say and that you would like to say. You don't have to say something but if you've got something= anything else that you'd like to add it'd be useful. If you want to.

<S04>:   Uh the class uh there was kind of test of listening what Sherlock said and that time I could listen what he said just one time and uh it was almost correct so I was really glad

<S00>:   Ohh okay, okay. So it's tough but it, it's +

<S04>:   Yeah tough but I can because I think I've been studying with Sherlock so I think I can listen that was good.

<S00>:   Okay okay any final thoughts?

<S06>:   No.

<S00>:   Okay, right, okay. Had you watched this before?

<S04>:   No but I've after the class.

<S00>:   Ah okay you went on to YouTube and watched it or something yeah. Okay okay right, thank you very much that's great.

Focus group 2 (Experimental group 2 – explicit teaching only)

<S00>:   Okay so um we're just gonna have if it's okay just a general discussion about the um classes and just so you know you're not being asked to judge the classes or anything like (<SS>: [Laughter]) that or to make any comments about the teacher or teaching or(<SS>: [Laughter]) anything like that really.

It's just your general views about the class content and I'm talking about the classes you did with Sherlock. (<S01>: ahh) (<S02>: ahh). The, the videos from Sherlock, you know (<S03>: yes), which obviously are based on the Sherlock Holmes stories as you know, and you can be as honest and open as you can't, there's nothing to worry about and um just, just to remember that when I transcribe it, you'll just be student A, Student B or whatever you won't have any names. Okay?

<S03>:   Okay.

<S02>:   Okay.

<S00>:   Right, so it's been a, I guess a few weeks since you finished doing the classes with Sherlock. (<S03>: yes, yes) (<S01>: yes) (<S02>: yes) Is that right? A few weeks? (<S01>: yes) Can you remember them?

<S02>:   Yeah.

<S03>:   Mmm yes [Laughing] think so.

<S00>:   Okay okay okay, um, can you just tell me any, any of you it doesn't matter who starts, can you tell me any general thoughts that you have about those classes.

<S03>:   General thoughts.

<S02>:   General thoughts?

<S00>:   General thoughts yeah, any general, general thoughts, any general comments.

<S01>:   Umm.

<S03>:   Umm, about the (<S00>: About the) Sherlock class?

<S00>:   Yeah, about the classes you did with Sherlock, yeah, (<S02> Uhh huh) when that was the Sherlock materials you used. (<S03>: Uhh yeah.) If you can remember.

<S04>:   It is my first time to watch the Sherlock movie. And [inaudible] err= and umm the Sherlock [laughs] speaks so quickly (<S02>: Ahh. Me too! Quickly. Too quickly too quickly) it's more difficult to, yeah, to catch what he saying (<S00>: mmm) than I thought (<S00>: Right) … I was a little bit surprise.

<SS>:   [Laughter]

<S00>:   Okay, okay.

<S04>:   Yes, is hard work.

<S00>:   Yes, okay.

<S03>:   First I think, I feel same feeling (<S00>: mmm) as S 04, (<S00>: mmm) ahh so quickly, (< S 02>: Yeah) so I can't, I can't catch (<S00>: mmm) him (<S00>: mmm) so first I was disappointed, ahh but, but thanks for the experience (<S00>: mmm) I decided to, umm, I decided to watch more of English movie, (<S05>: Ah yeah) so after that I, I watched a lot of English movie (<S00>: mmm) so I think it's good opportunity.

<S00>:   mmm, okay. So you went back and you watched other things (<S03>: Mmm yes) afterwards? Oh okay, okay that's good. What about the= what about you guys did you have the same feelings as this?

<S01>:   Yes, yes.

<S02>:   Same, same.

<S01>:   I think the movie of um, like eh daily life (<S00>: Mmm) situation is better I think (<S04>: oh ahh) for example ah [Inaudible] (<SS>: [Laughs] Inaudible]) the American dramas (<S03>: good, good).

<S00>:   Friends?

<S01>:   Oh yeah Friends. oh yeah something is better I think.

<S00>:   Right. Because?

<S01>:   Because mmm, such a drama or a movie includes a phrase which we can use in daily life so, maybe we can understand more easily (<S04>: Ahh yeah).

<S00>:   Okay, okay alright next question okay. Umm, so, what do you remember about the conversations in Sherlock that you studied? Can you remember anything about them?

<S02>:   Dirty dirty dirty (<S04>: dirty [inaudble]) [inaudible] (<SS>: Laughter) This area is clear +

<S06>:   And the clothes were wet [Laugher].

<S04>:   The Sherlock uh investigat= no, investigate the dead body (<S00>: Okay yes <SS>: [Laughter]). And uhh in lavatory Sherlock and Watson met for the first time and they Sherlock could, um em know the= where the Watson came from by just looking (<S00> Yes) watching.

<S00>:   Okay.

<S02>:   Sherlock said um his phone [inaudible] has no signal?

<S00>:   So you remember that (SS [Laughing]) Okay. Is there anything else? Anything you guys remember?

<S05>   Anything. Ummmm.

<S01>:   I just remember the situation in taxi. (<SS>: Ahh Yeah [Laughter]) Yeah but I don't remember much conversations.

<S00>:   No, okay +

<S04>   + Me too but in daily life umm British people they they use short= word (<S00> Yes) not long sentence (<S00> Yes) I just remember that. [Laughter].

<S00>   Okay okay, so that was gonna be my next question really. Is there anything from the conversations that you heard in the lessons or the things that you did in the lessons which you= maybe you remember hearing outside of the class in your daily life like you said people use lots of shortened expressions that kind of thing that you remember maybe you heard it in the Sherlock lesson and then you went outside and then you heard it or maybe you said it I don't know. Is there anything else?

<S01>:   I don't care about the things +

<SS>:   [Laughter]

<S04>:   Me too.

<S00>:   What do you mean? Can you say a bit more? What do you mean?

<S04>:   Yeah, uhh, I don't carefully listen to, to peoples conversations outside (<S00> No okey) to um, it's oh it's Sherlock I don't (<SS>: [Laughter]).

<S00>:   Okay so there's nothing that you heard and thought ah that's that same= you didn't notice anything, right, okay.

<S05>:   Me too.

<S02>:   Me too.

<S00>:   Okay but you noticed that people use lots of shortened expressions +

<S02>:   Ah yeah, shortened and sometimes I didn't understand the shortened what did they mean.

<S00>:   Yes, right okay, and do you think that after the lessons you understood a little bit more?

<S03>:   Maybe so.

<S02>:   Maybe.

<S00>   Yeah okay, of course you're not gonna understand everything but yeah okay, alright, was there anything else you remember from the lessons or the conversations that maybe you heard outside the class somewhere or you said it somewhere.

<S03>:   Umm no but uh, I could get used to the speed of (<S02>: mmm me too) Yes (<S01>: good point) it's what the movie.

<S00>:   Okay so can you say a little bit more about that, that's interesting, so speed.

<S03>:   Umm. Before I came here I heard British people speak more quickly, and the= the British peoples speak sounds more short short than the American peoples. And uh, yeah after came hear I, uh, also, hear the same thing. It is true and the and the class when I saw that= I watch the move I uh, I understand, uh, how they speak, speak quickly and uh yeah, um.

<S00>:   Okay okay +

<S01>:   + I think Sherlock movie was the quickest [Inaudible] for us.

<S02>:   Sherlocks speak, speaks= spoke too quickly. [Laughing] (<S03>: Yeah). So so after I asked the teacher to watch again. (<S00>: Mmm) By myself (<S00>: Mmm) so also then I could [laughing] [inaudible] so I repeat it.

<S00>:   Mmm, and when you repeated it did it come easier or was it kind of the same?

<S02>:   Uh kind of more get easier, but not, not so easy.

<S00>:   No, okay okay, and what do you think do you agree with this point about the speed? The speed thing?

<S05>:   Speed is so quickly, so we need= sometimes the teacher gave us but I think every time we need subtitles.

<SS>:   [Laughter]

<S00>:   Right yes, okay, okay. alright um thank you so my final thing is do you have any final thoughts about the classes that you wanted to add, anything else that you would like to say about them that maybe you forgot to say or you haven't said.

<S01>:   It was a good opportunity so I want to keep listening Sherlock or something.

<S04>:   Yes.

<S02>   Yes watching the English movie, so= effective to study English more.

<S05>:   In the= another class, (<S00>: Yes) we uhh, we often use document article (<S00>: Yes) letter (<S00>: Yes) so we uh so it is rare to watch some movie or drama in the class (<S00>: Oh okay) it was so fun.

<S00>:   Right okay.

<S04>:   We love to listen lecture in English but sometimes it is boring [Laughter] we can enjoy watching them I think.

<S00>:   And you knew= did you know= you knew about this series already? You had heard about it or watched it?

<S02>:   Uh Sherlock?

<S01>:   No first time.

<S00>:   Okay that's interesting. cos it's popular in a number of countries you see. Okay okay that's interesting. Thank you very much.

References

Alanen, R. 1995. 'Input enhancement and rule presentation in second language acquisition', in Schmidt, R. (ed.), *Attention and Awareness in Foreign Language Learning*. Hawai'i: University of Hawai'i Press, 259–302.

BBC. 2016. *English at University.* Available at: www.bbc.co.uk/learningenglish/english/features/english-at-university/ (Accessed 1 May 2017).

2017. '*Sherlock*: Most watched programme across all channels over festive season for second year running' . BBC Media Centre. Available at: www.bbc.co.uk/mediacentre/latestnews/2017/sherlock-most-watched (Accessed 7 April 2018).

Bergsleithner, J. M., Frota, S. N. and Yoshioka, J. K. (eds.) 2013. *Noticing and Second Language Acquisition: Studies in Honor of Richard Schmidt.* Hawai'i: National foreign Language Resource Center.

Biber, D., Johansson, S., Leech, G., Conrad, S. and Finegan, E. 1999. *Longman Grammar of Spoken and Written English.* London: Longman.

Bloemert, J., Paran, A., Jansen, E. and van de grift, W. 2019. 'Students' perspectives on the benefits of EFL literature education', *The Language Learning Journal* 47 (3): 371–384.

Carter, R.1998. 'Orders of reality: CANCODE communication, and culture', *ELT Journal* 52(1): 43–56.

2003. 'Language awareness', *ELT Journal* 57(1): 64–65.

Carter, R., Hughes, R. and McCarthy, M. 2000. *Exploring Grammar in Context: Grammar Practice and Reference Upper-Intermediate and Advanced.* Cambridge: Cambridge University Press.

Carter, R. and McCarthy, M. 1997. *Exploring Spoken English.* Cambridge: Cambridge University Press.2006. Cambridge Grammar of English. Cambridge: Cambridge University Press.

2017. Spoken grammar: Where are we are and where are we going?, *Applied Linguistics* 38(1): 1–20.

Carter, R. and McRae, J. (eds.) 1996. *Language, Literature and the Learner: Creative Classroom Practice.* Oxford: Routledge.

Carter, R., McCarthy, M., Mark, G. and O' Keeffe, A. 2011. *English Grammar Today: An A–Z of Spoken and Written Grammar.* Cambridge: Cambridge University Press.

Chirravoori, M. 2018. Sherlock Holmes fan.com. Available from: www.sherlockholmes-fan.com (Accessed 1 May 2018).

Choi, S. 2017. 'Processing and earning of enhanced English collocations: An eye movement study', *Language Teaching Research* 21(3): 403–426.

Cohen, J. 1969. *Statistical Power Analysis for the Behavioural Sciences* (1st edn). New York: Academic Press.

1988. *Statistical Power Analysis for the Behavioural Sciences* (2nd edn). London: Routledge.

Conan Doyle, A. 2008. *A Study in Scarlet.* Available at: www.gutenberg.org (Accessed 3 May 2018).

Council of Europe. 2001. *Common European Framework of Reference for Languages: Learning, Teaching, Assessment.* Cambridge: Cambridge University Press.

Davies, M. 2004. BYU-BNC (based on the British National Corpus from Oxford University Press). Available at: https://corpus.byu.edu/bnc/ (Accessed 2 May 2018).

DeVere, A. 2012. Sherlock transcript: 'A Study in Pink' (part 1). Available at: www
.ariandevere.livejournal.com (Accessed 1 December 2018).

Doughty, C. 1991. 'Second language instruction: Does it make a difference?',*Studies in
Second Language Acquisition* 13(4): 431–469.

Goh, C. 2009. 'Perspectives on spoken grammar', *ELT Journal* 63(4): 303–312.

Greenbaum, S. and Nelson, G. 1999. 'Elliptical clauses in spoken and written English',
in Collins, P. and Lee, D. (eds.), *The Clause in English: In Honour of Rodney
Huddleston.* Amsterdam: John Benjamins, 111–127.

Halliday, M. A. K. and Hassan, R. 1976. *Cohesion in English.* London: Longman.

Halliday, M. A. K. and Matthiessen, C. 2013. *Halliday's Introduction to Functional
Grammar* (4th edn). Oxford: Routledge.

Han, Z. H., Park, E. S. and Combs, C. 2008. 'Textual enhancement of input: Issues and
possibilities', *Applied Linguistics* 29(4): 597–618.

Indrarathne, B. and Kormos, J. 2017. 'Attentional processing of input in explicit and
implicit conditions', *Studies in Second Language Acquisition* 39(3): 401–430.

Izumi, S. 2002. 'Output, input enhancement and the noticing hypothesis: An experimental study on ESL relativization', *Studies in Second Language Acquisition* 24
(4): 541–577.

Jones, C. 2007. 'Spoken grammar: Is "noticing" the best option?', *Modern English
Teacher* 16(4): 155–160.

  2017. 'Soap operas as models of authentic conversations: Implications for material
design', in Maley, A. and Tomlinson, B. (eds.), *Authenticity in Materials
Development for Language Learning.* Newcastle upon Tyne: Cambridge Scholars,
158–175.

  (ed.). 2018. *Practice in Second Language Learning.* Cambridge: Cambridge
University Press,

Jones, C., Byrne, S. and Halenko, N. 2017. *Successful Spoken English: Findings from
Learner Corpora.* London: Routledge.

Jones, C. and Waller, D. 2017. The effect of input enhancement on vocabulary learning:
Is there an impact upon receptive and productive knowledge?', *TESOL
International Journal* 12(1): 48–62.

Lee, S. K. and Huang, H. T. 2008. 'Visual input enhancement and grammar learning: A
meta-analytic review', *Studies in Second Language Acquisition* 30(3): 307–331.

Lin, H. W. 2010. 'The taming of the immeasurable: An empirical assessment of
language awareness', in Paran, A. and Sercu, L (eds.), *Testing the Untestable in
Language Education.* Bristol: Multilingual Matters, 191–216.

Mackenzie, I. 2000. 'Institutionalised utterances, literature and language teaching',
Language and Literature 9(1): 61–78.

McCarthy, M. 2010. 'Spoken fluency revisited', *English Profile Journal* 1(1): 1–15.

McCarthy, M. and Carter, R, 1995. 'Spoken grammar: What is it and how can we teach
it?', *ELT Journal* 49(3): 207–218.

McCarthy, M. and McCarten, J. 2018. 'Now you're talking! Practising conversation in
second language learning', in Jones, C. (ed.), *Practice in Second Language
Learning.* Cambridge: Cambridge University Press, 7–29.

McRae, J. 1991. *Literature with a Small 'l'.* London: Macmillan.

Norris, J. M. and Ortega, L. 2000. 'Effectiveness of L2 instruction: A research synthesis
and quantitative meta-analysis', *Language Learning* 50(3): 417–528.

Pawlowski, A. and Han, P. 2010. 'British tourism hopes to cash in on Sherlock Holmes'. Available at: http://edition.cnn.com/2010/BUSINESS/01/18/sherlock.holmes.tour ism.london/index.html (Accessed 2 May 2018).

Petchko, K. 2011. 'Input enhancement, noticing and incidental vocabulary acquisition', *The Asian EFL Journal Quarterly* 3(4): 228–255.

Rebuck, M. 2011. 'Using the 11 "errors" of native speakers in the EFL classroom', *ELT Journal* 65(1): 33–41.

Ricento, T. 1987. 'Clausal ellipsis in multi-party conversation in English', *Journal of Pragmatics* 11(6): 751–775.

Richards, J. C. and Schmidt, R 2002. *Longman Dictionary of Language Teaching and Applied Linguistics* (3rd edn). Harlow: Pearson Education.

Schmidt, R. 1990. 'The role of consciousness in second language learning', *Applied Linguistics* 11(2): 129–158.

1993. 'Awareness and second language acquisition', *Annual Review of Applied Linguistics* 13: 206–226.

2010. 'Attention, awareness and individual differences in language learning', in Chan, W. M., Chi, S., Cin, K. N., Istanto, J., Nagami, M., Sew, J. W., Suthiwan, T. and Walker, I. (eds.), *Proceeding of ClaScc 2010 Singapore December 2–4*. Singapore: University of Singapore Center for Language Studies, 721–737.

Sharwood Smith, M. 1981. 'Consciousness raising and the second language learner', *Applied Linguistics* 2(2): 159–186.

1991. 'Speaking to many different minds: on the relevance of different types of language information for the l2 learner', *Second Language Research* 7(2): 118–132.

1993. 'Input enhancement in instructed SLA', *Studies in Second Language Acquisition* 15(2): 165–179.

Sharwood Smith, M. and Truscott, J. 2014. 'Explaining input enhancement: A MOGUL perspective', *International Review of Applied Linguistics in Language Teaching*, 52(3): 253–281.

Sherlock: Complete Series 1–4 and the Abominable Bride. 2016. London: British Broadcasting Corporation.

Short, M. 1996. *Exploring the Language of Poems, Plays and Prose*. Harlow: Longman.

Spada, N. and Tomita, Y. 2010. 'Interactions between type of instruction and type of language feature: A meta-analysis', *Language Learning* 60(2): 263–308.

Timmis, I. 2005. 'Towards a framework for teaching spoken grammar', *ELT Journal* 59 (2): 117–125.

2012. 'Spoken language research and ELT: Where are we now?' *ELT Journal* 66(4): 514–522.

2018. 'A text-based approach to grammar practice', in Jones, C. (ed.), *Practice in Second Language Learning*. Cambridge: Cambridge University Press, 79–108.

Warner, C. 2012. 'Literary pragmatics in the advanced foreign language literature classroom: The case of young Werther', in Burke, M., Csabi, S., Week, L. and Zerkowitz, J. (eds.), *Pedagogical Stylistics: Current Trends in Language Literature and ELT*. London: Continuum, 142–157.

Wilson, P. 2014. *Mind the Gap: Ellipsis and Stylistic Variation in Spoken and Written English*. Oxford: Routledge.

Wong, W. 2003. 'The effects of textual enhancement and simplified input on l2 comprehension and acquisition of non-meaningful grammatical form', *Applied Language Learning* 13(2): 17–46.

5   Haiku and Spoken Language: Corpus-Driven Analyses of Linguistic Features in English Language Haiku Writing

Atsushi Iida

This chapter reports on a poetic inquiry with English language learners in the Japanese English as a Foreign Language (EFL) university context. It focuses on the use of haiku – a Japanese poem containing seventeen syllables in a three-line 5–7–5 syllable pattern with the usage of a seasonal reference and a cutting word – and analyses features of spoken language in a corpus of English language haiku poetry written by Japanese second language (L2) learners. The chapter begins by reviewing previous studies of the use of haiku in L2 contexts. It then describes a quantitative, corpus-based study which involved the analysis of textual and linguistic features of English language haiku writing. The data, consisting of a total of 2,017 haiku poems written by 204 first-year engineering students at a Japanese public university, were submitted to statistical analyses. The results illustrate some specific features of English language haiku produced by Japanese L2 writers: haiku poetry is a short, descriptive text which presents each writer's emotional reactions to his or her daily life, and it also includes such spoken language features as the twelve verbs most frequently used in spoken discourse (Biber and Conrad 2010), evaluative and emotive adjectives, contractions and vague language. This study suggests that the task of composing haiku in English can play an important role in L2 learning in terms of raising learners' awareness of typical spoken forms in the target language.

Introduction

Haiku – a Japanese three-line poem containing seventeen syllables in a 5–7–5 syllable pattern with the usage of a seasonal reference[1] and a cutting word[2] – is used for different purposes in various contexts around the world. Nowadays, its usage is not limited to Japanese as a first language (L1). The application of haiku ranges from literacy practice and literary/cultural studies to therapeutic practice. In Japan, for example, haiku is officially introduced in an authorised textbook in the third-grade Japanese language course (*kokugo*) in order for 9-year-olds to develop their L1 linguistic awareness. Additionally, haiku writing is used for non-Japanese students to study Japanese literature and/or develop cultural knowledge in the United States (Stokely 2000). Haiku writing is also used as a therapy through which patients compose poems as a way to release their negative emotions (Sky Hiltunen 2005). In the field of applied linguistics, a principal theoretical framework is to use haiku as a form of literacy practice in the second language (L2) classroom (Iida 2010, 2012, 2017a, 2017b). While many teachers and researchers report on their own usage of haiku poetry from practical viewpoints, the linguistic forms in haiku have been somewhat under-explored. Of importance in L2 research is to clarify textual features of haiku poetry written by L2 learners and provide pedagogical suggestions for the teaching of haiku writing in the L2 classroom.

The aim of this chapter is to explore spoken forms within English language haiku poetry written by Japanese learners of English. Initially, it reviews previous research on L2 haiku writing. Following this, it describes a poetic inquiry into characterising English language haiku writing. The main objective of the current study is to identify features of spoken English in the genre of haiku poetry, which is primarily written. In doing so, this article intends to argue for the use of this poetic genre as a way for L2 writers to develop their L2 literacy and enhance their L2 written and spoken language awareness in the EFL composition classroom.

Haiku Poetry and L2 Writers

Many teachers believe that poetry writing is an effective literacy practice in the L2 classroom (Chamcharatsri 2013; Hanauer 2010, 2012; Hanauer and Fang-Yu 2016; Iida 2016a, 2016b, 2017a, 2017b, 2018). Previous research discusses the effect of poetry writing on L2 learning, and it is considered to be useful to express voice (Chamcharatsri 2013; Hanauer 2010, 2012; Iida 2010, 2012, 2016a, 2016b, 2017b, 2018), enhance L2 linguistic knowledge (Hanauer 2003, 2011; Iida 2012), develop L2 cultural awareness (Hanauer 2003) and broaden genre-specific knowledge (Hanauer 2011; Iida 2012).

Likewise, haiku writing, a sub-genre of poetry, is seen as an effective approach for L2 literacy practice. From a theoretical perspective, social-expressivist haiku pedagogy designed by Iida (2010) has great potential to transform the traditional Japanese EFL classroom into communicative contexts in which 'students learn to express their voice – the articulation of their personal needs, interests and ideas – in a social context that presumes an *audience* – the teachers, classmates and even the community at large' (28). This theoretical perspective has been supported t by several empirical studies. For example, Iida's (2012) study on cross-genre literacy development demonstrated the positive influence on academic prose of composing haiku in English. This intervention study, through which pre- and post-tests were administered to determine twenty Japanese EFL learners' progress in academic prose as a result of a six-week treatment of haiku writing in English, reported a significant increase in word counts and the use of verbs between pre- and post-tests, indicating that composing haiku made a contribution to written fluency in L2 academic prose. Another empirical study conducted by Iida (2016a) also showed the potential of teaching haiku writing in the L2 classroom. This poetic inquiry, which involved literary, linguistic and content analyses of a collection of ten haiku poems written by a Myanmarese student, documented some discursive identities in relation to his study abroad experience in Japan. This study revealed that haiku writing was an effective literacy and reflective practice and also illustrated the expressive ability of an EFL writer to communicate personal life stories through haiku writing.

In this way, previous research on L2 haiku writing has discussed the effect of writing poems on L2 literacy practice and development, but very few studies have focused on textual features of haiku poetry produced by L2 writers. The particular interest of this current study is to analyse and identify features of spoken language used in English language haiku writing (see also Chapter 2, this volume, for an analysis of spoken language features in fiction). Hence, this study addresses the following two research questions in order to illustrate how written haiku can be a useful way of raising awareness of common features of speech:

RQ1: What are the genre specific features of English language haiku written by Japanese L2 learners?

RQ2: What spoken language features are used in English language haiku produced by Japanese L2 learners?

Methodology

The current study involves a quantitative, corpus-based approach to examine textual and linguistic features of haiku poetry written by Japanese L2 learners. In order to investigate the research questions, the task of haiku writing was incorporated into the first-year college English course and introduced as a form of literacy practice.

Participants

Participants were 204 Japanese engineering students (163 male and 41 female) who registered in the first-year English course over five semesters during the academic years 2011–2014 at a 4-year Japanese public university. Their English language proficiency is 325 points on the TOEIC (Test of English for

International Communication), which is approximately equivalent to 410 points on the TOEFL (Test of English as a Foreign Language) paper-based test. In CEFR (Common European Framework of Reference for Languages) terms, this is A2 level (Council of Europe 2001). All participants were born and grew up in Japan and had studied English for 6 years under the Japanese educational system. Although they had no experience of writing poetry in English, they had experience of reading and studying haiku poetry in elementary school. In other words, haiku poetry was a culturally familiar genre to the participants.

Data Collection

Data were collected over five semesters in the six sections of the English as Liberal Arts course. The investigator designed and taught a fifteen-week unit in order for the participants to create their books of haiku. This project consisted of three stages. The first stage was to review the concept of haiku poetry. The participants reviewed the structure of haiku and the construction of meaning by reading both traditional Japanese haiku and some English poetry written by L2 learners. The second stage involved haiku writing. The participants reflected on their personal life experiences, chose and free wrote ten significant memories in their lives, composed one haiku for each memory, and revised it based on feedback from the investigator and classmates. The last stage was about book design. The participants were assigned to design, create and submit their original, hand-made booklets including a table of contents, an introduction and ten poems. Overall, a total of 2,017 haiku poems in the 204 books of poetry consisting of 25,675 tokens were collected.

Data Analysis

Drawing on methodological guidelines for exploring L2 poetry writing (Hanauer 2010; Iida 2012), data analysis involved computational analyses of the 2017 haiku poems written by the participants. Since each book of poetry was handwritten, it was first transcribed and transformed into an MS Word document. The ten poems in each book were given a single page with exactly the same font and spelling as in the original. In this way, the corpus of 2017 haiku poems including 25,675 tokens was created.

The analyses involved the examination of text size, lexical category, lexical frequency profile and lexical content in the corpus of L2 haiku writing. The computational analyses consisted of five stages and the L2 haiku writing corpus was analysed with different statistical software programs. First, the analysis of text size of the corpus of 2017 poems involved the basic statistics of text-size features including words per poem, lines per poem and words per line. This analysis allowed the computation of average, standard deviation, mean, maximum and minimum of each text-size characteristic.

The second analysis entailed looking at the linguistic categories in the corpus of L2 haiku writing. The Linguistic Inquiry and Word Count (LIWC) 2015 software program (Pennebaker et al. 2015) was used to analyse the linguistic categories. The analysis of linguistic categories was limited to the percentage of function words, pronouns (personal pronouns, first person singular/plural, second person, third person singular/plural and impersonal pronouns), articles, prepositions, auxiliary verbs, adverbs, conjunctions, negations, verbs, adjectives, comparisons, interrogatives, numbers and quantifiers. The analysis of these linguistic features was for establishing the usage of lexical categories in the corpus of L2 haiku writing.

The third analysis involved examining the lexical richness of the poetic texts. The Range software program was used to calculate the Lexical Frequency Profile (Laufer and Nation 1995). This software program divided the corpus into four categories depending on the frequency level: the first 1,000 words, the second 1,000 words, the third 1,000 words and words not in the lists. The outcome of this computational analysis provides the percentage and total words of the corpus depending on each category.

The fourth approach entailed lexical content analysis of the corpus of the 2017 poems using the Concordance software program (Watt 2009). It allowed for the production of a list of high-frequency words, their frequency of usage and their example contexts. In this analysis, the 20 most frequently used content words in the L2 haiku writing corpus were listed. In order to clarify spoken features in the L2 haiku writing corpus, the output from the program was compared to the most frequent 5,000 words used in the Corpus of Contemporary American English (COCA) (Davies 2008).

The last analysis involved the investigation of the usage of verbs, adjectives, contractions and vague expressions in the corpus of 2017 poems. With the concordance software program, all verbs and adjectives that had high-frequency usage over 30 were listed with their frequency of usage and their example contexts, respectively. In order to make these findings more meaningful, the results from the computational analyses were compared to the most frequent 5,000 words used in COCA. In relation to the usage of contraction and vague expressions, all words or phrases were listed with the order of high-frequency usage.

Results

This section presents the results of analysing a total of 25,675 words in the corpus of 2017 haiku poems in terms of the following four features: text size, linguistic categories, word frequency and content words.

Table 5.1 *Text length in L2 haiku writing corpus*

	Words per poem	Lines per poem	Words in first line	Words in second line	Words in third line
Average	12.55	3	3.64	5.12	3.80
SD	1.95	0	0.94	1.14	0.91
Mode	13	3	4	4	4
Max	19	3	6	9	7
Min	7	3	1	2	1

Table 5.1 shows the text size and length. L2 haiku poetry averages 12.55 words with 3.64 words in the first line, 5.12 words in the second line and 3.80 words in the last line. The standard deviation and mode also demonstrate that there is little diversity concerning the text length of each haiku poem in English.

Table 5.2 shows the results of the analysis of the percentage of words used in the total corpus of L2 haiku writing.

First of all, the usage of function words is limited to 37.31 per cent. This means that approximately two-thirds of the total words in the corpus were content words. Secondly, in relation to the usage of personal pronouns, first person pronouns form the most frequent category of all pronouns in L2 haiku poetry (5.68 per cent). On the other hand, the use of second person pronouns accounts for only 0.22 per cent of the total word count and that of third person pronouns is limited to 0.41 per cent of the corpus. This means that, although the participants had chances to compose haiku from different standpoints, they were inclined to write poetry primarily from their own viewpoints. As found in other corpus studies (e.g. O'Keeffe, McCarthy and Carter 2007; Timmis 2015), this result reflects a similarity to spoken data where 'I' and 'you' are more frequently used. Finally, the data present the low-frequency use of conjunctions, comparison, interrogatives, negations and quantifiers. This indicates that the L2 haiku poetry in this corpus is written in a direct manner with very little extensive use of complicated structural and grammatical patterns. This sample haiku poem illustrates this point:

> First snow in my town:
> Silent, cold, white, light morning
> Snowflake on window

Table 5.3 presents the number of words and the percentage of coverage in relation to three frequency levels of words. Of all running words, 79.66 per cent are found in the 1,000 most frequent word list, 89.05 per cent of the words are seen in the 2,000 most frequent words and 90.15 per cent of the words are in the 3,000 most frequent words. This means that high-frequency words are used in

Table 5.2 *Linguistic categories in L2 haiku writing corpus*

Linguistic categories	Percentage of total words in L2 haiku writing corpus
Total function words	37.31
Total pronouns	8.61
Personal pronouns	6.13
1st person singular	4.86
1st person plural	0.82
2nd person pronouns	0.22
3rd person pronouns	0.19
3rd person plural	0.22
Impersonal pronouns	2.47
Prepositions	10.46
Auxiliary verbs	4.96
Adverb	3.68
Conjunctions	4.13
Negations	1.38
Verbs	13.84
Adjectives	8.75
Comparison	1.39
Interrogative	0.57
Numbers	1.41
Quantifiers	1.80

Table 5.3 *Word frequency band and percentage of L2 haiku writing corpus*

Word frequency band	Number of words	Cumulative coverage (%) of whole L2 haiku writing corpus	Individual coverage (%) of whole L2 haiku writing corpus
1st 1,000	20,452	79.66	79.66
2nd 1,000	2,412	89.05	9.39
3rd 1,000	283	90.15	1.10
Not in the lists*	2,528	100	9.85
Total	25,675	-	-

the L2 haiku poetry in this corpus and that the usage of these words is seen as a function of general L2 proficiency. As for the words which are not listed in the 3,000 most frequent words, only 145 words (0.56 per cent) included in 2,528 words come from the participants' L1 use, including the names of places (e.g. *Kyoto*), food (e.g. *tempura*), characters of the game (e.g. *pokemon*) or specific objects (e.g. *tatami*).

Table 5.4 shows the results of a lexical content analysis including the content word, the frequency of usage, the example contexts of usage in the corpus of L2 haiku writing and its comparison to the rank in COCA. There are 20 content words listed from the order of higher-frequency usage.

In this L2 haiku writing corpus, some core themes and concerns of significant life memory seem to be repeatedly addressed across the participants and haiku poetry. For instance, many words and contexts involve social relationship to *school* or *friends*. In addition, there is a strong emotional factor in the corpus. As shown in the examples from the concordance, the words, *heart, like, hot* or *cold* are used as part of expressing each writer's emotions. Furthermore, such content words as *day, time* or *sky* are used to describe the moment or situation in each significant memory. Along with these emerging themes, the frequent use of seasonal references is also found in the list (e.g. *summer, snow*).

From a spoken language aspect, the 13 content words including *day, school, time, big, friends, heart, like, white, people, hard, new, good* and *one* in the L2 haiku writing corpus were found in the most frequent 500 words in COCA. Likewise, the top 19 words in the haiku corpus were seen in the most frequent 2,000 words in the spoken corpus. These findings imply that L2 haiku consists of various content words which people frequently use in spoken contexts.

Table 5.5 presents the list of verbs, the frequency of their usage, the example contexts of their usage in the L2 haiku writing corpus and their comparison to the rank in COCA. The 18 verbs are listed from the order of higher-frequency usage.

The results show some features in relation to the usage of verbs. One of the prominent features in the L2 haiku writing corpus is the high-frequency use of *be*-verb (*is, was, are, am*). Actually, the highest usage of verb is *is* at 393 times and second highest is *was* at 166 times. The second feature is frequent use of action verbs. Such action verbs as *go, went, look, play, run, make* or *come* are found in a list of high-frequency use verbs. The third feature is the usage of present tense in the corpus of L2 haiku writing. Only two words (i.e. *was, went*) are seen in the top 18 verbs in the corpus.

Compared to COCA, the 15 verbs used in the L2 haiku writing corpus (*is, was, go, are, want, went, look, get, have, do, make, come, see, take* and *am*) are found in the most frequent 100 words in the spoken corpus. In addition, the usage of *be*-verb is most frequent in the corpus of L2 haiku writing, which mirrors the same results in the use of spoken language in COCA.

Table 5.6 shows the list of adjectives, the frequency of their usage, the example contexts of their usage in the corpus of L2 haiku writing, and their comparison to the rank in COCA. There are 27 adjectives listed from the order of higher-frequency usage.

Table 5.4 *Lexical content in L2 haiku writing corpus*

Word	Frequency of usage	Example contexts of usage	COCA rank
day	190	A camp with my friends: Delighting us, but feeling A *day* to be short	90
friend	170	On hot, summer court: Hit, chase yellow ball with *friend* Until the sunset	266
school	162	A cherry blossom: Carpet the road to the *school* To make us happy	125
time	152	A hot summer day A three-point shoot, just in *time*: Cheer arises and gives scream	52
hot	136	Running in the rain Body got cold, but heart is *hot* Few way until goal	722
cold	127	Get food poisoning Stomachache terrible in class Break out a *cold* sweat	888
sky	112	Under the dark *sky*: Parade coming to climax Our mood at the peak	1150
summer	112	Not shiny gold prize One more point to the next stage: End of my *summer*	619
first	106	My *first* car driving: My right leg holds a brake pedal Just look at one spot	2064
big	102	My host family Warm, *big*, overwhelming hearts: Like this continent	162
heart	96	My new college life: *Heart* beating fast and wonders What the life looks like	461
like	95	The Waikiki beach: The transparent sea and beach I'd *like* to jump in	74
white	86	*White* cloud and blue sky, Burning sun, romping children. Shouting 'It's ocean!'	302
sea	83	Blue sky and blue *sea*: Learning, hearing, looking and Thinking war . . ., AWFUL	992
people	82	Big wave reach the ground Many *people* escaping: I can't move any more	62

Table 5.4 (*cont.*)

Word	Frequency of usage	Example contexts of usage	COCA rank
hard	79	A day of summer Keep standing everyday: A yellow *hard* worker	439
new	79	Cherry tree blooming: My school uniform change to suits First day of *new* life	88
snow	77	The end of the year A freshly pounded rice cake: It is white like snow	1795
good	75	Clear, warm, and *good* day Run, dance and play tug-of-war: Cheer my classmate loudly	110
one	74	*One* day, all year round Continue to take pictures Day of trajectory	51

Table 5.5 *High-frequency use of verbs in L2 haiku writing corpus and their rank in COCA*

Verb	Frequency of usage	Example contexts of usage	COCA rank
Is	393	I went on the stage In front of hundreds of people My heart *is* pounding	(2)
Was	166	Hear dry and strong sound: Forget time and strum guitar When I *was* 16.	(2)
Go	100	*Go* to pearl Harbor Submarine and battleship are seen Very big and strong	35
Are	89	The graduation Cherry blossoms *are* swirling Everyone is shining	(2)
Want	52	Play rugby in snow Ears turn red and hands don't move I *want* to go home	83
Went	49	I *went* on the stage In front of hundreds of people My heart is pounding	(35)

Table 5.5 (*cont.*)

Verb	Frequency of usage	Example contexts of usage	COCA rank
Look	48	The glaring sunlight Leisurely, slowly walking *Look* and move around there	85
Play	47	*Play* tennis hardly Body and ball hopping: Pleasant sweat drop	200
Run	46	*Run*, muscle training Keep doing hardwork, that's all: For the victory	202
Get	43	Summer part-time work *Get* many taste and much money *Get* more happiness	39
Have	43	I first live alone now Always awkward at housework I don't *have* any time	8
Do	36	Enter the high school For finding my new dream What will I do?	18
Make	36	I waste everyday Meaning to *make* an effort I can't understand	70
Come	35	Gray kitten has *come*: Cat crying wet in the rain I say '*Come* on in'	884
Enjoy	33	In an avenue I can feel the city's vibrant I *enjoy*ed the mood	67
See	33	Driving is very good! I can *see* many landscape A heart becomes bright	63
Take	33	'Can I *take* a shot?' In a Halloween costume I'm in high sprits	88
Am	31	I *am* serious In boat race competition I row very hard	(2)

* Although the corpus of L2 haiku writing presents all *be*-verb forms (*is, am, are, was, were*), they are all categorised into 'be' in COCA.

Table 5.6 *High-frequency use of adjectives in L2 haiku writing corpus and their rank in COCA*

Adjective	Frequency of usage	Example contexts of usage	COCA rank
many	150	Practiced *many* times The attainment of our goal Enjoy our concert	99
hot	140	A white small baseball Hit, catch, throw, chase in *HOT* ground To be champion!	722
cold	136	*Cold* gymnasium But, enjoy play various game: Everyone good smile	888
first	106	My eighteen winter Taking an entrance exam: My *first* trip alone	2064
big	102	A hot summer day; *Big* stadium, spectators Nothing I can hear	162
white	86	Fishing on the boat I fished a catfish first time Red skin and *white* teeth	302
new	79	*New* driver's license: Want to go somewhere Now, Soon By my car with friends	88
hard	78	The concert finished, *Hard* practices finished too, But I was very sad	439
all	77	In the rainy season Staying at home *all* the time My heart never clear	222
good	75	Baseball in hot day: Cicadas chirp in grounds With my *good* friends	2280
high	69	My club activity: Very hard in my *high* school But, much fun for me	141
beautiful	66	Temple in Kyoto History is felt on the place How *beautiful* place!!	995
long	55	Run towards the goal: To achieve my completion Running *long* distance	262
happy	53	School excursion This travel makes me *happy* I want to go again	748

Table 5.6 (*cont.*)

Adjective	Frequency of usage	Example contexts of usage	COCA rank
fast	45	Very hotter day Running a race with form a row Running *fast* and *fast*	1100
old	44	We spend pleasant time 'The meeting time almost here!!' Running the *old* street	152
dark	42	Hot but *DARK* summer Dog lies down no bark no move Tears on our faces	860
warm	42	Cool temperature But my mind is *warm*, happy; Made a lot of friends	1363
last	39	'See you tomorrow' Go home just as usual: *Last* day of high school	130
small	39	It is a *small* room Our big sound vibrate there: The last performance	203
cherry	37	A *cherry* blossom Carpet the road for the school To make us happy	-
clear	36	No cloud and *clear* sky Went Mt. Fuji with my family Look out over town!	564
fun	33	Under clear dry sky Six thousand meters swimming It's painful but *fun*	2100
best	32	Quite, shy, small, girl: The first friend with whom I talk Now, she's my *best* friend	310
shining	30	*Shining* sun hot day Pedal bike towards hell in breeze Hell in mountain	-
strong	30	*Strong* sunlight, 'Hateful!!' Footrace, relay race . . . 'Worthless' 'Oh, no . . . Come On Rain!'	459
every	30	Go home *Every* day Parents have quarrel *Every* day Hear of *Every* day	172

This corpus illustrates some features of adjectives used by Japanese L2 writers. First of all, such emotive adjectives as *beautiful, happy, warm* or *fun* are frequently used in the corpus of L2 haiku writing. This means that L2 writers are inclined to express their feelings. In addition, the usage of evaluative verbs is also found in the corpus. It implies that this group of Japanese L2 writers are inclined to reflect on and evaluate their experiences. Another feature of adjectives is related to temperature. Such words as *hot, cold* and *warm* seem to be used as part of expressing each writer's emotion or describing a particular moment in their significant moments. From a different viewpoint, an interesting feature found in this corpus is that the Japanese L2 writers tend to use an antonym of a specific word. For example, a pair of adjectives, *cold–hot, first–last, big–small* or *new–old* are frequently used in L2 haiku writing.

With comparison to spoken data, 14 adjectives are found in the most frequent 500 words and 20 are seen in the most frequent 1,000 words in COCA. Only two words (i.e. *cherry, shining*) in the top 27 adjectives in the L2 haiku writing corpus are not shown in the list of the most frequent 5,000 words in the spoken corpus. This indicates that Japanese L2 writers are inclined to use several basic and common adjectives which were often used in spoken contexts.

Table 5.7 presents the list of contractions, the frequency of their usage and the example contexts of their usage. A total of 22 contraction forms are seen in the L2 haiku writing corpus.

Although the use of contractions is limited among the participants, some phrases including *it's, don't, can't, I'm* or *let's* are frequently used in this corpus. In addition, the results show that the use of contraction is categorised into four types: subject-verb contractions (e.g. *It's, I'm, that's* or *I'll*), negative contractions (*don't, can't, didn't* or *couldn't*), wh-words contractions (e.g. *who's, where'll* or *what'll*) and 'let us' contractions (e.g. *let's*).

Table 5.8 presents the list of vague language, the frequency of its usage and the example contexts of its usage. Only nine words or phrases related to vague language are found in the L2 haiku writing corpus.

The most frequently used phrase is *a lot of*. Likewise, the use of *lots of* is not as high as *a lot of*, but it is seen seven times in the corpus. Another feature is the usage of *thing* and *things*. The use of *thing(s)* is found 32 times in the corpus. This reflects similar tendencies to those found in native-speaker spoken corpora (see also Chapter 2, this volume, for a discussion of vague language in literary dialogues). In addition, this corpus illustrates the use of such vague language as *I think, about, and so on*, or *feel like* among the participants, but it is not frequently used. These findings show that some Japanese L2 writers in this group are inclined to express their experiences less directly and leave ambiguity in describing each significant moment.

Table 5.7 *High-frequency use of contraction in L2 haiku writing corpus*

Contraction form	Frequency of usage	Example contexts of usage
it's	74	At last, reached the top But *it's* far to reach the stars: Journey never ends
don't	54	Stand around people '*Don't* talk fast and don't forget': Now it's time for speech
can't	42	My first time cooking: Savory smell from the pot I *can't* wait for eat
I'm	29	New experience New things to see on the ship *I'm* so excited
let's	19	Practice together: You are final competitor *Let's* fight full power
that's	9	Run, Muscle training Keep doing hardwork, *that's* all: For the victory
didn't	5	Last ball fall a floor We are defeated in battle *Didn't* forget moment
couldn't	4	Clearing of the festival They kick and hit our mascot I *couldn't* do anything
I'll	3	Summer vacation Practice hard, gag and laughing *I'll* never forget
won't	3	Parting with my friends: I look up when I walk So the tears *won't* fall
isn't	3	I'm thinking this way Only given to humans with music *Isn't* it privilege
you're	2	Hot night of summer: The flowers shining on a sky But, *you're* shining more
she's	2	Quite, shy, small, girl: The first friend with whom I talk Now, *she's* my best friend
they're	2	'Are you ready guys?' *They're* tired of waiting for me: Let's take the first step!
wasn't	2	The cold weather day Second robot convention *Wasn't* a tight game

Table 5.7 (*cont.*)

Contraction form	Frequency of usage	Example contexts of usage
there's	1	*There's* discovery; It has not gone there Fun and fun
gonna	1	A giant parfait Keep eating, but cold, sweet, full 'Are we *gonna* eat more?'
I'd	1	One day, I know that name *I'd* learn by chance look at TV: It name is 'Dubstep'
I've	1	I went home by bicycle I was too fast to turn corner *I've* collide with a wall
who's	1	Critter-clatter *Who's* jigging one's knees? The beginning tragedy.
where'll	1	White scenery pass: Where does the melting snow go? *Where'll* our future go?
what'll	1	'*What'll* I do today?' I am thinking about it: 'Oh, look at the time!!'

Table 5.8 *Frequency of usage of vague language in L2 haiku writing corpus*

Word/Phrase	Frequency of usage	Example contexts of usage
a lot of	21	Heartbeat very fast Let's make *a lot of* new friends Say! How do you do?
thing	16	Happy *thing*, hard *thing* Three years passed in no time Everything is wealth
things	16	To ride ferris wheel View from the top, all *things* small: It's short and short time
lots of	7	*Lots of* things to do Cooking, cleaning and laundry: But I don't hate them!!
I think	5	My heart is cold *I think* family is warm I live by my self
about	1	Dance in Festival: *About* thousand people come to see Everybody smiling

Table 5.8 (*cont.*)

Word/Phrase	Frequency of usage	Example contexts of usage
and so on	1	In the first day,
		The first place, people . . . *and so on*
		My heart was pounding
feel like	1	Practice every day
		At last I get Shodan*
		I *feel like* grow up

* *Shodan* (sho-dan) means the certificate of the first level which assesses someone's specific talent or skills such as Japanese martial arts (judo, kendo) or calligraphy.

Discussion

Drawing on methodological approaches for analysing poetic texts produced by L2 writers (Hanauer 2010; Iida 2012), the current study has addressed the two research questions:

RQ1: What are the genre-specific features of English language haiku written by Japanese L2 learners?

RQ2: What spoken language features are used in English language haiku produced by Japanese L2 learners?

In relation to the first research question, the data show that English language haiku comprises very short texts that use high-frequency vocabulary items in English language. The average text length was 12.55 words, 3.6 words in the first line, 5.1 words in the second line and 3.8 words in the last line. Also, approximately 90 per cent of the vocabulary items were found in the 2,000 most frequently used words in the English language. The L2 haiku writing corpus included some specific Japanese words (e.g. *pokemon, Kyoto, tatami*), but the participants' L1 usage was limited to only 0.6 per cent. The results suggest that this group of Japanese L2 writers can handle the task of composing haiku in English as a foreign language.

The data also illustrate some specific styles of English language haiku. The usage of first person pronouns and very little use of conjunctions, comparisons, interrogatives, negations and quantifiers means that English haiku is written primarily from each writer's personal viewpoint without an extensive range of grammatical and rhetorical items. The use of affective words indicates that English language haiku is based on L2 writers' emotional responses to their personal experiences. This is seen from the usage of content words, verbs and adjectives in the L2 haiku writing corpus. For example, such emotive words as *like, enjoy, happy, hard, fun* or *pleasant* were used to express their emotional reactions to each memory. As shown in the examples in the concordance, the words, *heart, hot, cold* and *warm* were used as part of expressing their emotional insight into their experiences (see Hanauer 2010; Pennebaker et al. 2015). This finding suggests that even low-level Japanese L2 writers have the ability to express themselves through haiku writing in the target language. It provides empirical support that poetry writing is a feasible and manageable task to different groups of L2 learners including advanced ESL learners (Hanauer 2010), low-intermediate EFL learners (Iida 2012, 2016a, 2016b) and even lower level.

With regard to the second research question, the results of computational analyses show several features of spoken language in the corpus of L2 haiku writing. As discussed above, almost 90 per cent of lexical items used in the L2 haiku writing corpus were seen in the 2,000 most frequently used words listed in General Service List (GSL), indicating that English language haiku consisted of the texts which native speakers of English use in their daily life and very few academic terms were used. More specifically, a prominent feature of spoken language was the usage of certain verbs. As shown in a study by Biber and Conrad (2010), almost 45 per cent of occurrences of lexical verbs in conversation came from the following 12 verbs, *say, get, go, know, think, see, make, come, take, want, give* and *mean*. The data in the L2 haiku writing corpus also illustrated the same tendency: seven verbs, *go (went), want, get, make, come, see* and *take* found in the top 18 verbs in the corpus; and the above 12 verbs accounted for 17.8 per cent of the occurrences of all lexical verbs (572 out of 3,215 verbs). Another principal feature of spoken language was seen in the usage of adjectives among this group of Japanese L2 writers. In the spoken context, the most common predicative adjectives used in conversation are evaluative and emotive (Biber et al. 1999; Timmis 2015). The current study also mirrors this perspective and adjectives such as *good, better, beautiful, happy, warm* and *fun* were frequently used in English language haiku writing. This finding provides evidence, from a spoken language aspect, that an English language haiku is a text which represents each writer's emotional voice reflecting on both internal and external worlds of human individual (Iida 2008, 2010).

In addition to the use of certain verbs and adjectives, this group of Japanese L2 writers tended to use contractions and vague language in English language haiku. This usage is limited to only 260 times for contractions and 68 times for vague language in the corpus, but this seems to be attributed to the structure of haiku poetry. Haiku consists of 5–7–5 syllable format and L2 writers are expected to follow this structural rule in composing poetry. In such a situation, using a contraction form not only helps them to adjust a poem into its poetic structure but also allows them to put a one-syllable word in the text in order to better express themselves. The use of contractions may be one useful technique to compose haiku in English among the Japanese L2 writers. Using vague language may also be due to the nature of haiku poetry.

Traditionally, haiku poetry leaves ambiguity by using metaphors or indirect phrases (Higginson 1985; Tweedie and Kolitsky 2002; Iida 2008), and a good haiku poem is considered as the one which 'should leave readers wondering' in the process of interpreting the text (Blasko and Merski 1998: 40). This core nature of composing haiku, 'reader-centredness' or 'multiple interpretations', might provide these Japanese L2 writers with linguistic choices to use such vague expressions in their English language haiku. In other words, the task of composing haiku in the target language could probably enable the Japanese students to transfer their L1 rhetorical and generic knowledge to their L2 writing. This perspective could lead to an alternative approach to L2 learning. In general, Japanese EFL students tend to think that they must always be accurate and correct when speaking and writing in the target language, but poetry writing could allow them to focus more on meaning than forms of language in the language learning process (Iida 2016a). In such a literacy practice, their attention to L2 learning would probably shift from 'accuracy' of forms to 'appropriateness' to meaning in English. Poetry writing can therefore allow students to generate 'meaningful' output by negotiating and articulating their own emotional voice through the practical use of language.

In this way, the overall analyses of the corpus of 2017 poems written by Japanese L2 learners allow for the identification of genre-specific features of English language haiku writing. In this study, there is only limited data that characterise haiku poetry written by L2 learners. It was also conducted with a specific group of Japanese L2 learners at one academic institution (i.e. low-level students). However, even when considering these limitations, this study provides more detailed and specific linguistic features of English language haiku than Iida's (2012) study in that it adds some aspects of spoken language to the general description of haiku poetry. More broadly, it also illustrates the ability of L2 writers to express their own emotional insight into personally significant life experiences in haiku writing.

Conclusion

The current study has examined genre-specific features of English language haiku written by Japanese L2 learners. The overall analyses of the corpus of 2017 haiku poetry have identified its linguistic features: English language haiku is a short, descriptive text which reflects each writer's emotional response to his or her significant and meaningful life experience. This study has also found some spoken language features in English language haiku writing, including the twelve verbs most frequently used in spoken discourse, evaluative and emotive adjectives, contractions and vague language. This indicates that, through the teaching of haiku writing, teachers could draw L2 learners' attention to typical spoken forms. Using such spoken language in a written discourse is probably attributed to the genre of haiku poetry: using a specific number of syllables, reader-centredness and leaving ambiguity in the text. These features can provide L2 writers with various linguistic and literary choices and enable them to use spoken language features in the process of constructing meaning and producing haiku. In other words, the task of composing haiku has great potential for L2 learners in raising awareness of specific spoken forms.

L2 poetry writing is still an unusual task (Chamcharatsri 2013; Iida 2016b) and may be challenging for EFL students. As discussed in this chapter, however, the task of haiku writing has great potential to transform the EFL classroom into a place where L2 learners can reflect on their past experiences, negotiate meaning, express their own voice, raise awareness of spoken forms and ultimately consider the meaning of life through English language learning. Composing haiku can be an effective literacy practice to make language learning more meaningful and practical than traditional L2 learning approaches which target only the acquisition of L2 linguistic knowledge (e.g. the accurate use of grammar and the correct form of lexical items) in the EFL classroom. Haiku poetry is also relatively quick for EFL students to compose in English and it is very achievable in class.

References

Biber, D. and Conrad, S. 2010. 'Corpus linguistics and grammar teaching'. Available at: longmanhomeusa.com/content/pl_biber_conrad_monograph5_lo.pdf   (Accessed 1 June 2018).

Biber, D., Johansson, S., Leech, G., Conrad, S. and Finegan, E. 1999. *Longman Grammar of Spoken and Written English*. Harlow: Longman.

Blasko, D. G. and Merski, D. W. 1998. 'Haiku poetry and metaphorical thought: An invention to interdisciplinary study', *Creativity Research Journal* 11(1): 39–46.

Chamcharatsri, P. B. 2013. 'Poetry writing to express love in Thai and in English: A second language (L2) writing perspective', *International Journal of Innovation in English Language Teaching* 2(2): 142–157.

Council of Europe. 2001. *Common European Framework of Reference for Languages: Learning, Teaching, Assessment*. Cambridge: Cambridge University Press.

Davies, M. 2008. *The Corpus of Contemporary American English (COCA): 560 million words, 1990–Present*. Available at: http://corpus.byu.edu/coca (Accessed 15 October 2018).

Hanauer, D. I. 2003. 'Multicultural moments in poetry: The importance of the unique', *Canadian Modern Language Review* 60(1): 27–54.

2010. *Poetry as Research: Exploring Second Language Poetry Writing*. Amsterdam: John Benjamins.

2011. 'The scientific study of poetic writing', *Scientific Study of Literature* 1(1): 79–87. doi:10.1075/ssol.1.1.08han

2012. 'Meaningful literacy: Writing poetry in the language classroom', *Language Teaching* 45(1): 105–115. doi:10.1017/S0261444810000522

Hanauer, D. I. and Liao, F. 2016. 'ESL students' perceptions of creative and academic writing', in Burke, M., Olivia, F. and Zyngier, S. (eds.), *Scientific Approaches to Literature in Learning Environments*. Amsterdam: John Benjamins, 213–226.

Iida, A. 2008. 'Poetry writing as expressive pedagogy in EFL contexts: Identifying possible assessment tools for haiku poetry in EFL freshman college writing', *Assessing Writing* 13(3): 171–179. doi:10.1016/j.asw.2008.10.001

2010. 'Developing voice by composing haiku: A social-expressivist framework for teaching haiku writing in EFL contexts', *English Teaching Forum* 48(1): 28–34

2012. 'The value of poetry writing: Cross-genre literacy development in a second language', *Scientific Study of Literature* 2(1): 60–82. doi:10.1075/ssol2.1.04iid

2016a. 'Poetic identity in second language writing: Exploring an EFL learner's study abroad experience', *Eurasian Journal of Applied Linguistics* 2(1): 1–14.

2016b. 'Exploring earthquake experiences: A study of second language learners' ability to express and communicate deeply traumatic events in poetic form', *System* 57(1): 120–133. doi:10.1076/j.system.2016.02.004

2017a. 'Expressing voice in a foreign language: Multiwriting haiku pedagogy in the EFL context', *TEFLIN Journal* 28(2): 260–276. doi:10.15639/teflinjournal.v28i2/260–276

2017b. 'Voicing in second language poetry writing: Implications to English as Liberal Arts Education in the Japanese University Context', in *The 6th JAILA Annual Conference Proceedings*. Available at: http://jaila.org/activity/taikai20170218/proceedings20170218/jaila-proc-006-05-20170218.pdf (Accessed 8 May 2018).

2018. 'Living in darkness at the time of the Great East Japan Earthquake: A poetic-narrative autoethnography', *Qualitative Inquiry* 24(4): 270–280. doi:10.1177/1077800417745917

Laufer, B. and Nation, P. 1995. 'Vocabulary size and use: Lexical richness in L2 written productions', *Applied Linguistics* 16(3): 307–322.

Higginson, W. J. 1985. *The Haiku Handbook: How to Write, Share, and Teach Haiku*. Tokyo: Kodansha International.

O'Keeffe, A., McCarthy, M. and Carter, R. 2007. *From Corpus to Classroom*. Cambridge: Cambridge University Press.

Pennebaker, J. W., Chang, C. K., Ireland, M., Gonzales, A. and Booth, R. 2015. *The Development and Psychometric Properties of LIWC 2015*. Austin, TX: IWLC.

Sky Hiltunen, S. M. 2005. 'Country Haiku from Finland: Haiku meditation therapy for self-healing', *Journal of Poetry Therapy* 18(2): 85–95.

Stokely, S. 2000. *Haiku and Beyond: A Study of Japanese Literature*. El Alma de la Raza Series, Denver Public Schools. Available at: http://etls.dpsk12.org/documents/Alma/units/HaikuandBeyond.pdf (Accessed 10 June 2018).

Timmis, I. 2015. *Corpus Linguistics for ELT: Research and Practice*. London: Routledge.

Tweedie, S. and Kolitsky, M. A. 2002. '3-D haiku: A new way to teach a traditional form', *The English Journal* 91(3): 84–88.

Watt, R. J. C. 2009. Concordance version 3.3 [computer software]. Dundee.

NOTES

1. A seasonal reference is not always shown in English language haiku.
2. A cutting word which can be seen as either an actual word or an exclamation mark including a colon or semi-colon has a specific rhetorical function: it is to divide one haiku into two parts; 'this creates an imaginative distance, although both sections remain, to some degree, independent of each other' (Iida 2010: 29).

6 Screenplays as a Pedagogical Medium for Cultivating EFL Learners' Metapragmatic Awareness of Speech Acts in Spoken English

Yan Zhao and Jiangfeng Liu

This chapter reports a thirteen-week action research project that was conducted with sixty-seven first-year non-English-major students taking a mandatory general English course in a Chinese state university. Using English professional screenplays as the source of authentic conversations, we designed and implemented an intervention that enabled the English as a Foreign Language (EFL) students to consider how the realisation of a speech act is mediated by a range of contextual factors. We achieved this by: (1) selecting screenplay extracts that reflect varied communication situations, (2) using conversation analysis and Hymes' (1974) SPEAKING model as guiding frameworks, (3) combining awareness-raising tasks with explicit instruction and (4) setting up weekly group work. From two iterative cycles of research, the following qualitative data were collected: (1) two open-ended questionnaires, (2) audio recordings of classroom interaction, (3) our own observation and reflective notes and (4) the conversations and self-reflection created by the students each week. The results show that English screenplays helped to develop the Chinese EFL students' metapragmatic awareness by providing rich conversational, social and literary contexts to a speech act. The screenplays also enabled the students' resourcefulness as social actors, fans of pop culture or creative individuals in their interpretation and formulation of varied second language (L2) speech acts. This holds implications particularly for EFL teachers in challenging circumstances such as the one where this study took place: large class sizes, limited class time and students having only limited access to naturally occurring English conversations. The findings also hold implications for

118

the establishment of an interactional learning space facilitated by English screenplays and teacher scaffolding.

Introduction

Pedagogy related to teaching the spoken pragmatics of English in Chinese EFL classrooms often focuses on the *form* of language usage which is directly matched to distinct *functions* in talk (Ren and Han 2016) such as the creation of polite or formal requests. However, little explanation is provided as for how such form–function mappings are shaped by contextual detail such as 'the identities of the speakers, their relationship to each other, or their location' (McConachy 2009: 118). Without such explanations, EFL students might see the form–function mappings as absolute rules – that is, 'correct choice' – rather than choices to be made by speakers based on their appraisal of the context, in other words, 'appropriate choice' (McCarthy and McCarten 2018: 17). This precisely illustrates the importance of 'metapragmatic' knowledge to spoken language (Bublitz and Hübler 2007), which can be briefly defined as the knowledge of *how* linguistic forms and conversational structure signal speaker motives or reveal distinguishing features of the context surrounding a conversation. By teaching metapragmatic knowledge, we can raise EFL learners' awareness of the 'different aspects of social contexts', 'personal identities' and 'broader language ideologies' (van Compernolle and Kinginger 2013: 284) that underlie a locally constructed second language (L2) conversation.

The above goal can sound daunting to EFL teachers especially when naturally occurring English conversations that are comprehensible and interesting to the students are scarce. In addition, in our own context of China, a firewall constrains students' access to foreign websites (unless through a VPN). This consequently limits the kind of critical self-study activities in which students can independently seek and examine authentic English spoken materials on the Internet. Furthermore, regarding non-English-major EFL courses in Chinese universities, large class sizes can be 'the norm' (Chen and Goh 2010: 339); instruction time is often 'limited' (Chen and Goh 2010: 337); and students can be 'accustomed to a teacher-centred way of learning' (Chen and Goh 2010: 342). In our case, weekly class time that can be devoted exclusively to spoken English would not exceed 45 minutes. To counterbalance the constraints mentioned above, we deployed English professional screenplays as a feasible pedagogical tool to raise Chinese students' metapragmatic awareness of spoken English. Echoing the view of Baker (2016: 71–72), we do not see screenplays as 'a working document', but as 'finished creative works in their own right', and hence they 'can be understood as literature'. They are, in essence, a form of play, whether they are adapted from literary works or not and so fit the of literature given in this book (see Chapter 1). Screenplays as a source of authentic English provide rich and engaging illustrations of varied speech acts embedded in context, hence showing how the realisation of a speech act is underpinned by the speaker's metapragmatic awareness of the 'social meanings' (Henery 2015) engendered.

This chapter presents our 13-week-long action research project. In action research, the teacher researchers, after identifying an immediate problem in their classrooms, plan and execute pedagogical solutions (McNiff 2013) so as to seek 'answers in their own classrooms' (Ellis 2008: 689). Subsequently, through the teacher researchers' rigorous observation made in the teaching processes and their ensuing reflection on the feedback received, they design and initiate an improved 'action-reflection cycle of planning, acting, observing and reflecting' (McNiff 2013: 56). The strength of action research closely fits our primary goal. Firstly, since the pedagogical potential of L2 screenplays in a spoken class has not been much explored, our action research is exploratory in nature. Our priority is not to quantitatively test the effects of different instructional methods on the students, but to improve our teaching practices *through* and *during* this action research project by closely monitoring every step in the procedure. This enables us to 'bring about lasting benefit to the ongoing process itself rather than to some future occasion' (Cohen and Manion 1994: 192). We envisioned that our findings, on the one hand, would provide critical insights into distinctive learning moments when the students react to the interventions in ways that are informative to L2 practitioners. On the other hand, we hope our findings could contribute to the methodology and research frame for utilising English screenplays as a critical tool to raise EFL students' metapragmatic awareness.

To situate our research – especially to justify the integrated sociolinguistic framework that we have designed to raise EFL learners' metapragmatic awareness and to illuminate the rationale behind our task procedures – it is necessary to review previous studies. Subsequently in the methodology section, the specific task procedures and the adjustments that we had made to our teaching practices during this action research are explicated. This is then followed by our discussion of the findings, which illustrate how English screenplays helped the EFL students develop metapragmatic awareness in empowering ways.

Previous Research

Although the 'practice of using literature in ELT is far from being a novelty' (Lima 2018: 226; Chapter 1, this volume), there is only a small collection of empirical studies that examine how literary texts can be used to teach pragmatics in EFL classes where the focus is on speaking. These studies make use of the interaction between stylistics and pragmatics (Sukhina 2011; Warner 2012; Lambrou 2015). That is, when interpreting a dialogue – either one created in literature or one occurring naturally in daily life – we can always trace the subtexts of the utterances and examine how these can be derived from linguistic, interactional or contextual detail. There is a small but growing collection of L2 classroom-based studies that have used films or soap operas as audiovisual resources to cultivate learners' awareness of the pragmatics of spoken language (Washburn 2001; Kambara 2011; Fernández-Guerra 2013; Abrams 2014, 2016; Tajeddin and Pezeshki 2014; Kaiser and Shibahara 2014; Bruti 2016). These studies illustrate the validity of using movie/TV dialogues to raise L2 learners' sensitivity to 'the relationship between language and its social implementation' (Abrams 2014: 59). In our action research, screenplays are proposed as an alternative to filmic audiovisual input. We acknowledge that audiovisual input hones language learners' listening skills and such input draws learners' attention to paralinguistic features (see Chapter 4, this volume, for a study using dramatised literature on television). On the other hand, screenplays foreground a written representation of an extended interaction, including visual description of gestures, movements and the setting. This particularly suits our teaching context where the EFL students' listening skills could greatly hinder their interpretation of a dialogue and their motivation to have their metapragmatic awareness enhanced.

Metapragmatic awareness entails increasing students' pragmalinguistic and sociopragmatic knowledge (Thomas 1995; Li and Gao 2017). As summarised by Ishihara and Cohen (2010: 43), 'sociopragmatics deals with sociocultural norms for linguistic behaviour in a given context while pragmalinguistics refers to the actual language forms used to convey the intended meaning'. Although film/TV dialogues are scripted, research has shown that such dialogues can provide reliable models of speech acts particularly from a pragmalinguistic perspective (Rose 2001; Tatsuki and Nishizawa 2005; Fernández-Guerra 2008; Jones and Horak 2014; Nuzzo 2015). Regarding sociopragmatics, film/TV dialogues, however, are found to exhibit some deviations from naturally occurring conversations within the realisation patterns of speech acts such as compliments and compliment responses (Rose 2001; Tatsuki and Nishizawa 2005). This can be attributed to diversified social norms or scenes depicted in films/on TV soap operas and to their inherent goal of creating dramatic tension. As eloquently explained by Abrams (2016: 26), 'a drama depicting 18th century England would illustrate/depict different social roles and pragmatic functions than a modern sitcom full of colloquial banter among young people'. Nonetheless, sociopragmatics deviations can be reduced by L2 teachers' judicious selection of film/TV resources.

Through a literary medium, our action research aims to add to the success recorded in L2 instructional studies on the teaching of speech acts by addressing the following two operational issues which have not received sufficient attention yet: (1) how to teach a variety of speech acts under a holistic sociolinguistic framework; and (2) how to integrate implicit awareness-raising activities with explicit instruction so as to cultivate learners' self-agency while raising their metapragmatic awareness of the target spoken language. These will be discussed below.

Firstly, many L2 pragmatics instructional studies target one or two specific speech acts which is/are deemed crucial to L2 learners achieving effective communication in a specific context. This could be a study abroad context where ESL students' L2 socialisation impacts on their welfare (Halenko and Jones 2011, 2017), or an English-mediated learning context (Taguchi et al. 2015) and the context of ESL/EAP group discussions (Hüttner 2014; Cheng 2016) where L2 students' access to learning resources and their 'power to impose reception' (Bourdieu 1977: 75) are at stake. Different from the above ESL situations, in a typical Chinese university EFL classroom like ours, students often do not have an immediate need to use spoken English that can critically impact on their social networking or academic advancement. However, metapragmatic awareness in spoken language is critically linked to communicative competence (Ren and Han 2016). The previously published draft of the *Guidelines on College English Teaching* in China indeed highlights the objective 'to enhance Chinese students' cross-cultural awareness and communicative competence ... so that they can effectively use English in their studies, daily lives, social interactions and future careers' (Wang 2016: 5). The key question is: how can we mediate between the lack of immediate demands on many Chinese EFL learners to 'produce pragmatically appropriate language in interactions' (Halenko and Jones 2011: 240) and the long-term importance of acquiring metapragmatic awareness and hence communicative competence?

As one solution, we propose that course materials on teaching the pragmatics of spoken English should cover 'a wide enough range of speech acts' (McConachy and Hata 2013: 295) to enable learners to see themselves as discerning, legitimate and empowered EFL speakers. Furthermore, we need to teach speech acts within manageable sociolinguistic frameworks. Taguchi (2011: 296) highlighted the necessity of devising an integrated instructional framework that no longer treats 'pragmatic competence as a constellation of bits of isolated pragmatic features that have to be taught independently from one another'. Without such a framework, L2 students' motivation and engagement in a spoken class is likely to decrease if they see the course predominated by instruction of a constellation of pragmatic rules when such rules have little bearing on their existing knowledge as conversationalists (in their L1) or discerning social participants, that is, a lack of 'learner authenti-cation' (McCarthy and McCarten 2018: 7). Hence, we propose to teach speech acts under conversational and contextual frameworks. First of all, conversation analysis (CA) concepts have been deployed in pedagogical interventions made in L2 spoken classes to raise learners' awareness of hidden meanings or interactional problems beneath a conversation (Barraja-Rohan 1997, 2011; Sayer 2005; Huth and Taleghani-Nikazm 2006; Wong and Waring 2010; Waring 2013; Filipi and Barraja-Rohan 2015; Nicholas 2015). For example, Barraja-Rohan introduced a number of CA concepts to her ESL students, such as 'response tokens', 'repair mechanism' or 'turn-taking sys-tem' (2011: 489) and managed to 'rais[e] [the] students' awareness of both the mechanisms and norms of spoken interaction' and to eventually transform the students into 'analysts of conversation and more effective conversation-alists' (p. 479). Apart from examining speech acts through CA concepts, McConachy suggests that a sociocultural framework is needed to guide EFL learners to actively evaluate 'a range of sociocultural variables' surrounding a conversation (2009: 117). A similar view is embraced by Bella, Sifianou and Tzanne (2015). They used Brown and Levinson's (1987) politeness model as a guiding framework to design classroom activities that stimulated L2 lear-ners to interrogate the sociocultural norms behind (im)politeness in conversa-tion, along the parameters of 'social power, distance and level of imposition' (Bella et al. 2015: 35). Although many L2 pragmatics instructional studies include explicit sociopragmatic instruction, much fewer of them have used specific frameworks to inform the design of such instruction. Apart from Brown and Levinson's politeness model mentioned above, McConachy pro-poses that Hymes' (1974) SPEAKING model – including Setting, Participants, Ends, Act sequence, Key, Instrumentalities, Norms and Genres – allows teachers to 'develop analytical questions for learners' (2009: 116). In another classroom study, Abrams (2016: 26) asked the students to conduct 'ethnographic analyses' of film scenes and dialogues. She used Hymes' (1972) 'Communicative Events' as the model to guide beginning L2 learners to critically analyse how pragmatic features are embodied in 'the local contextualization of interaction' (Abrams 2016: 26).

As for the second operational issue, we explore ways to complement explicit metapragmatic instruction with awareness-raising activities. It has been widely argued that explicit instruction is more effective than implicit approaches alone in enhancing EFL learners' metapragmatic knowledge (Halenko and Jones 2011; Nguyen et al. 2012; Nicholas 2015; Talandis Jr and Stout 2015; Cheng 2016; Ren and Han 2016; van Compernolle et al. 2016). On the other hand, implicit teaching approaches – which 'withhold explanation but provide input and practice opportunities where learners can develop implicit understanding of pragmatic forms and their uses' (Taguchi 2011: 291) – might play a stronger role in letting students reflect on their prior conversation experience in either their L1 or their L2 and to explore personal knowledge (Takahashi 2010; Abrams 2016). Takahashi (2010: 137), based on her extensive review of studies on L2 pragmatic intervention, concludes that explicit metapragmatic teaching 'does not allow learners to acquire substantial confidence in performing target speech acts'. Meanwhile, the potential of implicit intervention in nurturing agentive EFL speakers was observed by Abrams who stated that 'implicit instruction was more beneficial for pragmatic production on open-ended dialog tasks' (2016: 24). It has been suggested that L2 pragmatic learning is closely related to L2 students' cultural identities and motivation to align with target language's sociopragmatic conventions (Takahashi 2010; Nguyen et al. 2012; Abrams 2016). Hence, it is necessary for L2 teachers to acknowledge and utilise students' existing knowledge repertoire, students' 'interactional skills from their L1' (Abrams 2016: 25), their 'personal interactional preferences' and ability to observe and adapt (p. 39). The above can be achieved by integrating into teaching methods implicit approaches and inductive activities that acknowledge L2 learners' own 'informed choices' (Abrams 2016: 25) and accommodate 'individual variation' as in 'real-world interactions' (p. 39). In this action research, we combined explicit and implicit approaches, aiming to cultivate Chinese EFL students' metapragmatic awareness even when their pragmalinguistic knowledge was limited or their alignment with L2 socio-pragmatic knowledge varied.

Our action research was designed to answer the following research question:

RQ1: How can English screenplays be used to develop lower-intermediate Chinese EFL students' metapragmatic awareness in spoken English?

More specifically,

RQ2: How can English screenplays be used to promote the students' attention to both pragmalinguistic forms and sociopragmatic factors in their interpretation and formulation of varied speech acts?

Methodology

Context and Participants

Sixty-seven first-year non-English-major Chinese EFL students (21 males, 46 females) – mostly around 20 years old – participated in this action research from March to June in the 2017–2018 academic year. The students came from two academic disciplines: business management and finance. They were study-ing at a state university in China and their average English proficiency can be described as a low B1 using the Common European Framework of Reference for Languages (Council of Europe 2001). Our action research project was conducted in a compulsory general English course – the only English course the students were taking in the university. Before this project was initiated, the second author had already taught these students for one term. The two authors then designed this action research together, and the first author delivered the teaching component in this project, which lasted 45 minutes per week, constituting a quarter of the students' weekly English class time. The second author was a non-participant observer during these sessions (twelve altogether spanning thirteen weeks).

The Intervention

According to Burns (2005), an action research project includes multiple cycles of intervention. Within each cycle, 'systematic collection of data' is followed by 'analysis of what is revealed by the data, and reflection on the implications of the findings' (Burns 2005: 59). Consequently, 'normal pedagogical practices' become 'investigative tools' (Allwright 2003: 127). In this study, we conducted two cycles of investigation and reflection, each lasting six weeks, with one week in between where we reflected on the first cycle and discussed adjustments to be made to the second cycle.

We collected the following four types of qualitative data. Firstly, two open-ended questionnaires (Appendix 6A) were administered, each upon the respective completion of the two cycles (week six and week thirteen). We elicited from individual students their reflection on the learning experience and sought their feedback. Secondly, the second author took class observation notes while the first author (the teacher) took reflective notes soon after each class. Thirdly, with the consent of the students, audio recordings were made of each class to capture any interaction between the teacher and the students. Fourthly, weekly group homework (sixteen groups altogether, about four students per group) – that consisted in a collaboratively written dialogue, an audio recording of the group performing the dialogue and the group's written self-reflection on major problems encountered or key decisions made during the dialogue creation process – was assigned and collected in order to monitor the students' ongoing development.

Initially, the teacher used a mixture of English and Chinese when providing instruction or feedback; meanwhile the students were expected to use English whenever they could. However, we soon noticed that the L2 created a barrier when the students were required to share their metapragmatic observation in class. A few students with good spoken English started to speak much more while 'the masses' remained shy and whispered short responses. Also, when using the L2, students habitually prioritised the form of their contribution (e.g. the fluency of their utterances) rather than any critical or novel insight that they could offer. We soon decided that from week two Chinese would be the primary language for communication in the classroom when discussing metapragmatic observations. This adjustment saved us precious class time while also allowing us to enhance the complexity of the metapragmatic discussions in class. By using Chinese in this way, the teacher put herself on a more equal footing with the students and managed to cultivate a community of collaborative analysts. The students gradually became more inclined to draw from their personal knowledge as experienced L1 interlocutors to scaffold or even problematise their examination of pragmatic features in an L2 dialogue.

When transcribing the audio recordings of classroom interactions, we focused on the parts where extensive interactions happened between the teacher and individual students. We transcribed these parts verbatim in their original renderings upon which ensuing analysis was conducted. Translation from Chinese to English was only made when the segment was selected as an example to be presented in this chapter. For the two open-ended individual questionnaires and the weekly group self-reflection piece, students were given the choice of writing either in Chinese or in English. They chose Chinese most of the time. Data collection and data analysis were conducted at the same time. Through iterative data analysis processes, we examined students' sociopragmatic or pragmalinguistic reasoning and performance in relation to the targets of the week (Appendix 6B), especially how students' sociopragmatic and pragmalinguistic manifestations were stimulated or scaffolded by their deliberation on aspects of the chosen L2 screenplays (e.g. characterisation, dramatic tension or character relationship).

Study Design and Teaching Methodology

We applied two frameworks to designing the week-by-week syllabi in Cycles One and Two (Appendix 6B): (1) key CA notions; and (2) Hymes' (1974) SPEAKING model. Hymes developed the SPEAKING model to highlight the need to analyse conversations 'as a social, rather than linguistic, entity' (1974: 47). He proposed a set of fundamental sociocultural 'Components of Speech' which underlie the production and interpretation of any conversation (Hymes 1974: 53–62). Subsequently, Hymes created the 'mnemonic code word' SPEAKING, with each of the letters standing for a key component, namely: Setting; Participants; Ends; Act sequence; Key; Instrumentalities; Norms; and Genre (1974: 62).

The following steps were taken to design the teaching methodology in Cycle One.
1. To settle a unique sociopragmatic dimension for each week (Appendix 6B), we paired up one or two CA notions with one or two components from the SPEAKING model (we skipped 'Act sequence' in the model as it largely

overlaps with the CA concepts of 'Turn-taking' and 'Adjacency pairs'). Subsequently, each week we designed focused sociopragmatic questions which prompted students to consider how the target conversational feature (s) (i.e. CA notions) can be shaped by the target contextual factor(s) (i.e. SPEAKING components), as revealed in a screenplay dialogue. For example, how might the setting influence the turn-taking pattern in this conversation? And how does this observation help you to understand a particular speech act, as realised in this conversation?

2. To find suitable English screenplay materials, we searched on the Internet where professional screenplays of many well-known films and soap operas are available. We narrowed down a list of screenplays with which the Chinese students were most likely to be familiar or of which we had good knowledge. In this chapter, our analysis focuses on students' interaction with screenplays which fit into at least one of the following three categories: those that are based on best-selling novels or literary classics; those that have won prestigious screenplay awards; those that have been published for artistic value by an established publisher. We also aimed for a diversity of speaking situations. We located scenes in these screenplays which illustrate interactions that we believed would not cause much discomfort to the students when discussing target sociopragmatic features. Subsequently, we labelled all the speech acts in these scenes, which formed the basis for our final selection of the target speech acts for each week (Appendix 6B). Special attention was also paid to copyright issues. As obtaining copyright permissions for multiple screenplays can be a tremendous task, we followed the minimum standards of educational 'fair use' of 'non-coursepack materials' (Stim 2016: 242–247). In particular, any screenplay excerpt displayed on the student handouts had fewer than '1,000 words' (Stim 2016: 246) and no more than 'two excerpts' were ever taken from the same screenwriter (p. 247). We made one printed copy of each handout for a participating student, and throughout the entire course we made 'nine instances of such copying' altogether (Stim 2016: 247).

3. It has been widely argued that the teaching of L2 spoken pragmatics needs to be empirically informed (Ishihara 2007; Ishihara and Cohen 2010; Ren and Han 2016). Therefore, for each teaching week we drew on one or a few empirical studies (also detailed in Appendix 6B). These studies had informed our design of the awareness-raising tasks and the provision of explicit metapragmatic instruction.

4. Each week, we followed a sequence of implicit and explicit activities (Table 6.1). Drawing on Ishihara's (2007: 22) 'learners-as-researchers' model, we aimed to maximally raise students' metapragmatic awareness by guiding them to independently examine speech acts from varied sociopragmatic angles and to notice the functions of highlighted linguistic forms themselves.

Table 6.1 *The weekly sequence of explicit and implicit activities*

Before class: a student handout was distributed three days before each session. An outline of a
   sample is provided in Appendix 6C. The handout includes:
1) Explicit instruction explaining the target sociopragmatic lens or parameter: written in plain
   language and in Chinese.
2) Awareness-raising task with implicit instruction: students read the provided screenplay extracts
   and then, through group discussion, responded to questions which prompted them to examine
   the dialogues by using a specific sociopragmatic lens and by focusing on specific linguistic
   forms. This step is regarded as implicit instruction, as students needed to develop their
   metapragmatic knowledge by firstly performing independent analysis of the conversations.
During class:
1) Classroom discussion through implicit instruction: the teacher elicited student responses to the
   handout questions. The teacher would prompt the spokesperson of a nominated group to
   elaborate on the reasoning processes behind their findings.
2) The above was followed by explicit teacher feedback.
3) Explicit pragmalinguistic instruction: through zooming in on how target speech acts were
   realised in the screenplay extracts, the teacher explained the illocutionary force and drew
   students' attention to the linguistic forms which help to fulfil such force.
After class: students were assigned homework to be completed in groups. A summary of the weekly
   homework prompts is provided in Appendix 6D.
1) Knowledge-application by implicit instruction: in groups, students collaboratively created or
   completed a dialogue (e.g. continuation writing or blank-filling writing). The homework prompt
   set the target speech act(s) in a specific context and scenario. Here, the instruction is regarded
   implicit, as it let students generate their own understanding as for how the previously gained
   metapragmatic knowledge can be applied to the actual production of a situated conversation
   (Abrams 2014).

A major issue we noticed in Cycle One was that although the students' sociopragmatic awareness was effectively evoked, their pragmalinguistic performance showed visible deviations from L2 norms despite explicit teacher instruction. Abrams (2016: 37), based on her findings, suggests that 'sociopragmatic knowledge … precede[s] pragmalinguistic knowledge'. Hence, with our students' L2 sociopragmatic awareness already initiated in Cycle One, in Cycle Two we shifted more attention to explicit pragmalinguistic instruction, modelling and feedback. Without changing the implicit–explicit sequence displayed in Table 6.1, we made the following adjustments to Cycle Two.

Firstly, each session was made to revolve around one speech act only. Similar to Cycle One, a sociopragmatic parameter was settled. For example, the students may be directed to examine how the illocutionary force of a complimentary remark in a screenplay dialogue can be derived from the turn (CA concept) this remark occupies in the overall conversation and the social status of the interlocutors ('participants' in the SPEAKING model).

Secondly, in response to the students' mid-term suggestions, we also played in class some film/TV clips that correspond to the screenplay extracts. The students enjoyed such opportunities and they did capture paralinguistic detail such as tones and facial expression. However, they struggled to follow the video clips even after they had already studied the screenplay extracts. We believe this provided further justification for the pedagogical value of screenplays in an L2 spoken class especially one for lower-intermediate learners. Lastly, explicit feedback to the weekly homework was given to the whole class in the ensuing week. The feedback built on specific examples drawn from the submissions, particularly aiming to strengthen the students' pragmalinguistic reasoning processes behind the phrasing of a target speech act. Below, we discuss our findings; pseudonyms are used whenever individual students are referred to.

Results and Discussion

Our analysis reveals that English screenplays helped our students develop metapragmatic awareness by: (1) invoking their sociocultural knowledge which subsequently facilitated their sociopragmatic analysis; (2) building a creative space where students made meaningful sociopragmatic and pragmalinguistic designs; and (3) providing a literary medium through which examination of pragmalinguistic features is stimulated by discussions of subtext and characterisation.

Invoking Sociocultural Knowledge to Facilitate Sociopragmatic Analysis

Excerpts 1 to 3 show that the students, by responding to questions framed by the teacher, evoked their knowledge of pop culture or L1 sociocultural values, which helped them to interpret L2 pragmatic features in the screenplay dialogues. Excerpts 1 and 2 are drawn from a discussion in week two where the following sociopragmatic lens was deployed: how speaker relationship influences the adjacency pairs in a conversation. *Sherlock Holmes* (Johnson 2008) was selected, since the central characters have created a great sensation in China. Before this session, in groups the students had already examined two screenplay extracts: one depicting an interaction between Holmes and Watson and the other between Holmes and Irene Adler. As shown in Excerpt 1, the teacher started the discussion by referring to a few questions on the handout. Given the limited space here, some utterances are omitted in the excerpts below, which is signalled by a three-point ellipsis ('...'). Square brackets indicate that the original utterance was made in Chinese and here only the English translation is provided.

Excerpt 1: *Discussions on* Sherlock Holmes *characters*

1	T:	. . . Holmes and Irene, what's their relationship like? . . . Holmes and Watson, what's their relationship? And how different are these two relationships? Umm, who he likes more? Who he feels closer to? Okay? . . .
2	Jiajia:	[Umm, Irene is Holmes', umm what I mean is she is the only woman who hasn't been defeated by Holmes.]
3	T:	Emm, indeed.
4	Jiajia:	[So she is super smart, she got involved with Holmes because of a scandal. And, because Irene is super smart, she managed to escape from Holmes.]
5	T:	Okay.
6	Jiajia:	[So her feeling towards Holmes is mostly admiration.]
7	T:	So are they friends or are they enemies? Or are they both friends and enemies?
8	Jiajia:	[I think they're a bit like soulmates, it's like they somewhat admire each other.]
9	T:	[Soulmates then. Do they see each other a lot?]
10	Jiajia:	[No.]
11	T:	[Then how did they become soulmates?]
12	Jiajia:	[Because they're both super smart and resourceful, and they think they are similar.]
13	T:	Okay, now what's the difference between these two relationships, Holmes and Watson, Holmes and Irene? . . . What about group one, what do you think?
14	Ting:	[We think Holmes and Irene are both intelligent, so they admire each other.]
15	T:	Okay, what about Holmes and Watson? [So they see each other as totally different creatures?]
16	Ting:	[They're just close friends, the most typical type.]
17	T:	[So who does Holmes feel closer to? Who does he trust more?]
18	Ting:	[Should be Watson, because they live together, so they grow close in their daily life and work.]

Toward the second half of Line 1, the teacher established a focus on comparing these two sets of speaker relationships from 'the emotional dimension' (McConachy 2013: 104) and the perspective of social distance. Jaijia, a hardcore Sherlock Holmes fan, eagerly volunteered. However, at the beginning (Lines 2 and 4) Jiajia was mostly paraphrasing declarative knowledge rather than evaluating the differences between these two speaker relationships. Nonetheless, Jiajia's comments reveal that she oriented to distinct sociocultural frames (McConachy 2013) for describing interpersonal relations, such as gender ('the only woman'), rivalry ('hasn't been defeated by Holmes', 'escaped from Holmes') and intellectual power ('super smart'). In Line 6, Jiajia's comment developed by evaluating the emotional dimension between Irene and Holmes. To prompt Jiajia to elaborate on this evaluation from the perspective of social relations, the teacher offered an 'affiliation-disaffiliation' 'relational frame' (McLaren and Solomon 2015: 117), i.e. 'friends' or 'enemies'. Jiajia somehow problematised this simplistic opposition by attributing 'soulmates' to Holmes and Irene's relationship: are 'soulmates' 'friends'? Or could 'enemies' become 'soulmates' at a certain point? Later, when the teacher nominated another group to continue the discussion, Ting, as shown in Line 14, paraphrased and summarised Jiajia's comments previously made in Lines 8 and 12, a sign of peer scaffolding. It can also be seen that Ting applied her perceptions of particular social relations – for example, the affinity between *great minds* ('both intelligent', 'admire each other'), and what *close friends* are typically like – in an attempt to justify her differentiation between these two speaker relationships.

After Excerpt 1 interaction, the teacher scaffolded the class to label all the adjacency pairs in each *Sherlock Holmes* (Johnson 2008) dialogue. Subsequently, the students were invited to comment on the natures of the adjacency pairs by deploying the target sociopragmatic lens. Excerpt 2 presents Zhi's observation. He alluded to Jiajia's and Ting's earlier contributions – such as the 'tense' rivalry between Holmes and Irene and the 'confrontational' though 'casual' interaction between Holmes and Watson – and managed to link these to major illocutionary force (e.g. 'probing and challenging each other', and 'argued about trivial things in daily life'), which underlies the adjacency pairs in each dialogue.

Excerpt 2: *Discussion on* Sherlock Holmes *dialogues*

1	T:	[. . . Ok now let's look at question three okay? Now let me ask group eleven. What do you think?]
2	Zhi:	[The conversation between Holmes and Irene, basically they were probing and challenging each other. They were both trying to retrieve more valuable information from the other person, so they remained quite tense and alert. Meanwhile, the conversation between Holmes and Watson was quite casual though also confrontational. As for the content, they argued about trivial things in daily life. But Holmes talked about big crimes with Irene.]

Next, Excerpt 3 is drawn from a class discussion conducted in week twelve. It revolved around the first of the two *Love Actually* extracts (Curtis 2002) (see Appendix 6C). The teacher removed from this dialogue three different segments where disagreement is uttered. The teacher started the classroom discussion by eliciting the students' own renderings of the first disagreement that is expressed by Tony in reaction to Colin's excited announcement of his plan to spend the forthcoming Christmas in the States. Colin is hoping to meet up with 'babes' in the States who would be attracted to his British qualities (hence his humorous self-reference as 'Sir Colin'). The general tone (Key, a SPEAKING component) and the language style (Instrumentalities, another SPEAKING component) that this speech event (chit-chat between close friends) embodies were deemed familiar enough to the students that they would be able to infer the moves that Tony's disagreement with Colin's envisioned adventure are likely to involve (Preference organisation, a CA notion). This is the target socioprag- matic lens.

Excerpt 3: *Filling in a disagreement blank for a* Love Actually *dialogue*

1	T:	[... Next, so Tony disagrees with Colin's idea of spending the Christmas in the States, right? What would he say here? Firstly, you must know that this is a kind of, a very informal, a very relaxed chat, and a highly casual, colloquial and humorous chat. It has a lot of slang and bantering between these two close friends. ... One more clue, you know, in a conversation, what one speaker says right now often relates to what another speaker said earlier], okay? [Such as a word or something that was mentioned earlier in the dialogue] okay? .... [So here, Tony, when expressing his disagreement, he would use two words that were mentioned earlier by Colin, one is 'babes', the other is 'the States'. So, what would you fill in here? ... I'll give you 3 minutes to recollect your thoughts] ... Group thirteen, what did you fill in here?
2	Liu:	Emm, [what we wrote is] 'I agree with you, there are babes in the States but maybe American babes are too busy in Christmas to pay attention to Sir Colin?'
3	T:	Great, so you start with 'I agree with you'. [I'd like to hear how you had designed this disagreement, especially the moves that Tony follows to express his disagreement], okay?
4	Liu:	[On the task sheet you say Tony and Colin are buddies and they're both young males, so we spent a lot of time thinking how to make their talk humorous but also to the point. They wouldn't let each other spend a lot of effort guessing what one really thinks.]
5	T:	Humm. [So what moves did you finally design?]
6	Liu:	[First of all, Tony must express his disagreement in a clear manner, but he can't step over the line, in case Colin gets angry and beats him up.] ((Some students laughed)) [So we choose to use 'I agree with you' in the beginning, and we used 'maybe', and also the question mark in the second part.]
7	T:	Humm, [so to soften the tone. But did you also try to make this a bit light-hearted since Tony wouldn't want to sound too serious or pretentious?]
8	Liu:	[Emm, we can't find any slang, so we borrowed 'American babes' and 'Sir Colin' from Colin. But we don't think anyone would be very happy to hear disapproval, so Tony needs to find an excuse to dissuade Colin.]
9	T:	I see. Excellent. Thank you. [So buddies sometimes beat each other up?]
10	SS:	((Laughter))
11	Liu:	[You have to give each other some face, that's how good friendship is kept.]

Excerpt 3 suggests that Liu and his group applied their previous observations in life and their L1 interactional skills to internalise the target sociopragmatic lens. They also invoked specific sociocultural norms – for example, close friends 'can't step over the line' – as the frame of reference for their design of the preference organisation.

Furthermore, they borrowed two phrases from the original screenplay excerpt in an attempt to maintain the informal style (Instrumentalities). Under the teacher's prompting in Lines 3, 5 and 7, Liu somehow problematised the Key of this dialogue by commenting on the intricate relationship – and potential tension – among the goals of achieving light-heartedness, clarity and 'face'–for example, 'we spent a lot of time thinking how to make their talk *humorous* but also *to the point*' (Line 4), 'we don't think anyone would be very *happy* to hear *disapproval*' (Line 8). Liu also managed to coordinate his group's design of the Preference organisation with the Key they eventually tuned for their own rendering of the disagreement: that is, one that was peaceful and civilised.

Building a Creative Space Where Students Made Meaningful Sociopragmatic and Pragmalinguistic Designs

Screenplays not only stimulate students' metapragmatic analysis of dialogues but also foster a creative space through which L2 students produce fictional but personally meaningful conversations. This is illustrated in Excerpt 4 (Ting, Yang, Qi and Gang, week one homework dialogue), which was written by a student group in response to week one's homework prompt (see Appendix 6D), which required the students to create a *Harry Potter* conversation for an imagined scenario. The students were advised to imitate the screenplay format.

Excerpt 4: Harry Potter *continuation*

Harry opens the door and sees Ron and Hermione standing outside.

HERMIONE: Harry!
HARRY: Hermione? Ron? Come on in!
HERMIONE: Thanks.
HARRY: So ... What brought you two here?
HERMIONE: Harry, Ron and I are getting married!
HARRY: Wow! Congratulations!

After entering the house, they begin chatting on the sofa.

HERMIONE: I thought we could add some games in the wedding party.
HARRY: Yeah, that's a good idea.
HERMIONE: Harry, we'd imagine you could give a speech at our wedding as the best friend of Ron and me.
HARRY: Well ... It's my honor.
RON: You've got to tell the stories we've been through!
HERIMONE: Well ... I don't know how the audience is ever going to love that.

This group wrote in their self-reflection: '[We worked hard on the characterisation of Hermione. She must confidently announce to Harry her engagement with Ron, meanwhile she does feel a bit embarrassed seeing Harry]' (Ting, Yang, Qi and Gang, week one self-reflection). As shown in Excerpt 4, Hermione speaks to Harry and Ron in distinct ways; also, Hermione and Ron talk to Harry differently. These suggest the students' awareness of speaker distance and consequently level of imposition. The students employed linguistic devices that they had captured in the original screenplay of *Harry Potter and the Order of the Phoenix* (Goldenberg 2007). These include formulaic expressions for crafting varying tones of request or suggestion (e.g. *I thought; we'd imagine you could* ...; *you've got to* ...; *I don't know how somebody is ever going to* ...), discourse markers (*well; so*) and the use of vocatives to adjust illocutionary force. It can also be seen that Ron takes the fewest turns while Hermione the most, which resembles this trio's interactional patterns in the original screenplay. Finally, there is evidence that the students' reasoning behind tense went beyond grammatical correctness, as shown in their self-reflection below:

[Hermione says they are getting married. We initially wrote 'Ron and I are getting married!' But then we thought maybe the simple future tense is more appropriate ('Ron and I are going to get married!')? Eventually, after searching the Internet and doing some comparison, we decided that our original version is better as it can better show Hermione's confidence. That is, getting married is a solid thing, there wouldn't be any change to that.] (Ting, Yang, Qi and Gang, week one self-reflection)

Providing a Literary Medium through Which Examination of Pragmalinguistic Features is Stimulated by Discussions of Subtext and Characterisation

In week five, we examined two excerpts drawn from the screenplay of *Get out* (Peele 2014). The excerpts portray the first time that Chris (the central character) meets the parents of Rose (his girlfriend) in a family mansion. Before the discussion that is displayed in Excerpt 5 occurred, the teacher had explained to the students that this screenplay belongs to the horror genre and that the screenwriter creates a chilling atmosphere not through jump scares but through dialogues which indirectly show the characters' divergent speaking styles and hence simmering tensions.

As shown in Excerpt 5, the teacher focused on a particular speech event, i.e. small talk, and encouraged the students to examine the illocutionary force that dominates this small talk. In Line 25 Zhi zoomed in on the word 'ecology'. Subsequently the teacher, by asking the students to look for a colloquial synonym, elicited 'negative evidence' (McConachy 2013: 106) and hence

Excerpt 5: *Discussion on one* Get out *dialogue: 'Ecology' and 'Traumatic'*

22	T:	[Now I want you all to focus on their small talk, the part I've highlighted, can any group describe Rose's parents to me? What kind of impression do they leave on you? Find specific evidence . . . group eleven.]
23	Zhi:	[They're very formal.]
24	T:	[Yeah? Give us some examples.]
25	Zhi:	[Rose's dad mentioned 'ecology'.]
26	T:	[So what does it mean? Can you give me a synonym which is more colloquial?]
27	Zhi:	((Looking at the handout, thinking.))
28	T:	[Ok, I'll give you all a few minutes to check this, on your phone find a synonym . . . Group fifteen, do you have a synonym?]
29	Feng:	Biology?
30	T:	[Yes, we all know 'biology' from high school as a subject. Any other word? Group fourteen.]
31	Huang:	Nature.
32	T:	Good, [or 'environment', yeah? ((Meng put up her hand)) You have something to say?]
33	Meng:	[I know Rose's mom is a psychiatrist, and she uses the word 'traumatic', so maybe here the scriptwriter was alluding to her job, because 'traumatic' can be a jargon-like word?]
34	T:	Excellent, so Rose's parents use some big words in their small talk with Chris. Why? [Maybe they want to show their opinions in an intellectual way or maybe they consider themselves to be very well-educated . . .]

guided them to see how 'ecology' fulfils particular illocutionary force that corresponds with the speaker's 'formal' disposition. In Line 33, Meng volunteered. Meng previously told the teacher that she and her group had watched the film *Get out* together the night before (one with Chinese subtitles). Equipped with confident knowledge of the plot line, Meng speculated on the screenwriter's subtle means for shaping characterisation and made a critical observation on how the character's professional and social status can be implied by her lexical choice. Finally, the teacher, by building on the students' contributions, commented on how lexical choices – as a pragmalinguistic device – can contribute to an utterance's illocutionary force.

Discussion

This action research provides insights into how we can enhance lower-intermediate Chinese EFL learners' metapragmatic awareness of spoken English by using English screenplays as a source of authentic conversations in which a range of speech acts can be examined against rich and engaging conversational contexts. The findings also suggest that by guiding learners to examine speech acts through CA concepts and the SPEAKING model, there is much potential for the development of learners' sociopragmatic and pragmalinguistic knowledge and self-agency. We managed to create 'an interactional space' (Welch 2015) in our large-sized class *with* and *for* our students despite all the reality constraints. Indeed, the students were in position not only to comprehend the L2 screenplays and other explicit input from the teacher but also to make the necessary connections among their existing sociocultural knowledge, the target sociopragmatic lens or pragmalinguistic focus, and their personal experience. Screenplays can be a highly accessible form of literature for EFL students given their familiarity with film/TV genres, popular story themes, character archetypes and filmic depictions of tension and emotions. Hence, this interactional space created through L2 screenplays has allowed us to redefine for our EFL course 'what counts as knowledge, what counts as displaying knowledge, and who may define and display knowledge' (Heller and Martin-Jones 2001: 3). To be more specific, screenplays, like many other types of literature, stimulate the L2 students to invoke and engage with a multiplicity of knowledge (e.g. knowledge of film plots or characters, universal schema of storytelling, or stereotypes of specific social relations) which crosses linguistic, sociocultural, temporal or spatial boundaries. To make such knowledge-reconstruction processes explicit, we echo McConachy's observation that in classroom interaction it is crucial that 'the students are pushed to justify their interpretations' and elaborate on them (2013: 108).

Given that literature is naturally open to multiple interpretations, screenplays help to build a collaborative discussion space where teachers can scaffold students' reasoning processes by providing or eliciting alternative interpretations (without discouraging the students). This also helps to show that metapragmatic knowledge of spoken English 'goes beyond the level of a simple matching of forms to social context' (McConachy 2013: 109). The processes and results of our experience as outlined in this chapter contribute to the goal stated by Taguchi (2015: 41) that future L2 research on spoken language pragmatics needs to investigate how 'performing more complex tasks le[a]d[s] to more learning opportunities through [peer or classroom] interaction' that occurs in the 'reasoning' behind specific forms of a conversation.

Conclusion

Using English screenplays to raise Chinese students' metapragmatic awareness of spoken English was a new experience for us. Our greatest challenge when designing the course was to find screenplay materials that represent a diversity of narratives and scenarios and to adapt them into enhanced input (e.g. students' pre-class handouts). We intended to provide an alternative instructional approach to complement the L2 instructional research on the awareness of spoken English pragmatics which 'were conducted either in a laboratory ... or in a regular classroom by sparing a few class periods for target pragmatic features' (Taguchi 2015: 42). Our project required on average 3 hours of work from each student per week (pre-class review and group discussion, class time and group homework) over at least 10 out of this 13-week period. In addition, our task design and the teacher's provision of metapragmatic instruction is critically informed by our own analysis of the selected screenplay materials and our ongoing observation of the students' performance. The results of our experience also support Taguchi's (2015: 28) assertion that students benefit from a combination of explicit metapragmatic explanation and more implicit approaches 'inducing learners' attention to forms and having them evaluate the forms for appropriateness'. Through careful selection of screenplay dialogues that can relate to the students' existing knowledge repertoire and interests, we promoted the students' attention to the 'forms and context' of speech acts in spoken English (Taguchi 2015: 41).

This method provides a solution to our EFL context where often students do not have many opportunities to speak or listen to English in 'real-life social interaction' (Taguchi 2015: 42). In addition, we believe this study also provides a solution to teaching contexts where students do have access to L2 interactions out of class but experience disempowerment or feel a disconnection between their own sense of self and the L2 speaker images that they involuntarily evoke when participating in conversations. As suggested by the results of this action research, L2 metapragmatic awareness is central to the development of moti-vated and empowered L2 speakers (Ishihara and Cohen 2010), especially for L2 learners positioned towards the lower end of the proficiency continuum. Facilitated by a literary medium, we gave our students opportunities to be conversation analysts, screenplay commentators and screenwriters and made them see how their L2 pragmatic decisions are critically linked to their own sociocultural being and self-agency (Ishihara and Cohen 2010).

Major limitations of this action research are related to its exploratory nature. Firstly, we were unsure how the students' metapragmatic development during these thirteen weeks can be quantitatively measured. We were particularly con-cerned about whether the students' language proficiency would become an inter-fering factor, especially on their control and interpretation of pragmalinguistic features. Secondly, we did not prioritise specific linguistic features in this research, such as 'formulaic expression' or 'syntactic mitigations' (Taguchi 2015: 37).

Nonetheless, in the second open-ended questionnaire that we administered in week thirteen, many students commented that they picked up particular phrases from the screenplays, such as 'wanna bet' and 'why thank you', and discourse markers such as 'well' and 'anyway', as well as informal apologetic expres-sions such as 'my bad', or various syntactic formulae to make requests. However, only one student, Meng, commented that she had collected from 'the many interesting screenplays' a repertoire of expressions regarding 'how to express my views', 'how to apologize, how to praise, and make a request' (Meng, Questionnaire 2, answer to Question 3, English original). She subsequently wrote 'I have to say something is beginning to change when I talk with my foreign friends through microblog. I'm no longer puzzled and the atmosphere of our conversation is more relaxed' (Meng, Questionnaire 2, answer to Question 3, English original). Meng's encouraging comments made us reflect on the mutually supportive relation between EFL learners' metapragmatic awareness and their acquisition of linguistic forms in spoken English. Hence, future L2 research on spoken pragmatics which utilises screenplays as a pedagogical tool can refine our curriculum much further by matching the target sociopragmatic lens with specific linguistic forms which are used to fulfil target speech acts. Finally, future L2 classroom research that utilises literature and targets learners' spoken language awareness may follow individual students who embody distinctive literary identities (e.g. cartoon reader, film watcher, fanfiction writer). Insights into their learning trajectories throughout a literature-mediated spoken language course can inform future L2 pedagogy which employs literature as an empowering tool.

Acknowledgement

This action research project was funded by National Social Science Fund of China (17CYY020). We are also grateful for the great support provided to us by the School of Foreign Languages of the university where this classroom project took place.

Appendix 6A The Two Open-Ended Questionnaires Respectively Administered in Week Six and Week Thirteen

(Both questionnaires were produced in Chinese to ensure clarity and to elicit precise and detailed responses from the students. Below, only the English translation for each questionnaire is provided.)

Questionnaire 1 (week six)

In these 6 weeks, the main purpose of this course has been to examine and learn spoken English from the following two perspectives: (1) the context of a conversation; and (2) the structure of a conversation. We did not just focus on pronunciation or simply learn the words or phrases needed for get something done in spoken English. In addition, we have used English screenplays as the main resource to study English conversations.

Now, to improve this course and our own teaching practices, we would like to hear your thoughts regarding this learning experience and get some specific feedback from you. All the questions below are completely open-ended and your responses would not in any way affect our assessment/judgement of your group's homework. We would appreciate very much any comment from you as long as it is detailed, truthful and relevant to the question. You can answer the following questions in Chinese if it is more convenient.

1. In the past six weeks, in which aspect of spoken English have you made the biggest gain or achieved the most visible improvement? Please describe for us one or two *specific* examples.
2. Apart from taking this course, do you have any opportunities to speak or listen to English outside the classroom (e.g. watching English films or videos, listening to radio programmes in English, taking extra English-speaking courses, or chatting with foreign friends, etc.)? If yes, go to Question 3, if not, go straight to Question 4.
3. Does what you have learned in this course help you in any way to speak or comprehend English in the above occasions outside the classroom? If YES, could you describe for us one or two specific examples? If NO, go to the next question.
4. Regarding what you have learned in these six weeks, where do you think that you need more help? Where can you use more improvement?

Questionnaire 2 (week thirteen)

The instruction here is essentially similar to the one given in Questionnaire 1.
1. Could you describe for us two aspects of spoken English where you have made the biggest gains or experienced the most visible changes in the past twelve weeks in this course? Please use *specific* examples. We'd like you to avoid general descriptions, because only details can help us understand your experience and allow us to improve this course in the future.
2. You have done the pre-class handout tasks for ten weeks and you have also performed the group homework assignment for ten weeks. Regarding these experiences, could you describe for us one or two area(s) where your improvement is relatively slow or your performance is less than satisfactory? Please use *specific* examples, for example, your experience with a particular homework or with a particular pre-class task.
3. Are there any other comments that you would like to share with us? Or any thoughts that you haven't got the chance to express previously? As long as your comment is specific and relevant, we're sure this can help us to improve this course next year.

Appendix 6B The Week-by-Week Syllabi in Cycle One and Cycle Two

Week	CA notion(s)	SPEAKING component(s)	Speech act(s)	Screenplay resource	Key empirical research
CYCLE ONE					
1	Turn-taking	Setting	Offers of opinions; Suggestions	*Harry Potter and the Order of the Phoenix* (Goldenberg 2007)	Ishino (2017); Weatherall and Edmonds (2018)
2	Adjacency pairs & Response tokens	Participants	Evaluations; Requests; Commands	*Sherlock Holmes* (Johnson 2008)	Weatherall and Edmonds (2018); McCarthy (2003)
3	Repair mechanism	Ends	(Requests for) clarifications or further explanations	*An Education* (Hornby 2008)	Mason (2004)
4	Topic management & Sequential organisation	Genre	Telephone conversation and its essential speech acts	*Crazy, Stupid, Love* (Fogelman 2010)	Hutchby and Barnett (2005)
5	Preference organisation	Key & Instrumentalities	Varied illocutionary acts of Questioning; Small Talk	*Get out* (Peele 2014)	Reynolds (2011); Bilmes (2014)
6	Adjacency pairs	Norms	Compliments; Requests; Apologies; Complaints	None	Su (2010); Halenko (2016); Ren and Gao (2012)
CYCLE TWO					
8	Topic management & Sequential organisation	Setting & Participants	Requests	*Doctor Foster* (Bartlett 2017)	Usó-Juan and Martínez-Flor (2008); Li and Gao (2017)
9	Turn-taking	Setting & Participants	Compliments	*500 Days of Summer* (Neustadter and Weber 2006).	Wu and Takahashi (2016)
10	Repair mechanism	Ends	Requests for repetition or clarifications	*Still Alice* (Glatzer and Westmoreland 2012)	Kendrick (2015)
11	Adjacency pairs & Response tokens	Genre	Apologies	The excerpts from *Crazy, Stupid, Love* and *Doctor Foster* were recycled.	Chang (2010)
12	Preference organisation	Key & Instrumentalities	Disagreements	*Love Actually* (Curtis 2002)	Kreutel (2007); Cheng (2016)
13	Adjacency pairs	Norms	All the speech acts covered in Cycle Two	None	Halenko (2016); Yu (2011)

Appendix 6C An Outline of the Pre-class Handout Distributed in Week Twelve

(In the original handout, there are images to make it engaging for the students, and explanations were mostly done in Chinese. For copyright reasons, the two screenplay extracts drawn from *Love Actually* (Curtis 2002) are not reproduced below.

Lesson 12 How would we express disagreement in English?

1. State the inevitability of expressing disagreement in daily life. Then explain how the different moves that we follow to express disagreement (i.e. Preference organisation) can be influenced by:

   1) The general mood of the conversation (Key). Illustrated with examples, for example, a joking mood in contrast to a solemn mood.

   2) The formality and the variety of English used by the speakers (Instrumentalities). Illustrated with examples, for example, a formal workplace conversation where standard English is used versus an informal chat between friends where slang words are prevalent.

2. Describe a particular situation where disagreement needs to be expressed. Then list a variety of preference organisation (including linguistic devices for boosting or softening the tone) for expressing disagreement, as informed by Kreutel (2007) and Cheng (2016). Invite students to add in one more version of preference organisation which is not included above.

3. Display the two screenplay extracts drawn from *Love Actually* (Curtis 2002). Before each extract, explain the background story (as shown below); also explain the Key and the Instrumentalities represented by the interaction.

   1) Tony (mid-20s) and Colin (mid-20s) are close buddies working in London. Colin has not been lucky when it comes to chatting up British girls and has been feeling quite frustrated. But Colin is convinced of his charisma, so he blames the stuck-up girls in Britain. One day Colin gets this ingenious idea of spending the upcoming Christmas in America, Wisconsin to be exact, so that he can charm the girls there. Colin excitedly informs Tony of his envisioned grand adventure, but Tony isn't that impressed. However, Colin is determined to go.

   2) Harry (early 1950s), the boss of a successful design agency, goes shopping for Christmas gifts with his wife Karen (early 1950s) in a big department store in central London. As soon as Karen goes away picking up gifts for the parents and in-laws, Harry heads for the jewellery section, wanting to get a necklace as the Christmas gift for his young secretary. Harry sees exactly what he wants and wants to purchase it quickly. A male shop assistant (late 1940s) – in a suit, well-groomed and extremely polite – approaches Harry and offers to help. However, despite the multiple times that Harry indicates that he is in a hurry, the shop assistant just wouldn't let Harry get the necklace and insists on performing an extremely elaborate gift-wrapping procedure.

4. Draw students' attention to the parts of the disagreement already removed from each screenplay extract. Ask students to fill in for the missing utterances. Ask students to justify for each filling how they have settled on specific preference organisation based on the Key and the Instrumentalities of the dialogue (or of a part of the dialogue).

Appendix 6D   A Summary of the Ten Weekly Homework Prompts

Week one: creating a screenplay dialogue along the following plotline. One day in the distant future, Hermione and Ron visit Harry informing him of their engagement. They also share with Harry their ideas for the wedding ceremony and elicit suggestions from him. Students are guided to pay special attention to the turn-taking patterns in this dialogue and to how suggestions and opinion-giving can be phrased in distinctive ways by these characters due to different speaker relations or motives.

Week two: revising the dialogue created last week. Students are asked to differentiate the adjacency pairs made between Hermione and Harry and those between Hermione and Ron, paying particular attention to the speakers' expression or reception of opinions, evaluations and requests.

Week three: filling in six blank lines in a screenplay dialogue that is created by us. We draw inspiration (not words or exact content) from a scene in *Blue Valentine* (Cianfrance, Delavigne and Curtis 2010). A potential misunderstanding happens between the male protagonist and a woman whom he just meets for the first time but already loves at first sight. The man desperately tries to clarify his earlier action to the woman. To fill in the blank lines, students are required to indirectly show the man's underlying motive (i.e. to win her over) in his attempts to repair.

Week four: filling in eight blank lines in a screenplay phone conversation created by us. We draw inspiration from a scene in *He's Just Not that into You ...* (Kohn and Silverstein 2007). The female protagonist – who has been keeping herself to herself after a recent nasty break-up – receives a phone call from her male best friend. He invites her to a birthday party where she could make new friends. To fill in the blank lines, students need to focus on the topic management in this phone conversation and the essential sequences and the order in which they are to be realised.

Week five: creating a screenplay dialogue along the following plotline. The fictional 'you' go travelling with your parents to a foreign country, but your seats on the plane are not together. You decide to ask another passenger (foreign male, 40 years old) sitting nearby if he is willing to exchange seats with you. How would you phrase the initial request? What moves would you take to persuade him if he initially shows hesitation? Students need to make sure the dialogue is harmonious and the register not too casual.

Week eight: filling in three blank lines in a screenplay dialogue created by us. We draw inspiration from a scene in *The Ring* (Kruger 2001). A female reporter arrives at a small tourist town to investigate a cold case that happened 10 years ago. She tracks down the chief CIA investigator back then – who now runs a B&B – and wants to ask him a few questions. The ex-officer is not that cooperative in the beginning, so the reporter has to make three different requests for information in the conversation. To fill in for these three different requests, students need to consider the sequential moves and the progression of topics (i.e. topic management) that the reporter is likely to follow based on her appraisal of this speaking situation.

Week nine: filling in four blank lines in a screenplay dialogue created by us. We draw inspiration from a scene in *500 Days of Summer* (Neustadter and Weber 2006). The female and the male protagonists are neighbours. Although the man is introverted, he does like the woman. In this conversation, they bump into each other in the lift and the man initially plays cool by listening to trendy music, ignoring the woman. Nonetheless, she overhears the music and then starts to small talk with him facilitated by the usage of compliments.

Week ten: creating a screenplay dialogue of three turns. The fictional 'you' goes to Cambodia to be a volunteer English language teacher. However, your foreign flatmate likes to throw frequent parties at night. This has gone beyond your tolerance and you have to make a complaint to him/her. After your initial complaint, your flatmate seems confused and asks you to clarify. You are then forced to reformulate your complaint. Students are required to consider the illocutionary act behind the flatmate's request for clarification; they are also asked to consider how 'your' own agenda can be strengthened in the ensuing reformulation.

Week eleven: creating a screenplay dialogue of three turns. The fictional 'you', a fresh intern, inadvertently bad-mouths your manager, who unfortunately overhears it. Fearing the negative ramifications, you decide to apologise to your manager (the start of the dialogue). To create this short sequence, students are required to deploy the genre of apologetic conversations between a subordinate and his/her superior in an international workplace.

Week twelve: creating a screenplay dialogue of three turns. The fictional 'you' visits a foreign friend who, on impulse, cooks a Chinese meal for you. Although the taste could use much improvement, you hide the truth well. You two are having a great time chatting, then suddenly your friend tells you that he/she should replicate this meal for his/her Chinese girlfriend/boyfriend's parents next weekend. You think this could be a bad idea and feel obliged to say so. To create this short sequence, students need to make sure the protagonist's expression of disagreement does not disrupt the amiable atmosphere achieved so far and the register should be casual.

References

Allwright, D. 2003. 'Exploratory practice: Rethinking practitioner research in language teaching', *Language Teaching Research* 7(2): 113–141.

Abrams, Z. I. 2014. 'Using film to provide a context for teaching L2 pragmatics', *System* 46: 55–64.

2016. 'Creating a social context through film: Teaching L2 pragmatics as a locally situated process', *L2 Journal* 8(3): 23–45.

Baker, D. J. 2016. 'The screenplay as text: Academic scriptwriting as creative research', *New Writing: The International Journal for the Practice and Theory of Creative Writing* 13(1): 71–84.

Barraja-Rohan, A. 1997. 'Teaching conversation and sociocultural norms with conversation analysis', *Australian Review of Applied Linguistics* 14: 71–88.

2011. 'Using conversation analysis in the second language classroom to teach interactional competence', *Language Teaching Research* 15(4): 479–507.

Bartlett, M. 2017. *Doctor Foster: The Scripts*. London: Nick Hern Books.

Bella, S., Sifianou, M. and Tzanne, A. 2015. 'Teaching politeness?', in Pizziconi, B. and Locher, M. (eds.), *Teaching and Learning (Im)Politeness*. Berlin: Walter de Gruyter, 23–52.

Bilmes, J. 2014. 'Preference and the conversation analytic endeavor', *Journal of Pragmatics* 64: 52–71.

Bourdieu, P. 1977. 'The economics of linguistic exchanges', *Social Science Information* 16(6): 645–668.

Brown, P. and Levinson, S. 1987. *Politeness: Some Universals in Language Usage*. Cambridge: Cambridge University Press.

Bruti, S. 2016. 'Teaching compliments and insults in the EFL classroom through film clips', in Bianchi, F. and Gesuato, S. (eds.), *Pragmatic Issues in Specialized Communicative Contexts*. Leiden: Brill, 149–170.

Bublitz, W. and Hübler, A. (eds.) 2007. *Metapragmatics in Use*. Amsterdam: John Benjamins.

Burns, A. 2005. 'Action research: An evolving paradigm?', *Language Teaching* 38(2): 57–74.

Chang, Y. 2010. '"I no say you say is boring": The development of pragmatic competencein L2 apology', *Language Sciences* 32(3): 408–424.

Chen, Z. and Goh, C. 2010. 'Teaching oral English in higher education: Challenges to EFL teachers', *Teaching in Higher Education* 16(3): 333–345.

Cheng, T. 2016. 'Authentic L2 interactions as material for a pragmatic awareness-raisingactivity', *Language Awareness* 25(3): 159–178.

Cianfrance, D., Delavigne, C. and Curtis, J. 2010. *Blue Valentine*. Available at: www.raindance.org/wp-content/uploads/downloads/2013/03/blue-valentine.pdf (Accessed 3 July 2018).

Cohen, L. and Manion, L. 1994. *Research Methods in Education*. London: Routledge.

Council of Europe. 2001. *Common European Framework of Reference for Languages: Language, Teaching, Assessment*. Cambridge: Cambridge University Press.

Curtis, R. 2002. *Love Actually*. Available at: http://screenplaysandscripts.com (Accessed 3 July 2018).

Ellis, R. 2008. *The Study of Second Language Acquisition* (2nd edn). Oxford: Oxford University Press.

Fernández-Guerra, A. B. 2008. 'Requests in TV series and in naturally occurring discourse: A comparison', in Alcón Soler, E. (ed.), *Learning How to Request in an Instructed Language Learning Context*. Bern: Peter Lang, 111–126.

    2013. 'Using TV series as input source of refusals in the classroom', in Martí-Arnándiz, O. and Salazar-Campillo, P. (eds.), *Refusals in Instructional Contexts and Beyond*. Amsterdam: Editions Rodopi, 5–22.

Filipi, A. and Barraja-Rohan, A. 2015. 'An interaction-focused pedagogy based on conversation analysis for developing L2 pragmatic competence', in Gesuato, S., Bianchi, F. and Chen, W. (eds.), *Teaching, Learning and Investigating Pragmatics: Principles, Methods and Practices*. Newcastle upon Tyne: Cambridge Scholars Publishing, 231–252.

Fogelman, D. 2010. *Crazy, Stupid, Love*. Available at: www.imsdb.com (Accessed 3 July 2018).

Glatzer, R. and Westmoreland, W. 2012. *Still Alice*. Available from: www.sonyclassics.com/awards-information/stillalice_screenplay.pdf (Accessed 3 July 2018).

Goldenberg, M. 2007. *Harry Potter and the Order of the Phoenix*. Available at: www.dailyscript.com (Accessed 3 July 2018).

Halenko, N. 2016. 'Evaluating the explicit pragmatic instruction of requests and apologies in a study abroad setting: The case of Chinese ESL learners at a UK Higher Education institution', PhD thesis, Lancaster University.

Halenko, N. and Jones, C. 2011. 'Teaching pragmatic awareness of spoken requests to Chinese EAP learners in the UK: Is explicit instruction effective?', *System* 39(2): 240–250.

    2017. 'Explicit instruction of spoken requests: An examination of pre-departure instruction and the study abroad environment', *System* 68: 26–37.

Heller, M. and Martin-Jones, M. 2001. 'Introduction: Symbolic domination, education and linguistic difference', in Heller, M. and Martin-Jones, M. (eds.), *Voices of*

Authority: Education and Linguistic Differences. Westport, CT: Ablex Publishing, 1–28.

Henery, A. 2015. 'On the development of metapragmatic awareness abroad: Two case studies exploring the role of expert-mediation', *Language Awareness* 24(4): 316–331.

Hornby, N. 2008. *An Education*. Available at: www.bbc.co.uk/writersroom/scripts/an-education (Accessed 3 July 2018).

Hutchby, I. and Barnett, S. (2005). 'Aspects of the sequential organization of mobile phone conversation', *Discourse Studies* 7(2): 147–171.

Huth, T. and Taleghani-Nikazm, C. 2006. 'How can insights from conversation analysis be directly applied to teaching L2 pragmatics?' *Language Teaching Research* 10 (1): 53–79.

Hüttner, J. 2014. 'Agreeing to disagree: "Doing disagreement" in assessed oral L2 interactions', *Classroom Discourse* 5(2): 194–215.

Hymes, D. 1972. 'Models of interaction of language and social life', in Gumperz, J. J. and Hymes, D. (eds.), *Directions in Sociolinguistics: Ethnography of Communication*. New York: Holt, Reinhart & Winston, 35–71.

   1974. *Foundations in Sociolinguistics: An Ethnographic Approach*. Philadelphia: University of Pennsylvania Press.

Ishihara, N. 2007. Web-based curriculum for pragmatics instruction in Japanese as a foreign language: An explicit awareness-raising approach. *Language Awareness* 16(1): 21–40.

Ishihara, N. and Cohen, A. D. 2010. *Teaching and Learning Pragmatics: Where Language and Culture Meet*. London: Routledge.

Ishino, M. 2017. 'Subversive questions for classroom turn-taking traffic management', *Journal of Pragmatics* 117: 41–57.

Johnson, M. 2008. *Sherlock Holmes*. Available at: www.raindance.co.uk/site/scripts (Accessed 3 July 2018).

Jones, C. and Horak, T. 2014. 'Leave it out! The use of soap operas as models of spoken discourse in the ELT classroom', *The Journal of Language Teaching and Learning* 4(1): 1–14.

Kaiser, M. and Shibahara, C. 2014. 'Film as source material in advanced foreign language classes', *L2 Journal* 6(1): 1–13.

Kambara, W. 2011. 'Teaching Japanese pragmatic competence using film clips', *L2 Journal* 3(2): 144–157.

Kendrick, K. H. 2015. 'Other-initiated repair in English', *Open Linguistics* 1: 164–190.

Kohn, A. and Silverstein, M. 2007. *He's Just Not that into You ...* Available at: www.dailyscript.com (Accessed 3 July 2018).

Kreutel, K. 2007. '"I'm not agree with you": ESL learners' expressions of disagreement', *TESL-EJ* 11(3): 1–35.

Kruger, E. 2001. *The Ring*. Available at: www.horrorlair.com (Accessed 3 July 2018).

Lambrou, M. 2015, 'Pedagogical stylistics in an ELT teacher training setting: A case study', in Teranishi, M., Saito, Y. and Wales, K. (eds.), *Literature and Language Learning in the EFL Classroom*. Basingstoke: Palgrave Macmillan, 298–315.

Li, C. and Gao, X. 2017. 'Bridging "what I said" and "why I said it": The role of metapragmatic awareness in L2 request performance', *Language Awareness* 26(3): 170–190.

Lima, C. 2018. *Literature*, by A. Paran and P. Robinson. Reviewed in *ELT Journal* 72 (2): 226–227.

Mason, M. 2004. 'Referential choices and the need for repairs in covertly-taped conversations', *Journal of Pragmatics* 36: 1139–1156.

McCarthy, M. 2003. 'Talking back: "Small" interactional response tokens in everyday conversation', *Research on Language and Social Interaction* 36(1): 33–63.

McCarthy, M. and McCarten, J. 2018. 'Now you're talking! Practising conversation in second language learning', in Jones, C. (ed.), *Practice in Second Language Learning*. Cambridge: Cambridge University Press, 7–29.

McConachy, T. 2009. 'Raising sociocultural awareness through contextual analysis: Some tools for teachers', *ELT Journal* 63(2): 116–125.

2013. 'Exploring the meta-pragmatic realm in English language teaching', *Language Awareness* 22(2): 100–110.

McConachy, T. and Hata, K. 2013. 'Addressing textbook representations of pragmatics and culture', *ELT Journal* 67(3): 294–301.

McLaren, R. M. and Solomon, D. H. 2015. 'Relational framing theory: Drawing inferences about relationships from interpersonal interactions', in Braithwaite, D. O. and Schrodt, P. (eds.), *Engaging Theories in Interpersonal Communication: Multiple Perspectives*. Los Angeles: Sage, 115–127.

McNiff, J. 2013. *Action Research: Principles and Practice* (3rd edn). Abingdon: Routledge.

Neustadter, S. and Weber, M. H. 2006. *500 Days of Summer*. Available at: www.cinefile .biz/script/500daysofsummer.pdf (Accessed 3 July 2018).

Nguyen, T. T. M., Pham, T. H. and Pham, M. T. 2012. 'The relative effects of explicit and implicit form-focused instruction on the development of L2 pragmatic competence', *Journal of Pragmatics* 44: 416–434.

Nicholas, A. 2015. 'A concept-based approach to teaching speech acts in the EFL classroom', *ELT Journal* 69(4): 383–394.

Nuzzo, E. 2015. 'Comparing textbooks and TV series as sources of pragmatic input for learners of Italian as a second language: The case of compliments and invitations', in Gesuato, S., Bianchi, F. and Cheng, W. (eds.), *Teaching, Learning and Investigating Pragmatics: Principles, Methods and Practices*. Newcastle upon Tyne: Cambridge Scholars Publishing, 85–108.

Peele, J. 2014. *Get out*. Available at: https://scriptpipeline.com/get-out-and-call-me-by-your-name-screenplays (Accessed 3 July 2018).

Ren, J. and Gao, X. 2012. 'Negative pragmatic transfer in Chinese students' complimentary speech acts', *Psychological Reports* 110(1): 149–165.

Ren, W. and Han, Z. 2016. 'The representation of pragmatic knowledge in recent ELT textbooks', *ELT Journal* 70(4): 424–434.

Reynolds, E. 2011. 'Enticing a challengeable in arguments: sequence, epistemics and preference organisation', *Pragmatics*, 21(3): 411–430.

Rose, K. R. 2001. 'Compliments and compliment responses in film: Implications for pragmatics research and language teaching', *IRAL* 39(4): 309–326.

Sayer, P. 2005. 'An intensive approach to building conversation skills', *ELT Journal* 59 (1): 14–22.

Stim, R. 2016. *Getting Permission: Using & Licensing Copyright-Protected Materials Online & Off* (6th edn). Berkeley, CA: Nolo.

Su, I. 2010. 'Transfer of pragmatic competences: A bi-directional perspective', *The Modern Language Journal* 94(1): 87–102.

Sukhina, E. 2011. 'Enhancing heritage speakers' communication skills through drama and improvisation', in Ryan, C. and Marini-Maio, N. (eds.), *Dramatic Interactions: Teaching Language, Literature, and Culture through Theatre–Theoretical Approaches and Classroom Practices*. Newcastle upon Tyne: Cambridge Scholars Publishing, 244–269.

Taguchi, N. 2011. 'Teaching pragmatics: Trends and issues', *Annual Review of Applied Linguistics* 31: 289–310.

2015. 'Instructed pragmatics at a glance: Where instructional studies were, are, and should be going', *Language Teaching* 48(1): 1–50.

Taguchi, N., Naganuma, N. and Budding, C. 2015. 'Does instruction alter the naturalistic pattern of pragmatic development? A case of request speech act', *TESL-EJ* 19(3): 1–25.

Tajeddin, Z. and Pezeshki, M. 2014. 'Acquisition of politeness markers in an EFL context: Impact of input enhancement and output tasks', *RELC Journal* 45(3): 269–286.

Takahashi, S. 2010. 'The effect of pragmatic instruction on speech act performance', in Martínez-Flor, A. and Usó-Juan, E. (eds.), *Speech Act Performance: Theoretical, Empirical and Methodological Issues*. Amsterdam: John Benjamins, 127–142.

Talandis Jr, G. and Stout, M. 2015. 'Getting EFL students to speak: An action research approach', *ELT Journal* 69(1): 11–25.

Tatsuki, D. and Nishizawa, M. 2005. 'A comparison of compliments and compliment responses in television interviews, film, and naturally occurring data', in Tatsuki, D. (ed.), *Pragmatics in Language Learning, Theory, and Practice*. Tokyo: Pragmatics Special Interest Group of the Japan Association for Language Teaching, 87–97.

Thomas, J. 1995. *Meaning in Interaction: An Introduction to Pragmatics*. London: Longman.

van Compernolle, R. A. and Kinginger, C. 2013. 'Promoting metapragmatic development through assessment in the zone of proximal development', *Language Teaching Research* 17(3): 282–302.

van Compernolle, R. A., Weber, A. and Gomez-Laich, M. P. 2016. 'Teaching L2 Spanish sociopragmatics through concepts: A classroom-based study', *The Modern Language Journal* 100(1): 341–361.

Usó-Juan, E. and Martínez-Flor, A. 2008. 'Teaching learners to appropriately mitigate requests', *ELT Journal* 62(4): 349–357.

Waring, H. Z. 2013. '"How was your weekend?": Developing the interactional competence in managing routine inquiries', *Language Awareness* 22(1): 1–16.

Wang, S. 2016. 'daxue yingyu jiaoxue zhinan yaodian jiedu [Interpretation of the key points in the Guidelines on College English Teaching]', *Foreign Language World* 174: 2–10.

Warner C. 2012. 'Literary pragmatics in the advanced foreign language literature classroom: The case of Young Werther', in Burke, M., Csabi, S., Week, L. and Zerkowitz, J. (eds.), *Pedagogical Stylistics: Current Trends in Language, Literature and ELT*. London: Continuum, 142–157.

Washburn, G. N. 2001. 'Using situation comedies for pragmatic language teaching and learning', *TESOL Journal* 10(4): 21–26.

Weatherall, A. and Edmonds, D. M. 2018. 'Speakers formulating their talk as interruptive', *Journal of Pragmatics* 123: 11–23.

Welch, I. 2015. 'Building interactional space in an ESL classroom to foster bilingual identity and linguistic repertoires', *Journal of Language, Identity & Education* 14 (2): 80–95.

Wong, J. and Waring, H. Z. 2010. *Conversation Analysis and Second Language Pedagogy: A Guide for ESL/EFL Teachers*. New York: Routledge.

Wu, H. and Takahashi, T. 2016. 'Developmental patterns of interlanguage pragmatics in Taiwanese EFL learners: Compliments and compliment response', *The Asian EFL Journal* 18(1): 130–166.

Yu, M. 2011. 'Learning how to read situations and know what is the right thing to say or do in an L2: A study of socio-cultural competence and language transfer', *Journal of Pragmatics* 43: 1127–1147.

Part II

Literature and Speaking Skills

7   EFL Learners Reading and Discussing Poems in English

Tara McIlroy

This chapter explores Japanese EFL learners' responses to poems of different levels of familiarity. The aim of the project was to try to uncover learners' interactions with poetry and then to consider the benefits of speaking about poetry for second language learning. A Japanese poem by Kenji Miyazawa in English translation was used as a familiar text, and a Dylan Thomas poem as an unfamiliar poem. Four pairs of learners were asked to talk together about the poems and report on what they understood the poems to mean. They were also asked to give a personal response to the poems. It was anticipated that in speaking about the familiar poem, learners' background knowledge of the Japanese text would support a more detailed interpretation, while the unfamiliarity of the new poem would present barriers to understanding of meaning but could present opportunities for co-constructed meaning creation through speaking. Three sources of data are used in the chapter: (1) a bilingual questionnaire which identified learners' poetry-reading backgrounds; (2) the learners' conversations, used to explore spoken responses to the two poems; and (3) follow-up interviews. The results indicate that poetry-reading processes such as noticing, questioning and interpreting meaning occur with both types of poem. The results also suggest that speaking about poetry could be useful for the development of speaking skills such as elaborating, negotiating and also practising specific spoken language such as use of discourse markers and conversation skills. The results also suggest that poetry discussions may help learners to express their feelings in English, which could develop their familiarity with conversational strategies when using their speaking skills in future situations.

Introduction

Widdowson (1992: 72) suggests that reading poems for 'how they mean' can stimulate 'an engagement with the poem' and 'extend the range of possible response'. In a recent study of English poetry reading with Japanese learners, Nishihara (2016: 166) calls for more research using poetry in specific second language (L2) contexts, to 'show the diversity of learners' poetry reading practices'. Nishihara echoes the suggestion of other researchers (Paran 2008; Fogal 2015; Hall 2015; McCarthy 2015) interested in researching literature in language classrooms. Paran (2008), for example, notes a gap between what researchers and L2 instructors appear to know about their shared fields of study. To address the need for more research in specific educational contexts, and to add to growing research using poetry with L2 learners, this study analyses language from learners talking about poetry in English. Conversations are used to evaluate the potential of poetry for English language learning, thereby approaching the central question of this book, that is how can literature enhance awareness of spoken language and improve their speaking skills?

The conceptual framework for this study comes in part from the work of Rosenblatt (1978). In what she called aesthetic reading, the focus is on the experience of reading the text, as well as the relationship between reader, text and context. The reader brings his or her own background, skills, and knowledge to a text, and this is what helps the reading experience come to life. McRae (1991) describes engaging the imagination of the reader when approaching what he called representational language as found in texts such as poetry, advertising and songs. Representational language can be decoded or understood in a number of ways, with various possible interpretations. In Japan, allowing and encouraging the use of imaginative answers requires careful management, as it can be a new experience for learners in English. Poetry can provide a space for imaginative discussion and engagement which can have other, real-world applications in later contexts, such as conversations, which frequently include indirect uses of language (Carter 2004).

In Japan, poetry features strongly in first language (L1) literacy development, which means that Japanese students have had some exposure to poetry in elementary school, where they have read and written haiku (see Chapter 5, this volume, and A. Saito 2015; Y. Saito 2015; Takahashi 2015). High school curriculum content is based around the National Centre Test for University Admissions, used by all public universities as well as some private ones, which 'consists of four parts: an essay in modern Japanese; a passage from a novel in Modern Japanese; an extract from a literary text in Classical Japanese and a brief extract from a literary text in Classical Chinese' (A. Saito 2015: 48). As a result of test preparation, Japanese learners have had limited experience in giving extended personal reactions to any type of literature. One effect of this is its connection to skills such as speaking, since English learners in Japan may approach conversation thinking that they need to find a correct response.

The present chapter investigates the potential of poetry for the development of spoken language skills, in particular because talking about poetry encourages discussion, negotiation, elaboration and description. By speaking about poetry together, the process through which language awareness and speaking skills develop can be illuminated and better understood.

Previous Research

Much previous research using literature reading has been focused on developing a greater understanding of reading practices. Novice poetry readers will begin to read poetry with confusion or by summarising the poem using what Richards (1929) called a 'plain sense' reading. The meaning will be translated into ordinary English sentences, ignoring the poetic qualities of the poem and talking about the poem as if it is merely prose (Richards 1929: 12). If L2 readers are using these explanations to practise their elaborations as a type of language output activity, then this could be valuable as a tool to develop negotiating and interpreting skills and through this their speaking skills. Various texts may lead to development of speaking skills, including those which are relatively easy as well as those which present difficulties.

The current study builds on previous research, including that of Hoffstaedter (1987), who used think-aloud protocols with poems in English and German, and suggested that some poetry readers liked simple texts, some preferred complex texts, and a third 'characterization' (1987: 85) of reader liked a combination of both. Following from this, Hanauer conducted a number of empirical studies (1998a, 1998b) using poetry alongside other genres of writing to determine features of the poetry-reading process. In a review article of poetry-reading research, Hanauer (2001b) looked at empirical studies of poetry reading and recommended more specific contexts to help understand the poetry-reading process, particularly for language learners at different stages of their learning.

Hanauer (2001a) used the approach by Skehan (1996) to evaluate poetry-reading processes, considering the resulting conversations as evidence for language learning although he did not focus on speaking skills. Hanauer asked pairs of English learners to talk together about song lyrics, finding that they 'recognize aspects of aesthetic textual manipulation (such as rhyme) and used it in the actual meaning construction process' (2010: 35). According to Hanauer, poetry reading involves a series of stages: 'The second language learner seems first to notice and analyze linguistic form and from this enter into a process of interpretation and elaboration in relation to the understanding of the poem' (2010: 36). Hanauer's study did not involve asking learners about feeling and enjoyment, which some other researchers suggest is important (Mattix 2002; Hall 2003). Hall concludes that 'pleasure and understanding are equally important and mutually necessary for a successful literary experience' (2003: 397).

From the field of pedagogical stylistics and critical pedagogy, Zyngier's 'literary awareness' is also used as background to the current study. Literary awareness (Zyngier 1994) occurs when literary reading activities are used to promote students' understanding of textual features with the aim of helping them use those skills when reading future texts. The approach comes from studies in language awareness (Sinclair 1985; Carter 1993) which look closely at what language is and how it is used (see, e.g., Swain and Lapkin 1995 and Chapters 2 and 3, this volume). The stages of literary awareness are reaction, awareness and interpretation, with the latter being most desirable for language learning because it will allow learners to apply strategies to other texts autonomously and automatically. The practical application of this in speaking situations is related to the notion that conversations naturally occur so quickly that it is desirable to interpret and understand language immediately. When practising responses to literary texts in conversation, one result could be to gain fluency of response and greater flexibility in conversation. According to previous work done in literary awareness, the 'role that feelings play' (Zyngier and Fiahlo 2010: 14) should also be considered in L2 literature classes. Paran (2008: 467) suggests that literature-based activities should aim to focus on language as well as literature, combined with 'literary knowledge and skills'. Although there has been increased interest in poetry in the field of pedagogical stylistics, little crossover into classrooms worldwide has been seen (Zyngier and Fiahlo 2010: 15). As Fogal (2015) notes, pedagogical stylistics and other related approaches often begin more with the text than the learner.

Poetry discussions could provide opportunities for developing speaking skills such as elaborating and negotiating meaning. Eva-Wood (2004) built on the work of Earthman (1992), who saw elaboration as meaning construction. In her thesis focusing on novice L1 readers of poetry, Eva-Wood looked at engagement through what she called 'thinking and feeling' (2004: 182). For Eva-Wood, the engagement was signalled particularly through the elaborations which learners made in think-aloud protocols, notably in how much detail they noticed from the poems. As Eva-Wood (2004) showed, elaboration can be visual, verbal and text or real-world related. Her study focused on reading practices rather than speaking skills, although think-aloud protocols were used as a data collection method. Background knowledge, understanding of key themes and recognition of allusions are all 'the elements of a text that create a feeling of familiarity in the reader' (Jacobs 2015: 7). From this we may predict that when a text has been encountered before, it may encourage greater elaboration on meaning, while an unfamiliar text will be approached differently because of the lack of background knowledge to assist meaning construction.

Related to the practice of speaking skills and conversation, the current study draws on work by McCarthy and McCarten (2018), who propose that conversations should create opportunities to develop fluency and successful interaction. Practice occurs when learning is 'within learners' linguistic comfort zone' and allows the use of target strategies while allowing them to 'engage confidently in confluent conversational activity' McCarthy and McCartern (2018: 29) in the L2. While poetry can resist initial interpretation, it is argued in this chapter that it does provide opportunity for discussion and practice of conversation. While related studies have revealed important findings about poetry reading, this chapter's focus on speaking offers a different perspective. The current project builds on previous studies while offering a particular focus on speaking.

Responding to Poetry

Poetry draws attention to itself through the process of foregrounding (Leech and Short 1981; van Peer 1986), which is a result of the poetic function (Jakobson 1960). Reading poetry involves significant attention to surface linguistic forms such as word choice, sounds and word order. When learners talk together about poetry, it is natural that they will notice and respond to poetic features such as repetition, use of metaphor and other examples of poetic language. Responding to poetry, either in speech or in writing, can create opportunities for pushed output (Swain and Lapkin 1995; Swain 2005), since the foregrounded language seems to invite comment and discussion. The activity in this study was a discussion with a partner, requiring co-constructed meaning and justification of answers, allowing this to be considered a 'pushed' output activity. Output activities using poetry can include speaking and discussions. The act of being involved in the creation of language is the essential element, since 'the learner is in control' (Swain and Lapkin 1995: 99), in this case, in control of the conversation and giving opinions. Noticing (Schmidt 1990) can occur when learners come into contact with authentic materials or activities and find the gap in their current knowledge. One example of this is talking together, which can result in language-related episodes (LREs). LREs occur when learners talk about the language they are producing and may correct themselves or others as they are talking together (Swain and Lapkin 1995). LREs may also lead to learners questioning their language use or the language of the text or their interlocutor. While conversations about poems may not be grammar focused explicitly, the questions and discussions around meaning may result in LREs, which are said to be evidence of noticing. Asking questions, negotiating and explaining, describing, and finding alternative ways to elaborate on meaning can all be considered types of extended production through which speaking skills can develop. Particularly for Japanese learners, who have had many opportunities to read and listen to English, speaking opportunities can provide rich opportunities for output and noticing. As a result, the following research questions guide this chapter:

RQ1: What are some identifiable differences in how Japanese learners approach familiar and unfamiliar poems in English?

RQ2: To what extent did poetry discussion help these learners in developing speaking skills in English?

Methodology

Participants

In this study, eight Japanese university EFL learners (F:5, M:3) completed a poetry-reading protocol activity and a follow-up interview with the researcher. These volunteer participants came from the elective poetry class (N:63) and were randomly allocated pairs to complete a poetry-reading and speaking activity. All participants were third- and fourth-year undergraduates from an English department at a private university near Tokyo, Japan. The participants were taking an elective course entitled 'Creativity in Poetry and Song'. Participants self-reported their total TOEIC (Test of English for International Communication) scores (reading and listening), the mean and standard deviation were 737.5 and 63.19, respectively. The participants can be considered mixed-level with estimated CEFR (Common European Framework of Reference for Languages) bands of A2–B2, using their TOEIC scores as a guide (Tannenbaum and Wylie 2008). The number of years of learning English (six in school, followed by their university studies) and relatively similar educational backgrounds meant that they shared L1 literacy backgrounds and to some extent their L2 English learning background. All the participants were native Japanese speakers, but two had dual nationality (see student data Appendix 7A) and their responses are reported using pseudonyms. All students agreed to complete the baseline questionnaire for research purposes in the first part of the study, and in the second part students volunteered for the conversation activity and follow-up interview conducted outside of class time which did not affect their grade for the course.

Procedure

The study was conducted in two parts:

Stage one: baseline poetry questionnaire. Students in an elective poetry course (N:63) completed a background questionnaire in the first week of class (Appendix 7B). Students gave permission for this information to be used for curriculum planning and research purposes. The questionnaire was given in English and Japanese, and the results revealed that all students in the class had some limited background in reading poetry in Japanese, but limited experience speaking about poetry in English.

Stage two: paired conversations about poems and follow-up interviews. A speaking activity was created with learners being given the following instructions: 'Give a personal response to each poem. Say what you liked or didn't like about the poem.' English–Japanese dictionaries were permitted and the recording included individual reading and note-taking time. Participants took 30 minutes on the activity and were video-recorded. Participants were asked to use English as much as possible in their conversations. Conversations were transcribed without making grammar corrections. Participants had follow-up interviews with the researcher one week later, during which they read over the transcriptions of their conversations and were given the opportunity to talk further about the poems. Participants were reimbursed for their time using the university research funds

Materials

In the poetry conversation activity students were given two poems. The project employed guidelines by Day (1994) for selection of texts in reading classrooms, that is, readability, length, vocabulary level and topic. The first was a Japanese poem that was likely to have been encountered before, '雨ニモマケズ / Ame ni mo makezu' (Not giving in to rain) by Kenji Miyazawa (1896–1933) from an anthologised collection (Sakai 2010). The poem was published posthumously, and the English translation was taken from an English/Japanese collection of Japanese literature, in a chapter entitled 'Heart and Soul' (Sakai 2010: 222–225). The Miyazawa poem is thirty-five lines long and expresses the concept of an ideal person, searching for how to conduct his life. The overall message seems to relate to a central idea or conceptual metaphor that life is a struggle. Students were given the poem to read in English and Japanese and could use dictionaries.

The second poem was 'Do Not Go Gentle into That Good Night' by Dylan Thomas (Thomas 1951). The Thomas poem is a villanelle, with five three-line stanzas and a final four-line one. Lines one and three of the first tercet repeat alternately until both are repeated at the end of the final quatrain. It contains obvious manipulation of language using rhyme, repetition and rhythm for effect. The meaning of the poem hinges in part on its play on the meaning of the key word 'rage' and understanding of light/dark to mean life/death, and like the Miyazawa poem it relates to life as a struggle. Although it is a short poem, its meaning does contain some potentially confusing complexity, and it presents difficulties on first reading. This poem was unknown to the students and was expected to be significantly challenging. During the activity the students used the dictionaries quickly, writing translated words above the poems. The poems had not been pre-taught, but given the short length of the poems and that dictionaries were available it was expected that the activity would be within the students' language abilities.

By looking at the vocabulary profile of the Thomas poem, it is possible to predict its difficulty for L2 readers. Most of the vocabulary in the poem is not difficult for advanced learners in terms of reading and pronunciation. The vocabulary is simple, with use of short, high-frequency words. Lexical analysis using the online tool Lextutor (Cobb 2018) reveals that the poem is made up of 90.4 per cent high-frequency words, with 168 tokens and 98 different word types (type-token ratio: 0.58). In this poem, high-frequency words from the first 1,000-word level include 'age', 'dying', 'eyes', 'night' (83 per cent of the words in the poem). There are 7 per cent words from the second 1,000 list of most commonly used words, also considered to be high frequency. Examples are 'burn', 'light', 'wild', 'wise'. This is still too low for the text to be read comfortably without a dictionary (Laufer and Nation 1995). One off-list word, 'rage', is repeated throughout the poem and appears eight times (accounting for 4.8 per cent of the poem's total running words). That is to say, the high-frequency 1,000 and 2,000 list (90.4 per cent) and the single word 'rage' (4.8 per cent) accounted for 95 per cent of the running words of the poem. The following words appear once in the poem: 'blaze', 'forked', 'frail', 'grieved', 'height', 'lightning', 'meteors', 'rave' and account for the final 4.8 per cent of the running words. Difficulty in reading a poem goes beyond the word level, but the vocabulary profile suggests that the poem would be suitable for this group of learners.

Data Categorisation

Data categorisation of using the protocols was done was in three steps. In the first part, the data were prepared and organised; second, an adapted coding system was established; and next, coding reliability was accounted for. The qualitative analysis looking at the focus on speaking skills was completed after these three steps. The steps were as follows:

1. *Preparing the dataset.* All of the conversations were transcribed using a broad transcription with the focus on what was said and not focusing on details such as pauses, intonation, etc. Pseudonyms were used for all the subjects in the transcription.
2. *Adapting a coding system.* The protocols were analysed initially using a coding system created by Hanauer (2001a). An adapted coding system was developed, with categories of *noticing, questioning, interpretative hypothesis/elaboration, world knowledge* and *integrating world knowledge*. The first category, *noticing*, includes quoting or paraphrasing of words or phrases, noticing repetition and other literary features and noticing idiosyncratic uses of language. The second category is *questioning*, which is when a speaker asks a question directly relating to part of the poem. *Interpretative*

hypothesis means explaining a section or part of the poem which could be in response to a question from the partner. In the current study, this category combines with *elaborative statement*, which occurs when using a paraphrase of the original text. The fourth category is *world knowledge*, which means general knowledge and presents as a response to a question or interpretation. The fifth category is *integrating knowledge*, which occurs when two interpretative comments are linked. In the Hanauer study there was no category for feelings of like/dislike, so those were additionally coded in this study and are referred to as the category *emotional responses* (positive or negative). In the final section of this chapter, the conversations are used to illustrate how learners may have developed their speaking skills while talking together about the poems.

3. *Evaluating the reliability of the coding system.* The conversations were coded and then a second rater helped to confirm the coding system. The rater was an experienced university teacher at the same institution who was familiar with literature teaching and Japanese poetry. Twenty per cent of the data was used to confirm the coding system, and the method was to provide the second rater with lists of coded data and ask to confirm which of the codes could be suitable for each item. Some differences of opinion were resolved through discussion, and the reliability of the coding was found to be 93 per cent. One week after the data collection, I met each pair of students once more and we talked together about the transcripts of their conversations. This post-session discussion aimed to answer any lingering questions that the students may have had about the activity and the poem. What I found was that students were engaged and interested in the poetry they had read, and some had taken the opportunity to investigate them in greater detail in their own time.

Results and Discussion

This chapter discusses results and discussion in three main subsections, beginning with the results of the poetry questionnaire. The second subsection gives results of coding the conversations. The third subsection offers a qualitative analysis of conversation data with specific reference to the development of speaking skills. The focus of discussion is on how learners are able to use speaking for co-constructed meaning making, for example, while utilising specific discourse markers.

Results of the Poetry Questionnaire

In question one of the poetry questionnaire, 50/63 of the learners could quote and name famous poets and poetry, while thirteen could not. Most of the answers to question 1 ('What is your experience of learning about poetry before taking this class?') referred to elementary school or junior high school, and the poetry was from 国語 / kokugo (Japanese language) class. A typical answer describes the content of classes in elementary and junior high school:

詩についての学習はほぼ皆無です。数少ない詩の学習で行ったものとすれば、小学生の時に 学ぶ「金子みすず」など有名な詩人の一番有名な詩を習って来ました。その他には短歌や俳 句といったものは中学生まで毎夏の長期休暇の課題として考えたことがあります。

[There is almost no learning about poetry. If we studied with learning a few poems, I remember the most famous poems by Kaneko Misuzu in elementary school. Other than that, I thought about something like *tanka* and *haiku* as homework in the summer vacation at junior high school.]

In high school, literature learning became reliant on the teacher's interpretation of the text. One student explained the feelings of difficulty which emerged from this experience:

作品や作者の背景を先生が説明するのをただただ聞いていました。私が作品を読んで感じた ことと、先生が説明する作品のいいたいことが度々異なり、詩は難しいと思っていました。そのため、あまり楽しかったという印象はありません。しかし、作者の意図に関係なく自由に詩を読むことは好きでした。

[I just heard that the teacher explained the background of the work and the author. The things I felt when I read the work and the things I wanted of the work explained by the teacher were often different, I thought the poem was difficult. Therefore, I do not feel that I had much fun. However, I liked reading poetry freely regardless of the author's intention.]

From these answers we can infer that these learners have had some experience with poetry in Japanese, as expected. In high school this became more focused on the National Centre Test for University Admissions (requiring correct answers in multi-choice tests) and teachers were preparing students for this learning instead of using poetry to develop other skills.

The most frequently mentioned poets in question 2 were Kaneko Misuzu (18), Aida Mitsuo (14), Shuntaro Tanikawa (8), Matsuo Basho (6), Akiko Yosano (5) and Kenji Miyazawa (4), who are all famous poets in Japan. None of the students had ever taken a creative writing class before (question 4), and most experiences with writing about poems had been through diaries and writing haiku or tanka, two short forms of Japanese poetry. Frequent references to elementary school and the choice of poems/poets mentioned indicated that most of these memories were from their early childhood. Some students also mentioned English poets such as William Shakespeare or John

Lennon. Most students were interested in reading poems together with classmates and in writing poetry (question 6), which was also to become part of the course. While some comments about school experiences mentioned that the reading of poetry was sometimes tedious or boring for them at the time, overall the questionnaire showed students' favourable disposition to poetry and enthusiasm for the beginning of the course.

In question 7, students explained their current understanding of poetry, which revealed some thoughtful insights. English comments have been left as is (English translations are my own):

詩は、心の機敏さを言葉で形容し、その言葉にのせられた想いを読む者は汲み取りそして感じる.

[Poetry expresses the agility of the heart with words, and those who read these thought [*sic*] on those words can also feel them.]

詩は考えさせられる。[Poetry makes me think.]
　詩はこころで感じ、読む人によって印象が変わる詩があることを学びました. [Poetry is an affair of the heart, and I learned that people can change their thinking by reading it.]

Poetry is one of the most beautiful ways to describe feelings and minds in our hearts.
Poetry is free, we can express what we see, what we hear and what we feel.
I think poetry is escaping from reality. While I reading poetry or lyrics, I depart adventure in imagination world. When I come back to real world, I can feel something hot in my heart.

While some students were unable to remember quotes or poets, there was no one who left question 7 without an answer. All of the group could give a definition of poetry, even those who were unsure who or what poems they had read before. This seems to suggest that even though this group of learners were limited in their confidence to recall and quote poetic knowledge openly, they had a positive disposition from which to talk together about poems.

Coded Analysis of Poetry Discussion

The next section includes results from a coded analysis of protocols based on categories developed by Hanauer (2001a). The category *emotional responses* draws on a study on literary reading and emotional response (Zyngier and Fiahlo 2010). The aim of this section is to answer the first research question: *What are some identifiable differences in how Japanese learners approach familiar and unfamiliar poems in English?* The next section uses qualitative methods to highlight in particular the discourse markers as evidence of developing speaking skills and aims to answer the second research question, *To what extent did poetry discussion help these learners in developing speaking skills in English?*

In the coding used by Hanauer in his 2001 study, *noticing* is a category used often in L2 language acquisition studies (Schmidt 1990), which sees language awareness as a key stage in the L2 language acquisition process. *Noticing* is 'direct evidence of close textual reading' (Hanauer 2001a: 303) and occurs frequently when speaking about poems. *Questioning* is coded for any type of question and is a broad category. In this study, the next category is *interpretative hypothesis* and *elaborative statement*, which were two separate codes in the Hanauer study but were joined for this study, that is, 'direct evidence of the participant's process of construction of meaning' (Hanauer 2001a: 304). *World knowledge* does not involve direct analysis of the content of the poem but helps to bring in background knowledge. Finally, to address emotion in the responses, the last category is *emotional responses*, which can be positive or negative. Results of the coding are presented in Table 7.1.

The familiar Japanese poem prompted *noticing* more than the English poem. When searching for meaning with the English poem, there was also use of quoting and noticing as a strategy, which seemed to work to support students as they looked closer at the unfamiliar poem they were struggling to read. There could be several reasons for this, including the idea that the poem was familiar, close to students, and therefore they could approach easily (and talk more about it). Another possibility is, given that the familiar poem was read first, the students had more to say.

Poem 1 prompted many *emotional responses*, but many of the comments were about how the students did not like the poem. More specifically, they went straight to the message of the poem and said that they did not like the lifestyle that the poet was describing. One student went so far as to say that she hated the poem. They seemed to think that the poem was telling them what to do, not merely talking about the poet's own life. One student mentioned her feeling that the poem was associated with the Second World War, which could account for the negative feelings about the poem. In contrast to this, with the Dylan Thomas poem, responses were generally positive, even when students accepted that the poem was difficult and that the subject was death/dying.

Questioning was used in different ways depending on the poem. For the familiar poem, procedural questions were typical. There were more questions about meaning for the unfamiliar, Dylan Thomas poem: 'Do you understand?', 'What does it mean?' and 'You think?'. There were also some questions which used the words of the poem directly and were coded twice as examples of *noticing* and as *questioning*. From this, it can be assumed that the Thomas poem encouraged greater curiosity and co-construction of ideas, since the frequent questions were related directly to interpretation and the meaning of the poem.

Interpretative hypothesis occurred frequently when talking about the Miyazawa poem. Familiarity with the poem appeared to mean that topics, recurrent themes and connections with experience resulted in a more smooth interpretation. One example of this was the comment: 'When I read this poem

Table 7.1 *Results of using adapted version of Hanauer's (2001a) codes*

Code	Examples of responses to the familiar poem	Frequency	Examples of responses to the unfamiliar poem	Frequency
1. *Noticing*	The person like this is what I want to be	26	Every first sentence in each paragraph is 'night' 'right' 'bright' 'flight'	18
	Neither giving in to rain Nor giving in to wind		Good men, the last wave by, crying how bright	
2. *Questioning*	Did you understand?	21	Old people should rage and burn?	17
	How about you?		Do not go gently into that good night?	
3. *Interpretative hypothesis/ Elaborative statement*	For me, it's difficult for me to be like this man because this man is always keeping calm, he doesn't get angry. When I read this poem, I thought that this poem conveys the difficulty of life.	33	This means don't be gentle. Rage is angry. So it means people want to live.	9
4. *World knowledge*	I know it's famous, but I've never seen this poem before.	16	I think he is describing the fear of death between Christians and atheists.	8
	I think almost all Japanese people know all sentences.		Dying means, going to heaven.	
5. *Integrating knowledge*	It's interesting way to show living, but it's a little bit strict for us, I think.	7	The writer's father can go to heaven.	13
	I think almost all people want to be like this person, but actually this is difficult to be like this person.		This is describing the anger against God, and also it is describing the fear of death through the experience of his father's death, I think.	

Table 7.1 (*cont.*)

Code	Examples of responses to the familiar poem	Frequency	Examples of responses to the unfamiliar poem	Frequency
6. *Emotional responses (positive or negative)*	I just don't like that kind of long poem and it's kind of complicated. I hate this sentence: 'Never getting angry. Always keeping a calm face'	20	It's a little difficult but we can enjoy the rhythm and the shape. I like this because it is rhythmical.	6

I thought that this poem conveys the difficulty of life.' The student referred to the central theme of the poem directly to make an interpretative comment. In contrast, with the Thomas poem, explanations were attempted, but they were simple ('This means don't be gentle' and 'dying means going to heaven') and less frequent.

World knowledge was used but not extensively in the responses. Some examples showed an overall lack of knowledge, for example, 'I know it's famous, but I've never seen this poem before.' Related to the Thomas poem, there was some background understanding of religion, which was introduced by one student, Hiro, who wrote 'I think he is describing the fear of death between Christians and atheists.' This interpretation includes speculation, which is an important aspect of developing speaking skills. In answer to the first research question about different ways in which the learners approached the different poems, it would seem from this small sample that both types of poems prompted various types of interpretation, and that the difficult poem did result in frequent use of questions and noticing, providing opportunities for speculation. In the following section, the qualitative discussion elaborates on how speaking skills are used in discussions using the two poems.

Qualitative Analysis: Using Poetry to Develop Speaking Skills

To answer the second research question (*To what extent did poetry discussion help these learners in developing speaking skills in English?*), this section looks at the poetry conversations using a qualitative approach. The conversations can be seen as creative acts of co-constructed meaning making, where participants are involved in 'jointly-produced fluency' (McCarthy and McCarten 2018: 4) leading to successful interactions. *Interaction* is the combination of 'noticing and awareness', which should be evaluated through looking at the depth of understanding achieved during interactions in the target language. According to McCarthy and McCarten, 'the very act of interacting with and practicing the target elements is in itself conducive to better inductive skills and increased awareness' (2018: 9). They also describe successful materials as a 'springboard for personalization' (2018: 24) because they 'afford learners overt opportunities to personalize the language' (26). *Personalising* allows students to talk about their own experiences, their beliefs or culture. In the case of these conversations, the spontaneous interactions serve as opportunities to practise conversation in real time, where each partner's response adds to the developing understanding of the poem. In the following examples from the conversations, it is possible to investigate four conversational strategies (from McCarthy and McCarten 2018: 17):

1. *Managing the conversation*: referring back to earlier comments, beginning or ending the discussion.
2. *Constructing your own turn*: taking time to think of an answer, elaboration.
3. *Listenership*: responding to news or information, showing understanding.
4. *Taking account of others*: projecting shared understanding, telling new information.

The difference between the relatively familiar Japanese poem and the difficult, unfamiliar English poem can be seen in the conversations through the presence or absence of these elements.

Example 1: Katsuhiko and Hiro discuss the Japanese poem

KATSUHIKO: Let's start with Kenji Miyazawa. This is famous, right? What is the question? [looks at sheet]

HIRO: I know it's famous, but I've never seen this poem before.

KATSUHIKO: Really?

HIRO: To be honest with this poem, I don't like that kind of poem.

KATSUHIKO: Really? Why?

HIRO: I just don't like that kind of long poem and it's kind of complicated. It's based on that lifestyle. You know? I don't know how to explain but 'eating one and a half bowls of brown rice' and some vegetables every day. I don't like that kind of stuff

KATSUHIKO: Absolutely. Yes, yes, yes. This is the ideal of man, or humankind. So, those things. How can I say? Don't be rich.

HIRO: I know.

KATSUHIKO: It's interesting way to show living, but it's a little bit strict for us, I think. 'The person like this is what I want to be' I don't want to be like this.

In example 1, Katsuhiko and Hiro are using all four conversation strategies in this section of their conversation. Both students were in their third year, and Hiro had high English proficiency (810 TOEIC). Hiro knew that the poem was famous but did not recall having read it (Hiro spent some time overseas during junior high school and may not in fact have encountered it). 'This is famous, <u>right</u>?', Katsuhiko asks, using the conversation strategy of *managing the conversation*. He adds to this by referring to the activity 'What is the question?' When Hiro expresses that he only knows the name of the poem, Katsuhiko expresses surprise with 'Really?', asking for clarification and inviting further detail. Hiro uses hedging and *taking account of others* to show that he disagrees with the message 'to be honest . . . ', where the phrase functions as a preparation for his next comment, 'I don't like that kind of poem'. Katsuhiko uses 'yes, yes, yes', which is an example of *listenership*, along with 'absolutely' as a discourse marker to show understanding and agreement. Katsuhiko also uses the conversation strategy *constructing your own turn* with 'So . . . how can I say?' and Hiro replies with good *listenership*, 'I know', to show agreement. Hiro's use of 'I don't like that kind of stuff' is particularly noteworthy since McCarthy and McCarten refer specifically to the phrase 'that kind of stuff' as clear evidence of projecting shared understanding. Hiro employs this strategy to help share mutual feelings about the poem's message. He may be hesitating to criticise such a famous work. Hiro and Katsuhiko both agreed that the message of the poem seemed to be an old-style way of thinking and that they did not feel that the text appealed to young readers. The discussion allowed them to use discourse markers, hedging and conversation strategies to navigate their opinions about the poem. In the follow-up interview, Katsuhiko also talked about the poet a little more, explaining that Miyazawa was from Northern Japan (where he was also from) and that he liked the poet for that reason.

In the next example, a conversation about the more distant, difficult English poem by Dylan Thomas is discussed with reference to the four conversation strategies.

Example 2: Aya and Taka discuss the unfamiliar English poem

AYA: *dou yuu imi/* What does it mean? [speaking Japanese] Do not go gently into that good night?

TAKA: This is a father who is dying, or almost dying. If people are dying, they can't move or say nothing, so before this moment they should, or father should, express his
emotion. Like that. So, human must be die. This can't be changed. So before death you should express what you feel. Even you are dying, when you are, before you are dying, you should get anger [*sic*] about dying.

This part of the conversation, taken from Aya and Taka's protocol, shows a lengthy elaborative comment on meaning. Even though Taka has only just read the poem for the first time, he uses a long turn to explain and elaborate on his understanding of the poem. Taka's TOEIC score of 670 was low, despite being in his fourth year at the university, and in class he was sometimes a reluctant speaker. Although the poem is difficult to read and understand, it provided a chance for him to explain his interpretation. Aya begins the section by orienting or *managing the conversation* with her question. However, she does not respond to Taka's discussion with anything that could be considered *listenership*. Taka's response was given slowly and carefully, and in the video recording there were pauses which could have provided Aya with a chance to respond, *constructing her own turn* or showing understanding of Taka's ideas. Taka's repeated use of 'you' to mean a general 'us' could be seen as *taking account of others* in projecting shared understanding, but he does not seek clarification for his statements with questions, possibly revealing elementary use of developing conversation skills. In the rest of the conversation, the two discussed the positive and negative feelings they had about getting old, working too hard and feeling stress. They seemed to use the poem as a way into another, related conversation about feelings and their future working lives. Aya and Taka were the only pair of students who were in a mixed male–female pairing, and their conversation overall was somewhat surprisingly open about feelings. In the follow-up conversation one week later, both expressed interest in reading further poems about emotions and feelings, particularly in poems written in English.

Example 3: Maki and Takako discuss the unfamiliar English poem

TAKAKO: It's a little difficult but we can enjoy the rhythm and the shape. Each paragraph has three sentences and similar sounds. And my image of poetry doesn't have period, but this one does.

MAKI: But this poem it is used.

TAKAKO: Do you like this poem?

MAKI: But content is difficult, so.

TAKAKO: Yes.

MAKI: And I felt a little serious and scary because 'near death' so.

TAKAKO: 'Dark is right'. Difficult. But I like this because it is rhythmical. It's really poetry.

MAKI: Yes.

MAKI: Is this a famous poem?

TAKAKO: I don't know. But maybe this poetry is talking to us like and 'you' maybe 'you' is me, the reader. But it's difficult for us. Any other comments.

MAKI: I enjoyed.

Despite the resistance to understanding that this poem presents, in this protocol there is some co-constructed meaning. The two students use short turns to work past the difficulty of the poem. The section begins with 'it is a little difficult for us', which projects shared understanding. The next part of Takako's statement is 'we can feel the rhythm and the shape'. She connects her own feelings with those of others. *Noticing* of poetic language or punctuation was not done at all with the Miyazawa, but with this conversation Takako refers to 'rhythm' and 'shape', which are both clear identifying elements of the poetic genre. Both students ask one question each. Instead of answering the question 'Do you like this poem?', Maki says 'But content is difficult', which could be interpreted to mean that she is reluctant to say that she did not like the poem and uses 'but' as hedging. There is some use of the skill of *listenership* when Takako uses 'yes' to agree with Maki, and later Maki uses the same simple word to show agreement. Both students were seniors and would be finishing their studies at the end of the year. They seem willing to assist each other with the interpretation. Takako's later comment 'It's really poetry' suggests a positive disposition to poetry despite its difficulty. She continues with a personalising statement about 'me, the reader'. Takako uses the strategy of *managing the conversation* and tries to summarise once more. While they use some strategies in this excerpt, the difficulty of the poem is a clear barrier to understanding. In the follow-up interview, both Maki and Takako talked about the language in the poem, asking some questions about rhyme and the background of the poem.

Example 4: Yukino and Eika discuss the unfamiliar English poem

YUKINO: Do you like this poem?

EIKA: No. Because I can't understand this poem. Perhaps his or her father is dying. This is a poem for his father.

YUKINO: Also, his father is likely to die. Or almost dying. Or already dying.

EIKA: Almost dying.

YUKINO: So, you feel sad?

EIKA: I think it's positive.

YUKINO: Positive? Positive?

EIKA: 'That good night' sentence means that dying people can be better.

YUKINO: I know! Dying means, going to heaven.

EIKA: Heaven.

YUKINO: Like this [points to translation in dictionary]. So the writer is relieved. The writer's father can go to heaven.

In this protocol, the conversation about whether or not the students liked the poem is centred on an overall feeling about whether the poem's meaning is positive, or not. Noteworthy for this pair is that language proficiency levels were different (Eika: TOEIC 625/Yukino: TOEIC 790) with Yukino as the stronger of the two. Eika does not soften her answer to the question 'Do you like this poem?', answering 'No' instead of hedging. In a conversation, lack of hedging can be a barrier to smooth conversation. Yukino and Eika help each other reach a shared understanding that 'This is a poem for his father'. They construct their understanding through the use of a key phrase, 'that good night', and its associations. Eika suggested her interpretation 'I think it's positive' and assists Yukino in seeing and grasping the positive aspects of the test. If 'good' means 'heaven', then they can infer a positive meaning throughout. Yukino uses the speaking skill of *questioning* to seek clarification, that is, 'So, you feel sad?' and 'Positive? Positive?' which helps connect ideas and gather further details from Eika. When they reach an agreement about dying/heaven, Yukino uses 'I know!', which is an example of *listenership*. Yukino appears to take on the role of asking questions, that is, 'Do you like the poem?' and 'Do you feel sad?', which is evidence of *managing the conversation*. When needed, Yukino encourages Eika to use a dictionary. This pair show what could be useful when using multi-level classes and asking students of different proficiency to work together. That is, the stronger student has the opportunity to practise using questioning, explanation and other strategies to continue the discussion, while the weaker student has the benefit of learning from a peer. Overall, however, this conversation could have been different with more *managing the conversation* and *taking account of others*. In the follow-up interview, both suggested that they liked the poem and were interested in knowing more about its background.

To sum up this section, it was possible through these examples to look at the conversation data from the perspective of McCarthy and McCarten's four types of conversation strategies to see how much the poems allowed for practice of these forms. The Miyazawa poem, despite being less popular overall, appeared to present opportunities for discussion. The challenging Thomas poem, even though it used simple language, was difficult for the learners to approach and talk about smoothly. While these sections of dialogue are only selected as part of the overall conversations which students had, they do show how these two poems were read differently.

Conclusion

Encouraging discussion in a literature reading class can create 'room for genuine and natural dialogue . . . where students become independent readers, thinkers and agents in their own world' (Zyngier and Fiahlo 2010: 20). Poetry and related, creative texts such as advertising contain what McRae calls representational language (1991), which can be understood in different ways. The aim of this chapter was to investigate speaking skills and spoken language using poetry, understanding that L1 literacy practices in Japan already involve poetry such as haiku reading and writing, which means that the familiarity of poetry could lead to thought-provoking and evocative discussions. Poetry could be helpful to understand others' feelings, with the poem providing a convenient level of distance between speakers. For Japanese students who may favour indirect language or find emotional expression to be difficult in English, a poem could provide opportunities for practising the use of using common discourse markers, requests for clarification and strategies of hedging and using vague language when appropriate. While the present findings are necessarily tentative due to the small sample size, the present research could guide future studies. Poetry which is familiar could result in more use of conversation strategies overall, since the familiarity assists in engagement with the poem. Development of expertise in speaking and second language use involves incremental steps towards language proficiency which could be supported by this type of opportunity.

The first implication for teaching is that the study could support the view that poetry reading makes use of the tendency to seek growth and knowledge. According to Self-Determination Theory (SDT), we are all moved on by 'self-motivation', which helps create the positive conditions for learning (Ryan and Deci 2000: 68). When talking with a partner about a poem or other text, it is natural that we tend to search for meaning. Even if the outcome is that the student dislikes the poem, engagement of some kind has occurred. As SDT theory applies to second language learning (Noels et al. 2003), we can see that reading a poem and talking about it will lead to questioning and a search for understanding. In the case of this study, learners' ability to demonstrate an understanding of aesthetic qualities in poems, along with their noticing of textual manipulation (such as repetition, rhyme, metaphor, etc.) showed that these elements became part of the meaning construction process. While poetry does appear to 'make us think' (as suggested by one respondent to the baseline survey), it also allows for conversations which provide practice in natural conversation, developing co-constructed meaning and opportunities to practise good listenership.

The data in this study can also be seen as evidence of developing language learner language (Biber et al. 2009). Recent studies (see Fordyce 2009 and Jones 2016) have revealed the usefulness of looking at real language use and helping this inform classroom choices. When reading a new text and talking about it, there is the issue of ambiguity and guesswork, and if learners are not suitably equipped to deal with this, teachers could think about how to support learning and offer suggestions while expressing developing ideas.

Future studies could specifically focus on poetry and emotions such as shock, surprise, warmth, regret or other complex ideas, in order to encourage a range of responses among learners approaching poetry and other creative texts such as song lyrics. Recent research into empathy (Bal and Veltkamp 2013) has shown that reading fiction can influence empathy in readers, the benefits of which have practical applications outside of the classroom. In a class of students who come from different language backgrounds, the discussion of poems translated from the L1 would also open up possibilities for language and culture which longer stories or novels may not be able to provide. Greater focus on reading poems aloud could help to draw more attention towards the form and function of language, encourage the playful use of language through recognition of humour and also through writing poems in a similar style. A suitable extension of this activity could also be to give learners a set of guidelines by which to select poems, and then to ask them to find and report on their choice of poem. The baseline survey used at the start of this course could also be developed further to help gain insights into out-of-class learning histories and generate interest in other types of creative activities such as writing songs and performing poems.

Limited experience with poetry, in any language, may not mean that students have negative views of poems. These results seem to show that different types of poems can result in co-constructed meaning making, even with the difficult Thomas poem. For students who require practice in asking and answering questions, giving opinions and justifying them, or helping with conversation practice, poetry could be a useful resource. When learners search for meaning in poems, asking questions to their partners and themselves, they use various elaboration and conversation strategies. It was surprising to find that although the Miyazawa poem was well known, it was not well loved. The positive responses to the Thomas poem, despite its difficulty, were also somewhat surprising in that speculation and discussion were attempted. In considering future projects using poetry, uplifting and heart-warming topics could certainly be recommended to teachers, since students appeared to be interested in discussing poems. Overall, discussions showed the potential for poetry as a possible resource to develop L2 speaking skills.

Appendix 7A Baseline Questionnaire: Week 1

(Answers in English or Japanese are OK) 英語でも日本語でも良いので答えて下さい。About poetry/詩について
1 今まで行ってきた詩の学習についての経験を教えてください。What is your experience of learning about poetry before taking this class?
2 有名な詩人や俳人を知っていますか? その人物のことで知っていることをできるだけ細かく教えて下さい。Do you know any famous poets? Write some details.

3 詩や詩人から好きな言葉がありますか? Do you know any quotes from poems or poets?
4 今までクリエイティブライティングのクラスを受講したことがありますか? もしあ
るのであれば、できるだけ細かく教えて下さい。Have you ever taken a creative writing
class before? Yes or No
5 自分の自由な時間に今までどのようなものを自主的に書いたことがありますか?
What kind of writing have you done in your spare time before? Diary 日記 Poetry 詩や俳句
Song lyrics 歌の詩   Other その他あればなるべく細かく
6 このクラスで何を学習したいですか? あてはまるものすべてチェックして下さい。
What would you like to learn from this class? Tick all that apply.
  o 有名な詩人について Learn about famous poets
  o 他国の詩人について Learn about poets from other countries
  o 詩を書くこと Write poems
  o 詩についての意見をクラスメイトとディスカッション Discuss poems with classmates
  o 様々な詩をクラスメイトと読む Read poems with classmates
  o 歌や音楽を使っての学習 Use songs and music
  o 詩人の人生について
  Learn about poets` lives
  Other . . ..
7 「詩は、」で始まる段落を書いて下さい。自分の意見やアイディアを書いてくれても
Write what you think poetry is. Opinion and individual ideas are OK.で, 詩は ... *Poetry is* . . . .

Appendix 7B Participant Information (names are pseudonyms)

Pair	Student number	Male/ female	Ethnicity	Age	Grade	Language ability (self-reported TOEIC score)
1	Katsuhiko	M	Japanese	21	junior	725
1	Hiro	M	Japanese/ British	20	junior	810
2	Maki	F	Japanese	22	senior	755
2	Takako	F	Japanese	21	senior	785
3	Eika	F	Japanese/ Filipino	21	senior	625
3	Yukino	F	Japanese	20	junior	790
4	Taka	M	Japanese	21	senior	670
4	Aya	F	Japanese	21	senior	740

References

Bal, P. M. and Veltkamp, M. 2013. 'How does fiction reading influence empathy?An
experimental investigation on the role of emotional transportation', *PLoS ONE* 8
(1): 1–8.

Biber. D. Johansson. S. Leech. G. Conrad. S. and Finnegan. E. 1999. *Longman Grammar of Spoken and Written English*. London: Longman.

Carter, R. 1993. 'Language awareness and language learning', in Hoey, M. (ed.), *Data, Description, Discourse*. London: HarperCollins, 139–150.

2004. *Language and Creativity: The Art of Common Talk*. London: Routledge.

Cobb, T. 2018. Compleat Web VP [computer program]. Available at: www.lextutor.ca /vp/comp/ (Accessed 15 May 2018).

Day, R. 1994. 'Selecting a passage for the EFL reading class', *English Teaching Forum* 32(1): 5–15.

Earthman, E. A. 1992. 'Creating the virtual work: Readers' processes in understanding literary texts', *Research in the Teaching of English* 26(4): 351–384.

Eva-Wood, A. L. 2004. 'Thinking and feeling poetry: Exploring meanings aloud', *Journal of Educational Psychology* 96: 82–91.

Fogal, G. G. 2015. 'Pedagogical stylistics in multiple foreign and second language settings: A synthesis of the research', *Language and Literature* 24(1): 54–72.

Fordyce, K. 2009. 'A comparative study of learner corpora of spoken and written discursive language: Focusing on the use of epistemic forms by Japanese EFL learners', *Hiroshima Studies in Language and Language Education* 12: 135–150.

Hall, G. 2003. 'Poetry, pleasure and second language classrooms', *Applied Linguistics* 24(3): 395–399.

2015. *Literature in Language Education* (2nd edn). Basingstoke: Palgrave Macmillan.

Hanauer, D. 1998a. 'The genre-specific hypothesis of reading: Reading poetry and encyclopaedic items', *Poetics* 26(2): 63–80.

1998b. 'Reading poetry: An empirical investigation of formalist, stylistic, and conventionalist claims', *Poetics Today* 19: 565–580.

2001a. 'The task of poetry reading and second language learning', *Applied Linguistics* 22(3): 295–323.

2001b. 'What we know about reading poetry: Theoretical positions and empirical research', in Steen, G. and Schram, D. (eds.), *The Psychology and Sociology of Literary Texts*. Amsterdam: John Benjamins, 107–128.

2010. *Poetry as Research*. New York: John Benjamins.

Hoffstaedter, P. 1987. 'Poetic text processing and its empirical investigation', *Poetics* 16 (1): 75–91.

Jacobs A. M. 2015. 'Neurocognitive poetics: Methods and models for investigating the neuronal and cognitive-affective bases of literature reception', *Frontiers in Human Neuroscience* 9: 1–22.

Jakobson, R. 1960. 'Linguistics and poetics', in Sebeok, T. A. (ed.), *Style in Language*. Cambridge, MA: Massachusetts Institute of Technology, 130–147.

Jones, C. 2016. 'Teaching spoken stance markers: A comparison of receptive and productive practice', *The European Journal of Applied Linguistics and TEFL* 5(2): 83–100.

Laufer, B. and Nation, P. 1995. 'Vocabulary size and use: Lexical richness in L2 written production', *Applied Linguistics* 16(3): 307–322.

Leech, G. and Short, M. 1981. *Style in Fiction*. Harlow: Pearson.

Paran, A. 2008. 'The role of literature in instructed foreign language learning and teaching: An evidence-based survey', *Language Teaching* 41(4): 465–496.

McCarthy, K. 2015. 'A critical review of cognitive approaches to literary interpretation and comprehension', *Scientific Study of Literature* 5(1): 99–128.

McCarthy, M. and McCarten, M. 2018. 'Now you're talking! Practising conversation in second language learning', in Jones, C. (ed.), *Practice in Second Language Learning*. Cambridge: Cambridge University Press, 7–29.

McRae, J. 1991. *Literature with a Small 'l'*. London: Macmillan.

Mattix, M. 2002. 'The pleasure of reading poetry in a second language: A response to David Hanauer', *Applied Linguistics* 23(4): 515–518.

Nishihara, T. 2016. 'Of learning and poetics: Exploring strategies used by L2 Japanese English learners', in Burke, M., Fiahlo, O. and Zyngier, S. (eds.), *Scientific Approaches to Literature in Learning Environments*. London: John Benjamins, 151–168.

Noels, K., Pelletier, L. G., Clement, R. and Vallerand, R. J. 2003. 'Why are you learning a second language? Motivational orientations and self-determination theory', *Language Learning* 53(1): 33–64.

Richards, I. A. 1929. *Practical Criticism*. New York: Mariner Books.

Rosenblatt, L. 1978. *The Reader, the Text, the Poem: The Transactional Theory of the Literary Work*. Carbondale: Southern Illinois Press.

Ryan, R. M. and Deci, E. L. 2000. 'Self-determination theory and the facilitation of intrinsic motivation,social development and well-being', *American Psychologist* 55(1): 68–78.

Saito, A. 2015. 'Bridging the gap between L1 and L2 education', in Teranishi, M., Saito, Y. and Wales (eds.), *Literature and Language Learning in the EFL Classroom*. London: Palgrave, 41–60.

Saito, Y. 2015. 'From reading and writing: Creative stylistics as a methodology for bridging the gap between literary appreciation and creative writing in ELT', in Teranishi, M., Saito, Y. and Wales (eds.), *Literature and Language Learning in the EFL Classroom*. London: Palgrave, 61–74.

Sakai, T. 2010. *An Anthology of Notable Japanese Literature*. Tokyo: JASRAC.

Schmidt, R. W. 1990. 'The role of consciousness in second language learning', *Applied Linguistics* 11(2): 129–158.

Sinclair, J. M. 1985. 'Language awareness in six easy lessons', in Donmall, B. G. (ed.), *National Congress on Languages in Education Assembly (York, July 1984)*. NCLE Papers and Reports, 6. London: Centre for Information on Language Teaching and Research, 33–36.

Skehan, P. 1996. 'A framework for the implementation of task-based instruction', *Applied Linguistics* 17(1): 38–62.

Swain, M. 2005. 'The output hypothesis: Theory and research', in Hinkel, E. (ed.), *Handbook of Research in Second Language Teaching and Learning*. Mahwah: Lawrence Erlbaum, 471–483.

Swain, M. and Lapkin, S. 1995. 'Problems in output and the cognitive processes they generate: A step towards second language learning', *Applied Linguistics* 16(3): 371–391.

Takahashi, K. 2015. 'Literary texts as authentic materials for language learning: The current situation in Japan', in Teranishi, M., Saito, Y. and Wales (eds.), *Literature and Language Learning in the EFL Classroom*. London: Palgrave, 26–40.

Tannenbaum, R. J. and Wylie, E. C. 2008. 'Linking English-language test scores onto the common European framework of reference: An application of standard-setting methodology'. Available at: www.ets.org/Media/Research/pdf/RR-08–34.pdf (Accessed 20 May 2018).

Thomas, D. 1951. 'Do not go gentle into that good night'. Available at: www.poets.org /poetsorg/poem/do-not-go-gentle-good-night (Accessed 20 April 2018).

van Peer, W. 1986. *Stylistics and Psychology: Investigations of Foregrounding.* London: Croom Helm.

Widdowson, H. 1992. *Practical Stylistics: An Approach to Poetry.* Oxford: Oxford Applied Linguistics.

Zyngier, S. 1994. 'At the crossroads of language and literature: Literary awareness, stylistics, and the acquisition of literary skills in an EFLit context', PhD thesis, University of Birmingham.

Zyngier, S. and Fiahlo, O. 2010. 'Pedagogical stylistics, literary awareness and empowerment: A critical perspective', *Language and Literature* 19(1): 13–33.

8   An Analysis of Collaborative Dialogue in Literature Circles

Scott J. Shelton-Strong

Sociocultural and social cognitive theories have begun to make a lasting imprint on English Language Teaching (ELT) and learning as it is undertaken and understood today across a range of contexts (Steffensen and Kramsch 2017). This chapter reports on a study conducted with English language learners involved in Literature Circles (LCs) over an extended period and centres on an analysis of the discourse generated within these post-reading, group discussions. The chapter begins by contextualising LCs as a vehicle for reader response and collaborative engagement within an ecological perspective to second language (L2) development. Drawing on sociocultural theory (Lantolf, Thorne and Poehner 2015) and its application to collaborative engagement in a language learning environment, the discourse presented undergoes an ecologically grounded, dialogical analysis. This analysis interprets examples from the group conversations as affordances for language development identified as an emergent phenomenon, co-constructed and mediated by the support of peers, the shared reading experience and relevant scaffolding. The current study suggests that this dynamic combines collaborative interaction and interpersonal communication with ecosocial processes to promote spoken L2 development, where deep processing of shared interpretation, critical evaluation, collective noticing and expression of affect are externalised within the discussions.

Introduction

As mentioned in Chapter 1 (this volume), literature as a resource for English Language Teaching (ELT) and learning has long been recognised for its potential to inspire and engage language learners (Brumfit 1985; Brumfit and Carter 1986; Collie and Slater 1987; Carter and Long 1991; McRae 1991; Carter and McRae 1996) and continues to generate strong interest in our field (Paran 2008; Cohen 2009; Hall 2015; Teranishi, Saito and Wales 2015; Bloemert et al. 2019). Today, a new generation of researchers, teaching practitioners and learners are discovering innovative ways to use literature to heighten spoken language awareness and afford opportunities for the development of speaking skills (see, e.g., Chapter 7, this volume).

In this chapter I will focus specifically on Literature Circles and the affordances they provide for L2 (spoken) language development (L2-LCs henceforth). Van Lier (2004b) defines affordances as opportunities for language learning constructed within the learner's relationship, or engagement, with the learning environment. Those identified here, it is argued, emerge from within the interaction of the small social/learning groups engaged in collaborative, peer-directed discussions (mediated by a shared reading experience) which define participation in L2-LCs.

The aim of this chapter is to analyse this interaction, through dialogue, and examine ways in which the language used to explore and develop a deeper understanding of the shared reading experience is co-constructed, leading to the emergence of affordances for L2 (spoken) language development (Lantolf et al. 2015; Steffensen and Kramsch 2017). The dialogue produced in this context is interpreted as spoken language used as a social form of thinking and learning, where linguistic knowledge and understanding are jointly constructed through the shared exchanges, which involve collaborative reflection, interpretation and personalisation of the shared reading experience (Mercer 2004).

The later discussion will centre on an analysis of this dialogue, in which learners engage in 'languaging', or the act of engaging in discussion, problem solving or the negotiation of meaning to produce meaningful, comprehensible language in the context of L2 learning (Swain 2006: 96–97). Steffensen and Kramsch (2017: 7) suggest this involves both multisemiotic exchanges and extra-semiotic exchanges, or what Thibault (2011: 3) conceptualises as a 'whole bodied achievement'. This analysis is grounded within a 'sociocultural theory of mind' (Swain 2000: 103), whereby language used with a collaborative aim is considered a powerful mediator, fostering the emergence of opportunities for language development (van Lier 2000; Mercer 2004). The chapter ends with a summary of the outcomes of this discussion, highlighting the benefits and affordances relating L2-LCs to L2 language learning and development.

Bearing this in mind, language learning, and by extension (spoken) language development in this study, is viewed as a dynamic process mediated by cultural, social and linguistic artefacts, and situated at the confluence of sociocultural and social cognitive theories (Bandura 2001; van Lier 2004b; 2007; Lantolf et al. 2015; Steffensen and Kramsch 2017).

Previous Research

Literature Circles (LCs) are a relatively new addition to the ELT landscape. Modelled on adult book clubs (Daniels 2002), these were first introduced in the early 1990s into first language (L1) language arts classrooms in the USA to promote reading and experiential learning, achieved through a combination of learner-led inquiry, awareness-raising and explicit instruction (Daniels and Steineke 2004). These were later adapted to ELT contexts, with early research showing benefits for L2 learners, such as increased motivation and a willingness to interact with one another and use the target language (Furr 2004), enhanced communicative competency (Kim 2004) and increased confidence in self-expression, fostered within the intimacy of the self-regulated, post-reading discussions (Chiang 2007).

L2-LCs are defined as collaborative, peer-led discussion groups supported by focused, extensive reading where learners engage in reading the same piece of literature, with a small 'l', indicating the use of any potentially interesting novels, short-stories or poetry rather than only the established cannon of classical literature (McRae 1991), and focus their reading and discussion through the preparation of specific roles (Daniels 2002; Furr 2004).

These roles constitute an important element of scaffolding, particularly when used in L2 language learning contexts (see Furr 2004 and Hsu 2004 for role sheet examples). Table 8.1 below exhibits examples of standard roles and their paired strategies.

The use of role assignments within the framework of L2-LCs has been found to be particularly effective, as they scaffold participation, distribute reading focus and strategies, provide models for inquiry and encourage the development of natural patterns for group interaction to emerge (Shelton-Strong 2012). According to Daniels (2002: 99), 'these roles aim to "create" positive interdependence by giving group members clearly defined and interlocking but very open ended tasks'. While role assignments provide scaffolding for focused reading and effective inquiry, learners are encouraged to exercise autonomy when noticing language, choosing examples from the text, formulating questions and identifying topics for discussion (Furr 2004; Hsu 2004).

Roles of this nature in L2 classrooms have been argued to support learner confidence and efficacy in task completion, and to enable peer-support through collaboration (Dörnyei and Murphey 2003: 118–122). As learners experiment with regular rotation of the different roles used in L2-LCs (see Table 8.1), the development of the social skills and cognitive strategies involved, such as questioning, visualisation, connecting and inferring are supported (Furr 2004; Maher 2015). This, in turn, can lead to the development of deep connections and rich discussions, as self-expression is supported and personal agency is invested in the collaborative engagement.

Table 8.1 *Standard roles and paired strategies*

Standard roles used in L2-LCs	Paired strategies of L2-LC roles
Discussion director or the Questioner	Questioning, noticing and analysing – maintains the interaction of the discussion through questions and invitations to participate
Word master	Noticing the writer's expression and style – responsible for choosing new, important or interesting words and multiword expressions to share, define and contextualise
Passage person	Determining importance – chooses key passages, explaining reasons for choice, and offers and elicits comment
Connector	Making connections – connects real-life people and events with the story content and prepares questions to invite similar comments
Cultural collector	Making connections and comparisons – looks for cultural similarities and differences between story and own culture and brings them to light, inviting comments through questions to circle members
Artistic adventurer	Visualising – draws or creates something to represent an element of the story, sharing and communicating the rationale to the group
Summariser	Reads for gist and essence, synthesises events – responsible for giving or eliciting an oral summary of the reading.

Research suggests that as learners participate within the L2-LC framework, (spoken) language development and collaborative learning is fostered and facilitated via active engagement in the group discussions (Kim 2004; Shelton-Strong 2012; Armstrong 2015; Nishikawa 2015). This is facilitated in part through prior attention to language use and meaning, while learners lay the groundwork for the discussions through reading and role preparation. However, it is the ideas and interpretations *developed and exchanged within* these discussions which are considered to be of particular relevance, as it is within this shared process that dialogue and social interaction occur, and through which affordances for (spoken) language development and collaborative learning emerge.

One of the findings often discussed in L2-LC research is the potential to transform relatively shy or reticent learners into collaboratively engaged participants (Furr 2004; Sambolin and Carroll 2015). A number of factors are pertinent here, including the agency and independence fostered through choice and responsibility as an active group member (Daniels 2002; Dörnyei and Murphey 2003: 105), response to the rich representational language found in literature (McRae 1991: 109) and engagement with the role assignments that scaffold, support and focus the reading and group discussions.

A subtler reasoning for this transformation comes from a self-determination theory (SDT) perspective (Deci and Ryan 1985), a meta-theory which seeks to understand human motivation and personality. One of the mini-theories which makes up SDT points to the basic psychological needs of autonomy, competence and relatedness (BPNT), which are likened to 'nutrients that are essential for growth, integrity, and well-being' (Ryan and Deci 2017: 10). In terms of L2-LCs, the socially supportive context of the discussion circles (relatedness), the full agency learners have within these to act and make connections (autonomy), and opportunities to express their views and generally feel supported in these (competence) may help to understand how learners gain the necessary confidence to engage more fully.

To date, much of the research into L2-LCs, across a range of educational and cultural environments, has focused on the affordances interrelated to group dynamics (LeBlanc 2015; Maher 2015; Sambolin and Carroll 2015), the motivation to read and use the target language (Furr 2004; Fredericks 2012) and opportunities for incidental learning through extensive reading (Chiang 2007; Ro 2017). However, further research to achieve a clearer understanding of the potential for (spoken) language development and second language acquisition (SLA) to be fostered within this learning environment, and the principles underpinning this process, is needed.

Theoretical Underpinnings

Social cognitive and sociocultural theories have been increasingly recognised as essential references as researchers discuss and seek to gain a deeper understanding of L2 language development (Steffensen and Kramsch 2017: 4).

Sociocultural theory (SCT) holds the view that learning first manifests itself in the social realm before this is internalised by the individual through engaging in inner speech, and in collaboration with (more competent) peers (Lantolf et al. 2015). The aspect of SCT most commonly referred to when we attempt to explain the phenomenon of collaborative learning is the Zone of Proximal Development (ZDP). This is defined by Vygotsky (1978: 86) as 'the distance between the actual developmental level (of a learner), as determined by independent problem solving, and the level of potential development as determined through problem solving under adult guidance, or in collaboration with more capable peers'.

Donato (2000: 45) describes collaborative L2 learning from an SCT perspective as a developmental process through which language is acquired via the mediation of resources, such as print material, physical environment, gestures and classroom discourse. Applied to the L2-LC model, this development is theorised to be mediated via object (text, for example), others (the group) and self (the learner), where language is not only the medium of communication and the source of private thought but also a cognitive tool to regulate inner-speech, and in addition, externalised socially as it is developed through inter-action (Swain and Watanabe 2013; Lantolf et al. 2015).

Similarly, social cognitive theory argues that exposure to language alone is insufficient for SLA, while participatory agentic action is suggested to be necessary for development, adaptation and change (Bandura 2001: 4; Batstone 2010: 18; Duff and Kobayashi 2010: 76–77). Participation and agency, in preparation for, and later sustained within, the post-reading discussions, are deemed important aspects of the L2-LC framework. This agency, as mentioned earlier, is encouraged by the choices afforded to learners, such as their focus in the reading, the topics initiated for discussion, and the direction of these taken within the discussions. This agency is carried over into the extended learning community, where learners develop their voice as group members, within the combined 'social-interactive and cognitive-reflective work' of the learner-led collaborative discussions (van Lier 2007: 47).

From an ecological perspective (van Lier 2000; Kramsch 2002), language is viewed as a socially constructed tool (Swain 2000; Larsen-Freeman 2010), and within the social setting of the group discussions, learner involvement and development are supported and enhanced through collaboration with others in the group. Specifically, within the L2-LC framework, learners are immersed in discussions about language and ideas, based on their perception of events and themes while they interact with what they are reading, and later through the interpretations of their classmates. As pointed out, while this collaborative construction of affordances has been associated with an expert/novice para-digm, other interpretations include peer support. Ohta (2001: 76) argues that co-construction of knowledge and emergent expertise is attained through groups joined in collaborative efforts.

One example of this is the opportunity that arises for learners to uncover gaps in understanding, fluency and linguistic knowledge (Green 2005) and act on these through negotiation. Within the ecology of collaborative discussion circles, this can lead to the restructuring of existing hypotheses of how the target language works (Swain et al. 2009). This negotiation can foster the emergence of interlanguage development, and as we will see in the later analysis of learner dialogue, real-time adjustments are often co-constructed. This is an important point, as it reflects the essentially dialogic and co-constructed nature of conversation itself. Van Lier (2000) frames learner activity on this plane as not only facilitating learning, but also importantly, as constituting *evidence* of learning. Oxford (2017: 148–152) validates this position and highlights the powerful association which binds together learning and performance, and envisions these as inextricably interlinked. This holds impor-tance in regard to how learner interaction and the affordances for (spoken) language development in L2-LCs are interpreted in our later discussion.

There is currently a broad consensus that L2 learning (including a focus on spoken language development) is essentially a holistic enterprise, which develops dynamically (Ohta 2000; van Lier 2007: Larsen-Freeman 2016). The growing influence of the ecology metaphor on SLA is derived from the hypothesis that there are any number of factors which combine to drive learning processes, including affordances in the learning environment and those produced through learner agency and collaborative efforts (Larsen-Freeman 2007: 784; Steffensen and Kramsch 2017). Such views lend strength to the argument that factors supportive of SLA emerge from active participation within the framework underpinning L2-LCs. These include the fostering of social interaction, creative communication behaviours, the willingness to communicate, sharpened cultural perceptions, attention to and conscious noticing of language, implicit processing of patterns, positive attitudes and motivation, a learner-managed environment and perceived self-efficacy (Dörnyei 2009; Schmitt and Celce-Murcia 2010).

This holistic perspective of L2 learning, with a nod towards a dynamic systems approach, positions L2-LCs to reflect current views regarding SLA as dependent on interrelated variables, including context and environment, as created by agency (Larsen-Freeman 2007; Dörnyei 2009; Dörnyei and Ushioda 2011; Steffensen and Kramsch 2017). It is this agency of the learner, including his or her role in creating speaking opportunities, and the willingness to speak, that is considered so influential in actively creating social learning environments which, in turn, may shape future learning outcomes (Dörnyei and Ushioda 2011: 34; Kalaja et al. 2011).

In a very specific way, it can be argued that a ZDP which supports L2 development (Lantolf et al. 2015: 7–9) emerges as an outcome of the collaborative engagement of learners as active participants within the L2-LC framework. This learning dynamic is mediated by the literature read, the collaborative dialogue drawing on personal interpretations of the text, as well as influences from outside the text, and within the group, as learners engage in discussion to communicate and engage with the ecosocial and linguistic demands of the L2-LC.

So far, we have examined in some depth the theoretical underpinnings of sociocognitive and sociocultural perspectives, and how these interface with and validate the adaptation of LCs to an L2 learning context (L2-LCs). To follow, I would like to briefly touch on three of the more practical elements involved, which could be considered the three pillars of the L2-LC framework: independent extensive reading, reader response theory and collaborative learning (Daniels 2002). These underpin many of the potential benefits associated with L2-LCs such as (spoken) language development through negotiation and interpretation of meaning, exposure to and focused noticing of language form and use, and the strengthening of social-learning systems through collaboration.

Independent Reading

Extensive independent reading is a key feature of L2-LCs and has long been recognised to play an important role in long-term L2 acquisition, providing opportunities for cultural and linguistic enrichment, personal involvement and motivation to engage with the target language (Nation 2003; Webb 2007; Brown et al., 2008; Carrell and Grabe 2010, 2015; Macalister 2015; Jeon and Day 2016). However, schemes encouraging extensive reading to support language learning, but which fail to direct or integrate it with opportunities for debate and discussion, have been criticised (Chen 2018). Green (2005: 311) suggests that: 'Extensive reading, if done in interactive mode, supports the negotiation of meaning in texts, helps prevent the fossilization of interlanguage structures, and provides contexts in which learners can encounter and debate ideas, and analyse and practice language features found in texts.' This combination of extensive reading and opportunities for debate and discussion is one of the principal defining features of L2-LCs.

Reader Response

Reader response theory (Rosenblatt 1968, 1978) explores the possibilities of multiple interpretations of literary works, which are formed and influenced through the knowledge and personal experience the reader brings to the text. It is argued that through this personal response, meaning is emergent, co-constructed and developed, as readers cognitively and affectively engage with what they read. Proficient readers are thought to be active readers who question, infer, connect, hypothesise, analyse and visualise while interacting in concert with the text (Keene and Zimmerman 1997; Tomlinson 1997). These strategies are fostered explicitly within the L2-LC framework, through the clearly defined roles guiding reading and interaction (see Table 8.1), and through peer and teacher modelling. This inquiry in response to the text is externalised within the collaborative interaction of the discussions, where a sense of efficacy is thought to increase through exposure to peer modelling of these cognitive skills (Schunk and Hanson 1985 in Bandura 1997: 234). Educational psychology argues that this sense of efficacy strengthens motivation, fosters academic success and aids in building intrinsic interest (Bandura 1997: 175).

Collaborative Learning

For effective collaborative learning to take place, it is argued that predictable and controllable structures must be in place if productive outcomes are to be attainable (Dörnyei 1997; Daniels 2002). Mindful construction and mediation are required so that learners can enjoy the freedom to explore language learning within a secure but dynamic framework (van Lier 2004a: 92). Drawing on group dynamics (Schmuck and Schmuck 2000), the following factors have been identified as key to successful group work:

1. Clear expectations
2. Mutually developed norms
3. Shared leadership and responsibility
4. Open channels of communication
5. Diverse friendship patterns
6. Conflict resolution mechanisms.

Collaborative learning is defined by deciding and working towards common goals with others, a balanced distribution of responsibilities and the joining together to accomplish greater things than could be achieved on one's own (Barfield 2016). This is achieved through dialogue, social interaction and collective decision-making with others in a group. Here, there are clear connections to sociocultural theories of L2 learning (Lantolf et al. 2015) where emphasis is placed on the crucial role of mediation (principally by language) and the understanding of learning as being socially constructed, before it is internalised through social interaction and relevant scaffolding.

Upon close examination of the L2-LC framework, the factors necessary for successful collaborative learning to occur are easily identifiable. Further, when groups work together over an extended period (as the groups in the current study) these factors tend to gain in strength and can have lasting positive implications for the learner.

Against this background, the research questions guiding this study are as follows.

RQ1: What examples of collaborative interaction foster language development and acquisition within the dynamic of the learner-led group discussions based on focused extensive reading?

RQ2: To what extent do examples within the post-reading discussion suggest that the text read has elicited personal reactions, leading to interpretation and cultural or personal connections, which could promote heightened attention, collaborative noticing and engagement?

Methodology

This study was conducted over a period of three eight-week terms, with the discussions used for analysis recorded in the first two terms. The participants in this study attended a private language learning centre in Hanoi, Vietnam. The group consisted of three female and five male students between 15 and 17 years of age, all of whom were Vietnamese. The average level of proficiency was approximately at the Common European Framework of Reference for Languages (CEFR) B2 level (Council of Europe 2001). Class was held twice a week for a total of 4 hours, half of which were used for the L2-LC discussions and feedback. Approximately three-quarters of the class had studied at this language centre previously and were accustomed to being involved in pair and group work within a broad Communicative Language Teaching (CLT) methodology. However, none had been involved in L2-LCs prior to this study. In order to safeguard the identity of these students, pseudonyms have been used.

The Context of the Literature Circles

Over a period of approximately twenty-four weeks, these students read and discussed an essay[1] and two works of fiction[2] by George Orwell in unabridged versions. These texts were chosen for their intrinsically interesting plots, characters and settings, and for the powerful (representational) language used. McRae (1991: 3) describes representational language as that which demands from the reader an engagement of the imagination so that its potential meaning can be made (see also Chapter 7, this volume). While the reading and role preparation were conducted independently, outside of class, the discussion groups met at the onset of each class twice a week.

Initially, preceding the first L2-LC cycle, I discussed the basic framework underpinning the activity with the class, and expectations for the different stages in the reading and discussion cycle were set for performance and behaviour. To serve as a model for their own reading, and for the later discussion, questions and elements to be noticed, such as those suggested on the role sheets, were brought to the attention of the class. Pre-reading activities were conducted related to the story topic, context and genre to raise interest and initiate appropriate schemata, before a short excerpt of the reading was prepared, which for the first session, was done in class. From feedback at the conclusion of this trial discussion, procedural issues and related difficulties, such as making appropriate enquiries or invitations to participate, were discussed and ideas for improvement were elicited from the students, or suggested. This type of feedback became a regularly occurring feature at the conclusion of the discussions.

Following this introduction, reading and role preparation were done independently, outside of class. The discussion circles took place regularly, ending with feedback concerned with attention to language, reflection on both the story content and group interpretation, occurring within the time remaining after the discussions had ended. Following this, reading for the next discussion was negotiated and new roles were allocated or chosen.

As the discussions became progressively interactive, these learners became more confident to lead and contribute as well as to offer original ideas, or help as required, should the discussion falter. From my observations and notes, as well as from unsolicited comments from several class members, there were indications that, as the reading and discussion cycles progressed, both reading and speaking fluency increased incrementally.

Although the groups engaged with material written for an L1 readership, proving a challenge at many levels, they were able to follow the plot, understand the characters and place the story within the larger context of the external world. Their eager and energetic involvement, supported by careful role preparation, demonstrated their motivation to meet the challenges posed by the unabridged material. Aided by the scaffolding built into the role preparation, and provided within the peer-led discussions, the groups proved capable of navigating the layers of meaning in the literary texts and expressed enjoyment and satisfaction in collectively and individually reaching an understanding of these.

Data Collection and Analysis

The principal methods used to facilitate the data collection and analysis, apart from personal observations and field notes, were recordings and transcriptions of sustained learner-led dialogue within the L2-LCs on two occasions, with two discussion groups. Building on the work of Kim (2004), these transcripts underwent an interpretative dialogical analysis (Riessman 2008; Scotland 2012) in which excerpts of the dialogue were coded and categorised into four principle areas of reader responsiveness. These categories emerged from within the content and purpose of the dialogue, and the direction of its development. This focus reflects the affordances created through a personal response to literature, which has been suggested to foster personal growth, language awareness and motivation (Rosenblatt 1968; Carter and Long 1991; McRae 1996).

As a case study involving a small number of individuals within a classroom setting, individual and inter-group contribution was explored in-depth, with a focus on interaction, collaboration through dialogue and self-regulation. The discussions were learner-led and self-managed, allowing for close observation of how these developed, and the language used to develop these discussions.

Through post-discussion feedback and on-task observation, I was able to make reasoned inferences by combining my knowledge of the students as their teacher, with that of the role of the researcher. I thus made inferences through the lens of my understanding of how the L2-LC framework is theorised to provide opportunities for (spoken) language development through sustained engagement, collaboration through dialogue and group dynamics.

This aided in creating a broad overview of a genuine 'real-life' task (freely discussing a shared experience following individual preparation), which in turn allowed for a more detailed investigation used to highlight meaningful characteristics implicitly or unequivocally linked to the development of spoken language and personal growth within the learning community. This development is hypothesised to emerge from sustained participation in reading and discussion with peers, and supported by minimal teacher intervention.

Results and Discussion

In this section, four extracts undergo an analysis within the following four categories, which emerged from the learner interaction within the post-reading discussions. The headings used make reference to the type of learner engagement demonstrated as the dialogues are developed, and how these relate to the learner-led response to the story. The headings are:

1. Literal comprehension
2. Interpretation
3. Personal connection and cultural observation
4. Evaluation.

Literal Comprehension

The discussions normally began with the discussion leader asking questions to initiate the conversation. These were often in reference to general comprehension, but also of a general summative nature to provide a background for the discussion. These were open to response by any of the group members. At this point, several discussions into the book, the groups have attained a discernible cohesiveness and are openly supportive (or challenging) when attempting to reconstruct their understanding of the text.

The following is an example of group 1 working collaboratively to define, literally, one of the major elements which make up the fabric of the story they are reading. They have previously read and discussed four chapters in book one of Orwell's *1984*. This excerpt is taken from the discussion of chapter 5. L1 /L2 has been added after each pseudonym to allow me to refer to 'line one', 'line two' etc. in the discussion.

Extract 1

Group 1: Discussing chapter 5 of Orwell's *1984*

MINH (L1):   Ok, so first question is um, tell me, what is the, um, tell me what Big Brother's original idea is.
THUY (L2):   About what?
DUC (L3):   About what?
MINH (L4):   Yeah, about the original idea, BB's, you know ...
THUY (L5):   In chapter 5?

MINH (L6):   Yeah, the idea about destruction of the language.

THUY (L7):   Yeah, I have that one right here, I think on the whole, the . . . aim is to um, well, they, the Big Brother wants to destroy the words, reduce and simplify them.

MINH (L8):   How do they reduce the words?

THUY (L9):   How?

MINH (L10):   How, yeah.

THUY (L11):   Well, uh, they cut off, they cut off.

MINH (L12):   (to Lin) Do you remember?

LIN (L13):   The chapter is so long I cannot remember.

MINH (L14):   No? Cannot?

LIN (L15):   Yeah.

THUY (L16):   Well they cut off, there's like something, and there's something and, people can use a lot of words to describe something – yeah, a lot of levels to describe them, but they only use . . . but now they cut off most of them and only use some very simple words.

MINH (L17):   Yeah.

THUY (L18):   If they want to describe something else like the opposite meaning or (indistinguishable words between Lin and Minh), they only use two simple words to uh, you know . . .

LIN (L19):   Describe . . .

THUY (L20):   Describe it, you know like . . .

LIN (L21):   So, uh, give us some examples

DUC (L22):   um, just like excellent . . .

MINH (L23):   Yeah,

DUC (L24):   . . . it becomes uh, you know, double plus and you know . . .

THUY (L25):   . . . plus good

DUC (L26):   good.

DUC (L27):   Double plus good, and you know, double speak.

THUY (L28):   Double speak.

DUC (L29):   And also the opposite sign.

In this part of the conversation, initiated by Minh, the group works together to define what Minh frames as 'Big Brother's original idea.' The leading question is open (L1), but somewhat vague, and as he is asked for clarification, he is prompted to define it further (L6). This is a good example of learner interaction, which reflects the ethos of L2-LCs. Through questions generated by a need for clarity, learners are led to rephrase and paraphrase ideas in order to convey their ideas more clearly. This reprocessing or negotiation of meaning often leads to interactional adjustments, arguably leading towards acquisition, as input, focused attention and language production combine (Long 1996: 451; Makey 2007: 12–13). Collective interaction of this nature, connecting cognitive and social processes, have been argued to be fertile ground from which language development emerges (van Lier 2000: 258; Lantolf and Thorne 2006). In her eventual response, Thuy appears to have taken note of this information while reading, or has it at the tip of her tongue, as reference is made to 'having that one right here' (L7). She then goes on to give a clear description in response to the question asked and later attempts to provide an example to the follow-up question (L11).

Thuy had used the word 'reduce' as part of her definition of how language was being destroyed. Minh noticed this and used it in his follow-up question, 'How do they reduce the words?' This type of interaction is typical of the noticing suggested to occur within collaborative dialogue and may lead to eventual internalisation and automatisation as language is noticed, attended to and practised (Swain 2000). At this point Minh attempts to bring Lin into the conversation unsuccessfully (L12). However, Thuy redoubles her effort to continue with her previous thought and appears to engage in a form of 'private speech' (Smith 1996 in Donato 2000: 31), or externalised private verbalisation (Swain 2000) as she works through the difficulty of clearly expressing her idea (L16). This is thought to represent mediation of one's thoughts while speaking and may serve as a tool to navigate uncertain linguistic terrain while a solution is being sought (Donato 2000: 33). Thuy eventually manages to give an example to illustrate her meaning (L18). This prompts Minh to seek further clarification, pushing the group to produce more concrete, concise language. Duc enters the conversation at this point, and offers a literal example of how words are reduced and simplified in the story, reminding everyone how 'excellent' becomes 'double plus good', defining this language, and demonstrates that he recalls this works for negative words also (L22-29).

The collaborative effort of the group provided them with opportunities to actively engage in meaningful discussion supporting each other's contributions, while working to reconstruct the literal meaning of a rather complicated idea. Minh, in the role of discussion leader, asked demanding questions and pushed his classmates to produce clear, unambiguous examples. This led to extensive individual language production mediated by recollection of the text, learner's thoughts, responses and questions from other members. It also demonstrates how within the individual and collective ZDP, these learners helped to extend understanding and support each other to use the target language.

Interpretation

While involved in discussion, interpretations were often made, reaching past literal comprehension, while making inferences and what might also be seen as a collaborative negotiation of meaning. This allowed for deeper meanings to be co-constructed through the interactive participation of the group in response to the text. McRae (1991) described this as a process of seeing through language. He suggested that as readers recall and reflect in this way, it may signal language learning moving from the referential plane towards a declarative awareness of the representational qualities of the language.

Fillmore (1979 in Dörnyei 2009: 286) defines fluency as the ability to speak both clearly and with reason, appropriately and creatively. In this excerpt, which follows on from the previous, the learners hypothesise why language is manipulated in *1984* and make cross-reference to elements in the story to support their ideas, exercising fluency and developing an understanding of a major theme in the novel.

Extract 2

Group 1: Discussing chapter 5 of Orwell's *1984*

MINH (L1):	What do you think about that? That kind of language?
DUC (L2):	I like this because I don't remem ..., I don't need, you know, learn too much new words.
MINH (L3):	Yeah – but because you are stupid?
DUC (L4):	Yes, I'm stupid (laughs).
MINH (L5):	So, what is the aim of this, um treatment?
DUC (L6):	They want people to be stupid.
THUY (L7):	Yeah and the um, the party they want to ...
LIN (L8):	So, well, people use many, people use uh, complicated words when they think, and when they understand and they can feel things around them – I think that the aim of this treatment is, of this um, idea of Big Brother ...
MINH (L9):	Idea ...
LIN (L10):	... is to, um, well ...
MINH (L11):	... narrow their thoughts.
LIN (L12):	Yeah, make people become more stupid.
DUC (L13):	Yeah.
THUY (L14):	Yeah, because they only have to use ...
MINH (L15):	So but yeah, yeah, I agree, but what is the purpose of making people more stupid?
THUY (L16):	Well – what else?
LIN (L17):	They can control the people easily.
MINH (L18):	Yeah.
THUY (L19):	When the people, what I mean, when they are not thinking of anything else and do not have to think about what is going on around them, they have to ... yeah, whatever ...
MINH (L20):	But, but the direct, uh, direct effect is, uh, to prevent people have thought crime, you know, thought crime.
DUC (L21):	Because they don't have enough words to commit that.
THUY (L22):	Yeah – Because they don't have enough words to describe what they are thinking.
LIN (L23):	Yeah. / Thuy – Yeah.
DUC (L24):	Yeah!
DUC (L25):	So they don't know what they are thinking ...
DUC (L26):	Yes!
MINH (L27):	Maybe.
DUC (L28):	I'm good!

Here, Minh requested his classmate's opinions in reference to the 'double-speak' that had been referred to previously (L1). In response, Duc employs irony to explain that it might be a good idea as there are fewer words to learn (in reference to his position as a language learner, perhaps). Minh wonders if this might be because Duc is 'stupid', to which Duc laughingly agrees (L4).

The banter stops quickly here though as Minh again asks what the purpose might be for doing this (L5). At this point the whole group engages in unearthing the aim of reducing the language as a ploy to keep people from using complicated words to express feelings and understanding. Through further discussion they agree that the aim is to keep people from being aware and that 'thought crime' is used as a deterrent to restrict the use of words needed to express feelings and to describe what they are thinking. It is agreed as a result of this lack of expressive language, people are left in total ignorance of their own thoughts, which allows Big Brother to control the population more easily (L6–28).

This is an example of affective response to literature which enables learners to hypothesise and co-construct meaning within the collaborative framework of L2-LCs through use of imagination and interconnecting ideas. We can see the students involved in genuine attempts to put meaning into words. Lin, who was relatively silent in the initial part of this conversation, increases her participation and is supported several times as she attempts to express her thoughts clearly. It is also clearly motivating to them to collectively bring together ideas to coherently express a solution to the problem posed by Minh's initial enquiry. The end of the conversation gives an indication that they are satisfied with their collaboration and with the ideas put forward. Employing the metaphor of participation as language development (Donato 2000: 41), it can be argued that learning is evident here as meaning is developed collaboratively, mediated by the understanding achieved through reading, and emergent in the collective discourse.

Personal Connections and Cultural Observations

Group members responded to elements in the story, which evoked reactions to personal or collective cultural experiences, and realities in their own lives and environment. There were many occasions when these students were able to draw parallels between situations in the novel and collective interpretation of their country's past. As learners noticed language describing evocative situations while preparing for their discussion, initial connections were made. These, which were later explored more fully in the discussion, provide an example of language being deeply processed. First noticed through attentive reading, and later cross-referenced and attended to again in the discussion, the attention necessary to further acquisition may be exercised (Gass and Mackey

2007). In this extract, the politics of *1984* are discussed and related to the past and present policies of Vietnam. The roles of culture collector and connector are especially active here.

Extract 3

Group 2: Discussing chapter 5 of Orwell's *1984*

TRANG (L1): I don't know if you talked about in chapter 4, but about to reduce things in the ministry of plenty, they reduced everything more and more because everything was raised – but in Vietnam at the same time, in the past, like they had a card to ... they had to write everything in and they had to queue in line to buy everything cheap in the poor, poverty ...

DAO (L2): They didn't have money back then, just a card to ... the, the work give us the card for us to buy, to purchase things.

HUY (L3): So we wasn't ... wouldn't overbuy anything, because of the conditions of the economy they don't have enough so we can't buy too much.

TRANG (L4): And so much was, like I said, very poor poverty especially in food so they must buy in group quantity in the special holiday like TET or something or when someone is sick.

HUY (L5): You know, I think that time is like, this time. There is a ration for everything – they rationed everything, you know, you could only buy this much, this much meat, or buy this much rice per month, or ...

ANH: I don't think (*unintelligible*) doesn't have meat ...

TRANG (L6): Or they steal in the lunch ...

HUY (L7): Yes, but I think, I think that the announcement of the ministry of plenty in chapter five, I think it is ridiculous, ridiculous, everybody can see that everything is getting reduced and they still, and they still dare to say that things are getting better and better when they are lying and lying.

DAO (L8): I think that's the point, they lie about everything – at least our government is half honest not to say that we have nothing!

EVERYONE: (*laughter*)

HUY (L9): Yes, but the lie, but the, our government can lie because the lies are still reasonable but this lie is unacceptable!

DAO (L10): Yes.

ANH (L11): Yes.

In this excerpt, the themes of induced poverty through government restrictions, rationing of goods and the truthfulness of politicians are all connected to realities through examples in the text. Trang begins by making reference to a previous discussion and connects the rising prices and reduction of goods available, manipulated by the government in the novel, with the ration cards used in her country's past (L1). Dao attempts to clarify the definition given (L2), which is taken up by Huy, who provides an example of why this might have been (L3). He uses self-correction, changing 'wasn't' to 'wouldn't' and creatively used his developing knowledge of prefixes to construct 'overbuy' as he attempts to convey his meaning. Trang takes up the mention of 'conditions of the economy' and makes reference to her original turn to provide an example of how, in poverty, people had to collaborate to obtain sufficient goods for times of celebration or illness (L4).

Here, Huy affirms his belief that there is a connection between his country's past and the situation of rationing in the novel. He continues in this line and expresses emotional involvement in the story. Frustration is evident as he doubles on words like 'ridiculous' and 'lying' to describe the politics and the government's false claim announcing improvements, while the public can see how rationing is increasing (L7). Dao makes his interpretation of this evident, stating that this represents the total falsehood of the political situation in 1984, and brings humour in to suggest that their real government is honest enough to tell the truth about their predicament, to which all share laughter (L8). Huy, however, insists emotionally, that while their government might get away with lying, the lie expressed in the novel is unreasonable and unacceptable, with which all agree (L9-L11).

Here the group skilfully interacts with one another to take an initial observation connecting rationing in Vietnam with the continual reductions made by the 'Ministry of Plenty' in the story. As the conversation developed, the theme was explored in depth, with specific examples being offered. Culturally, there were similarities that were noted to have occurred possibly through government mismanagement and misinformation. Real emotion and energy were invested outlining these injustices. The group communicated easily, providing examples of rich language, and supported each other through elaboration in reference to previous utterances. This positive evidence within recasts has been linked to L2 learning (Gass and Mackey 2007: 184).

This meaningful dialogue presented a number of opportunities to explore the world created within the text and how it may or may not reflect the external world. As these connections were elaborated on, learners invested humour and emotion and collaboratively made observations while making reference to what they had read and how it affected them. Through this deep, personal involvement, learners are seen to move far beyond mechanical language practice. Here they are fully immersed, speaking, thinking and interacting with one another in English, conceptualising ideas, connecting them, enriching their understanding of the world and sympathising or showing frustration with it. Rosenblatt (1978: 14) makes reference to an aesthetic mode of reading (opposed to an efferent, or literal mode), through which personal experience is used to reach an understanding, utilising the affective domain. This demonstrates how response to literature can motivate personal involvement, which may encourage L2 learning through deep, memorable processing, making the language one's own (Carter and McRae 1996: Chen 2018).

Evaluation

In the L2-LCs, participants often exercised criticality. While making judge-
ments concerning character traits, intentions, the plot and where it was heading,
inferences were made relating to how meaning was dependent on a number of
interrelated elements, and evaluations were made. These evaluative comments
were often insightful and involving. In this final excerpt, the second group has
been discussing why Winston keeps a diary. It is suggested that he does this to
secretly express his feelings. It is also suggested that he is confused. As he may
be the only person not brainwashed, the group wonders if he believes there was
a different world before, or if it has truly been as it is now all along.

Extract 4

Group 2: Discussing chapter 5 of Orwell's *1984*

TRANG (L1):	So, what do you think about the character of Winston?
HUY (L2):	The character of Winston?
ANH (L3):	*Laughter* ... I read about the Winston think about the character of another character, sorry ...
HUY (L4):	About Winston, I think he has a little rebellion from the inside, yeah. He's one of the few people in the story who is able to, to overcome what the party, the party tries to put, tries to put in his mind and bang! A rebellion from the inside.
ANH (L5):	Anyway, I think he's brave.
HUY (L6):	Bravery, yeah.
ANH (L7):	Bravery.
TRANG (L8):	Brave.
HUY (L9):	Yeah, I can imagine that writing a diary is an act of bravery.
TRANG (L10):	No, I think it's not kind of bravery, because it's an idea in his mind and he put it in his own diary and only himself.
ANH (L11):	Most people are brainwashed, you know, and I think he can't say about his idea for, for, uh, to anyone so he just can uh, write it in his diary.
HUY (L12):	You must remember that there's a telescreen ...
ANH (L13):	Yeah.
HUY (L14):	... if he caught, if he is caught writing in his diary he will be arrested, and executed.
DAO (L15):	I think he's kind of in-between, uh, not brave enough to, uh, go, uh, public like Goldstein, but not too coward to do nothing like uh, Mr. Parson.
ANH (L16):	I think he uh, he uh, work for party, so he can understand what the punishment, he will ... he would be punished if uh, if they found, if they found ...
DAO (L17):	found out.
ANH (L18):	Found out, yes, found out, so I think he's brave.
HUY (L19):	He's kind of brave.
ANH (20):	Kind of brave.

The character of Winston is key to the novel, and the group try to conclude what he might be like. Differing opinions are offered and rejected, accepted or modified. Huy recognises Winston as a rebel and explains why he fits that description (L4). Anh offers an appropriate adjective, brave, to add to the description. Huy offers the adverb, which Anh mistakes as a correction, repeating it. Trang offers the adjective again, and Huy takes it up and uses it in a very well formed utterance, concluding with the formulaic: 'an act of bravery'. A discussion then ensues to evaluate if writing a diary is indeed a brave thing to do (L10–14). Anh and Huy join to provide reasons why it may be in this situation. Dao evaluates Winston in comparison to two other characters in the text. However, Anh insists that Winston understands the risks he takes, but has trouble remembering the particle for 'found out' to complete his idea, embedded in a conditional utterance. Dao provides the missing word, which Anh takes up and repeats twice. There seems to be a compromise in the end, that he is indeed, 'kind of brave'.

This part of the conversation illustrates how the collaborative framework functions to allow for divergent opinions to be elicited, expressed, evaluated, accepted, discarded and, in this case, modified through mediation of reference to the text and expressed through learners stretching their language to express meaning. Dealing with ideas in this way takes learners beyond a simple evaluative sentence, along the lines of 'I think he is brave.' Discussions such as these, held in small supportive groups, provide a safe arena for learners to try out new ways of expressing themselves, here mediated by the text and opinions from others in the group. Not only is it agreed upon that yes, Winston is 'kind of brave', but opportunities for extensive inter-group languaging took place and were acted upon. Learners worked together to define bravery in this context, and examples were provided in different ways to support this. Here learners are involved in critically evaluating literature within a supportive environment, where explicit reference to the text is made and opportunities for implicit learning are developed through dialogue, reinforcing and expanding on language collaboratively created (Green 2005). It has been argued that learner dialogue such as this demands a deeper processing of language as it is discussed, focusing attention on this language and possibly an evaluation of its effectiveness, as language hypotheses are tested and gaps in interlanguage noticed. This is suggested to 'have a potentially significant role in language development' (Swain 2000: 99–100), as awareness increases opportunities for noticing, which may foster SLA.

Conclusion

In this chapter, the effectiveness of literature as a resource for (spoken) language development has been explored within the framework of L2-LCs collaborative reader response groups, and evaluated through an analysis of sustained learner dialogue.

To determine the extent to which (spoken) language development was fostered within the L2-LC discussions, the research questions will be reviewed with a summary of the findings given here in response to these. These questions focused on examples of collaborative interaction to foster language development, and how these suggest different ways in which interaction with the reading material encouraged personal and cultural interpretation, language awareness and collaborative engagement.

In summary, drawing on sociocultural theory applied to L2 learning, the analysis of the post-reading dialogues has shown in different ways how affordances for language learning were developed within the learner-led discussions. Mediated by focused engagement with the rich, representational language of literature, learners brought their personal interpretations and own reflections to these discussions. The participants self-managed the exploration and development of the various themes as they emerged, and used their agency to make relevant, real-world connections, initiate a playful approach to languaging, critically examine interpretation from different angles, and participate in the social use of language to collectively explore these interpretations. It is an important finding in this study, that within the ecology of this collective response to the literature, and through the learner-directed group discussions, affordances for the development of (spoken) language emerged and were engaged with.

Within this dialogic interaction, we see examples of the learners rephrasing and paraphrasing their ideas as they attempt to express what they mean, or when they work at negotiating the meaning embedded in the text with others. The use of private speech to mediate one's thoughts in preparation for public talk, collaborative scaffolding among group members as events and themes from the story are reconstructed, recalling words and defining them, as well as examples of self-correction, were also observed. Deeper processing, or absorption, was evident as the groups became involved in critical evaluation, expression of irony, personalisation of language, and through the emotions or affect evident in many of their responses. While the groups were fully immersed in using the target language to engage in dialogue (including inner thoughts or private speech), they interacted with one another in skilful, often playful ways, giving rise to affordances from the reading and preparation for discussion, which encouraged personal and cultural interpretation, language awareness and collaborative engagement.

Exercising the agency and autonomous engagement that L2-LCs encourage, the learners not only spoke to one another with purpose but discussed at length rather complex layers of meaning, which required a socially mediated and collective response. This dialogue in turn created rich, coherent, extended discourse of the kind that has been hypothesised to be fertile ground for (spoken) language development. It is this collective development of socially constructed language that scholars have argued is crucial to L2 learning (Swain 2000; van Lier 2007; Dörnyei 2009; Lantolf et al. 2015; Steffensen and Kramsch 2017).

Throughout this chapter I have argued that the L2-LC framework is instrumental in creating opportunities for (spoken) language development, particularly through collaborative dialogue. The current study suggests this development is emergent and interrelated to the affordances of the L2-LC model, in step with a sociocultural view of language learning as well as an ecological perspective on the way in which languages are learned through dialogue and collaboration. This importance of dialogue and discussion in language education is underscored by the direction of current theory (Lantolf and Poehner 2014; Larsen-Freeman 2016; Steffensen and Kramsch 2017), wherein language development is no longer viewed through a conduit metaphor, or as a simple cause and effect continuum, but rather as a socially engaged system of semiotics within which we interact to function and develop as agents, as we navigate our journey towards becoming more competent users of a second or additional language.

The limitations of this study include the limited number of participants and quantity of dialogue which underwent analysis. Another limitation may relate to the proximity of the roles of researcher as teacher, and any conflict of impartiality this may have produced. Nevertheless, strong arguments for the potential of the L2-LC framework remain. It uses literature as a resource for (spoken) language development to generate meaningful, collaborative, learner-led inquiry and response, and at the same time, through the collaborative post-reading dialogue, provides the social learning context and the agency necessary to afford opportunities for L2 language learning, growth and development.

References

Armstrong, M. 2015. 'Using literature in an EFL context to teach language and culture', *The Journal of Literature in Language Teaching* 4(2): 7–24.

Bandura, A. 1997. *Self-Efficacy: The Exercise of Control*. New York: W. H. Freeman and Company.

————. 2001. 'Social cognitive theory: An agentic perspective', *Annual Review of Psychology* 52: 1–26. Available at: www.annualreviews.org (Accessed 8 November 2018).

Barfield, A. 2016. 'Collaboration', *ELT Journal* 70(2): 222–224. doi:10.1093/elt/ccv074

Batstone, R. 2010. 'Issues and options in sociocognition', in Batstone, R. (ed.), *Sociocognitive Perspectives on Language Use and Language Learning*. Oxford: Oxford University Press, 3–23.

Bloemert, J., Paran, A., Jansen, E. and van de Grift, W. 2019. 'Students' perspective on the benefits of EFL literature education', *The Language Learning Journal* 47(3): 371–384.

Brown, R., Waring, R. and Donkaewbua, S. 2008. 'Incidental vocabulary acquisition from reading, reading-while-listening, and listening to stories', *Reading in a Foreign Language* 20(2): 136–163.

Brumfit, C. J. 1985. *Language and Literature Teaching: From Practice to Principle.* Oxford: Pergamon.

Brumfit, C. J. and Carter, R. A. 1986. *Literature and Language Teaching.* Oxford: Oxford University Press.

Carrell, P. L., and Grabe, W. 2010. 'Reading', in Schmitt, N. (ed.), *An Introduction to Applied Linguistics.* London: Hodder Education, 215–231.

Carter, R. and Long, M. N. 1991. *Teaching Literature.* Harlow: Longman.

Carter, R. and McRae, J. (eds.) 1996. *Language, Literature and the Learner: Creative Classroom Practice.* Harlow: Longman.

Chen, I. 2018. 'Incorporating task-based learning in an extensive reading programme', *ELT Journal.* Advance online publication. doi.org/10.1093/elt/ccy008

Chiang, M. H. 2007. 'Improved reading attitudes and enhanced English reading comprehensionvia literature circles', *Lagos Papers in English Studies* 1: 168–183.

Cohen, R. (ed.) 2009. *Explorations in Second Language Reading.* Virginia: TESOL.

Collie, J. and Slater, S. 1987. *Literature in the Language Classroom: A Resource Book of Ideas and Activities.* Cambridge: Cambridge University Press.

Council of Europe. 2001. *Common European Framework of Reference for Languages: Learning, Teaching, Assessment.* Cambridge: Press Syndicate of the University of Cambridge.

Daniels, H. 2002. *Literature Circles: Voice and Choice in Book Clubs and Reading Groups* (2nd edn). Portland, ME: Stenhouse.

Daniels, H. and Steineke, N. 2004. *Mini-Lessons for Literature Circles.* Portsmouth, NH: Heinemann.

Deci, E. L. and Ryan, R. M. 1985. *Intrinsic Motivation and Self-Determination in Human Behavior.* New York: Plenum.

Donato, R. 2000. 'Sociocultural contributions to understanding the foreign and second language classroom', in Lantolf, J. P. (ed.), *Sociocultural Theory and Second Language Learning.* Oxford: Oxford University Press, 27–50.

Dörnyei, Z. 1997. 'Psychological processes in cooperative language learning: Group dynamics and motivation', *The Modern Language Journal* 81: 482–493.

    2009. *The Psychology of Second Language Acquisition.* Oxford University Press.

Dörnyei, Z. and Murphey, T. 2003. *Group Dynamics in the Language Classroom.* Cambridge: Cambridge University Press.

Dörnyei, Z., and Ushioda, E. 2011. *Teaching and Researching Motivation* (2nd edn). Harlow: Pearson.

Duff, P. A. and Kobayashi, M. 2010. 'The intersection of social, cognitive, and cultural processes in language learning: A second language socialization approach', in Batstone, R. (ed.), *Sociocognitive Perspectives on Language Use and Language Learning.* Oxford: Oxford University Press 76–93.

Fredericks, L. 2012. 'The benefits and challenges of culturally responsive EFL critical literature circles', *Journal of Adolescent & Adult Literacy* 55(6): 494–504. doi:10.1002/JAAL.00059

Furr, M. 2004. 'Literature circles for the EFL classroom'. Available at: www .eflliteraturecircles.com/litcirclesforEFL.pdf (Accessed 8 November 2018).

Gass, S. M. and Mackey, A. 2007. 'Input, interaction, and output in second language acquisition', in van Patten, B. and Williams, J. (eds.), *Theories in Second Language Acquisition*. London: LEA, 175–200.

Green, C. 2005. 'Integrating extensive reading in the task-based curriculum', *ELT Journal* 59(4): 306–311.

Hall, G. 2015. *Literature in Language Education* (2nd edn). Basingstoke: Palgrave.

Hsu, J.-Y. 2004. 'Reading without teachers: Literature circles in an EFL classroom', *The Proceedings of 2004 Cross-Strait Conference on English Education*: 401–421 Available at: https://files.eric.ed.gov/fulltext/ED492558.pdf (Accessed 8 November 2018).

Jeon, E.-Y. and Day, R. R. 2016. 'The effectiveness of ER on reading proficiency: A meta-analysis', *Reading in a Foreign Language* 28(2): 246–265.

Kalaja, P., Alanen, R., Palviainen, A. and Dufva, H. 2011. 'From milk cartons to English roommates: Context and agency in L2 learning beyond the classroom', in Benson, P. and Reinders, H. (eds.), *Beyond the Language Classroom*. Basingstoke: Palgrave, 47–58.

Keene, E. and Zimmerman, S. 1997. *The Mosaic of Thought*. Portsmouth, NH: Heinemann.

Kim, M. 2004. 'Literature discussions in adult L2 learning', *Language and Education* 18(2): 145–166. doi.org/10.1080/09500780408666872

Kramsch, C. (ed.) 2002. *Language Acquisition and Language Socialization: Ecological Perspectives*. London: Continuum.

Lantolf, J. P. and Thorne, S. L. 2006. *Sociocultural Theory and the Genesis of Second Language Development*. Oxford: Oxford University Press.

Lantolf, J. P. and Poehner, M. E. 2014. *Sociocultural Theory and the Pedagogical Imperative in L2 Education: Vygotskian Praxis and the Theory/Practice Divide*. New York: Routledge.

Lantolf, J. P., Thorne, S. L. and Poehner, M. E. 2015. 'Sociocultural theory and second language development', in van Patten, B. and Williams, J. (eds.), *Theories in Second Language Acquisition*. New York: Routledge, 207–226.

Larsen-Freeman, D. 2007. 'Reflecting on the cognitive-social debate in second language acquisition', *The Modern Language Journal* 91: 773–787.

2010. 'The dynamic co-adaption of cognitive and social views: A Complexity Theory perspective', in Batstone, R. (ed.), *Sociocognitive Perspectives on Language Use and Language Learning*. Oxford: Oxford University Press, 40–53.

2016. (an author in) The Douglas Fir Group. 'A transdisciplinary framework for SLA in a multilingual world', *The Modern Language Journal* 100(S1): 19–47. //doi.org/10 .1111/modl.12301

LeBlanc, C. 2015. 'Investigating high school students' self-efficacy in reading circles', *The Language Teacher* 39(1): 15–21.

Long, M. 1996. 'The role of the linguistic environment in second language acquisition', in Ritchie, W. C. and Bhatia, T. K. (eds.), *Handbook of Second Language Acquisition*. New York: Academic Press, 413–468.

Macalister, J. 2015. 'Guidelines or commandments? Reconsidering core principles in extensive reading', *Reading in a Foreign Language* 27(1): 122–128.

McRae, J. 1991. *Literature with a Small 'l'*. London: Macmillan.

1996. 'Representational language learning: from language awareness to text awareness', in Carter, R. and McRae, J. (eds.), *Language, Literature and the Learner: Creative Classroom Practice*. Harlow: Longman, 16–40.

Maher, K. M. 2015. 'EFL literature circles: Collaboratively acquiring language and meaning', *The Language Teacher* 39(4): 9–12.

Mercer, N. 2004. 'Sociocultural discourse analysis: Analysing classroom talk as a social mode of thinking', *Journal of Applied Linguistics* 1(2): 137–168.

Nation, I. S. P. 2003. *Learning Vocabulary in Another Language* (3rd edn). Cambridge: Cambridge University Press.

Nishikawa, M. 2015. 'How facilitator styles affect overall dynamic of group discussions in EFL contexts', *JACET Journal* 59: 151–167.

Ohta, A. S. 2000. 'Rethinking interaction in SLA: Developmentally appropriate assistance in the zone of proximal development and the acquisition of L2 grammar', in Lantolf, J. P. (ed.), *Sociocultural Theory and Second Language Learning*. Oxford: Oxford University Press, 51–78.

2001. *Second Language Acquisition Processes in the Classroom: Learning Japanese*. Mahwah, NJ: Erlbaum.

Oxford, R. L. 2017. *Teaching and Researching Language Learning Strategies: Self-Regulation in Context* (2nd edn). New York: Routledge.

Paran, A. 2008. 'The role of literature in instructed foreign language learning and teaching: an evidence-based survey', *Language Teaching* 41(4): 465–496. doi:10.1017/S026144480800520X

Riessman, C. K. 2008. *Narrative Methods for the Human Sciences*. Thousand Oaks, CA: Sage.

Ro, E. 2017. 'How learning occurs in an extensive reading book club: A conversation analytic perspective', *Applied Linguistics*. doi.org/10.1093/applin/amx014

Rosenblatt, L. M. 1968. *Literature as Exploration*. London: Heinemann.

1978. *The Reader, the Text, the Poem*. Carbondale: Southern Illinois University.

Ryan, R. M. and Deci, E. L. 2017. *Self-Determination Theory: Basic Psychological Needs in Motivation, Development, and Wellness*. New York: Guilford Press.

Sambolin, A. N. and Carroll, K. S. 2015. 'Using literature circles in the ESL college classroom: A lesson from Puerto Rico', *Colombian Applied Linguistic Journal* 17 (2): 193–206. doi.org/10.14483/udistrital.jour.calj.2015.2.a02

Schmitt, N. and Celce-Murcia, M. 2010. An overview of applied linguistics', in Schmitt, N. (ed.), *An Introduction to Applied Linguistics* (2nd edn). London: Hodder Education, 1–14.

Schmuck, R. and Schmuck, P. 2000. *Group Processes in the Classroom* (8th edn). Dubuque, IA: William C. Brown.

Scotland, J. 2012. 'Exploring the philosophical underpinnings of research: Relating ontology and epistemology to the methodology and methods of the scientific, interpretive, and critical research paradigms', *English Language Teaching* 5(9): 9–16. doi:10.5539/elt.v5n9p9

Steffensen, S. and V. Kramsch, C. 2017. 'The ecology of second language acquisition and socialization', in Duff, P. A. and May, S. (eds.), *Encyclopedia of Language and Education: Language Socialization* (3rd edn). Cham, Switzerland: Springer. doi.org/10.1007/978-3-319–02327-4_2–1

Shelton-Strong, S. J. 2012. 'Literature circles in ELT', *ELT Journal* 66(2): 214–223. doi:10.1093/elt/ccr049

Swain, M. 2000. 'The output hypothesis and beyond: mediating acquisition through collaborative dialogue', in Lantolf, J. P. (ed.), *Sociocultural Theory and Second Language Learning*. Oxford: Oxford University Press, 97–114.

2006. 'Languaging, agency and collaboration in advanced language proficiency', in Byrnes, H. (ed.), *Advanced Language Learning: The Contribution of Halliday and Vygotsky*. London: Continuum, 95–108.

Swain, M., Lapkin, S., Knouzi, I., Suzuki, W. and Brooks, L. 2009. 'Languaging: University students learn the grammatical concept of voice in French', *The Modern Language Journal* 93: 5–29. doi:10.1111/j.1540-4781.2009.00825.x

Swain, M. and Watanabe, Y. 2013. 'Language: Collaborative dialogue as a source of second language learning', in Chapelle, C. A. (ed.), *The Encyclopedia of Applied Linguistics*. Oxford: Wiley-Blackwell, 3213–3225. doi:10.1002/9781405198431.wbeal0664

Teranishi, M., Saito, Y. and Wales, K. (eds.) 2015. *Literature and Language Learning in the ELF Classroom*. London: Palgrave Macmillan.

Thibault, P. J. 2011. 'First-order languaging dynamics and second-order language: The distributed language view', *Ecol Psychol* 23(3): 210–245. doi:10.1080/10407413.2011.591274

Tomlinson, B. 1997. 'The role of visualisation in the reading of literature by learners of a foreign language', PhD dissertation, University of Nottingham.

van Lier, L. 2000. 'From input to affordance: Social-interaction learning from an ecological perspective', in Lantolf, J. P. (ed.), *Sociocultural Theory and Second Language Learning*. Oxford: Oxford University Press, 155–177.

2004a. 'The semiotics and ecology of language learning: Perception, voice, identity and democracy', *Utbildning & Demokrati: Tidskrift för didaktik och utbildningspolitik* 13(3): 79–103.

2004b. *The Ecology and Semiotics of Language Learning: A Sociocultural Perspective*. Boston: Kluwer Academic.

2007. 'Action-based teaching, autonomy and identity', *International Journal of Innovation in Language Learning and Teaching* 1(1): 46–65.

Vygotsky, L. 1978. *Mind in Society: The Development of Higher Psychological Processes*, ed. M. Cole, V. John-Steiner, S. Scribner and E. Souberman. Cambridge, MA: Harvard University Press.

Webb, S. 2007. 'The effects of repetition on vocabulary knowledge', *Applied Linguistics* 28(1): 46–65. doi:10.1093/applin/aml048

NOTES

1. 'Shooting an Elephant'.
2. *1984* and *Animal Farm*.

9   Exploring Literary Texts as a Tool for Developing L2 Oral Proficiency

Gary G. Fogal and Richard S. Pinner

Numerous publications have examined the impact that studying literature has had on second language (L2) development across modes, including its usefulness for advancing language awareness (Lin 2010), academic writing (Fogal 2019), reading comprehension (Paesani 2006) and general academic performance (Badran 2012). However, limited studies – and with varying results – have explored the utility of studying literary texts for enhancing L2 oral proficiency. Moreover, the sparse literature on this topic blurs an already narrow conception of how literary texts impact L2 oral proficiency and thus invites further research. To address this concern, the present classroom-based study examined changes in L2 learners' lexical complexity (operationalised as lexical density, diversity and sophistication) after a semester of studying English literature within the context of a discussion and presentation course. Data were collected from a first-year class in an English literature department at a private university in Japan and comprised audio recordings of classroom interactions, classroom observations, post-semester interviews with learners and evidence-based reflections compiled by the course instructor. To examine changes in lexical complexity, a pre-test post-test research design was used, and a Wilcoxon signed-rank test was employed to compare changes in lexical complexity over time. Results showed that learners made no statistically significant gains in oral proficiency. This study discusses pedagogical concerns related with this outcome and offers suggestions for balancing classroom attention on literature, the learner and the language of the text. This work also contributes to advancing research methods related to investigating the efficacy of studying literary texts for developing L2 oral proficiency.

Introduction

Commentary on the efficacy of classroom-based literary studies to inform second language (L2) development has enjoyed frequent attention in the literature, with a notable focus on the potential such studies have to advance linguistic competency. This attention to potential has been widespread among researchers and across time and informs part of the impetus for this edited volume. This pedagogical potential is underscored in Boyd and Maloof (2000), Carter (2007), Hall (2007), Paran (2008) and more recently Hall (2015) and Fogal (2015), among others. These studies highlight, to varying degrees and by concentrating on different aspects of the relationship between L2 learning and literature studies, a lack of substantive evidence that confirms the utility of studying literature for advancing L2 development. As Paran (2008: 490) suggests, evidence is at the stage of emergence and 'we still need more empirical studies into what happens in literature and language classrooms'. As discussed in Chapter 1 (this volume), research and the resulting evidence on how learners' oral proficiency develops as a result of studying literature is no exception. As outlined in the section 'Previous Research', the investigation of changes in oral proficiency in said context remains underdeveloped, and claims about its efficacy lack extensive support. This chapter addresses, then, Paran's call by focusing on changes in L2 learners' oral proficiency as a result of discussing literary texts (see also Chapter 7, this volume, for a study focused upon discussion of literary texts). While the term proficiency lends itself to a range of interpretations (Housen, Kuiken and Vedder 2012), for the purposes of the present chapter it is operationalised as a measure of linguistic accuracy associated with lexical complexity. In doing so, we acknowledge that this is a limiting definition; this study does not, for instance, investigate non-linguistic features that contribute to developing L2 oral proficiency including, for example, learner characteristics or turn-taking – the latter associated with the cultural norms of a target language. In the 'Methodology' section, we provide a rationale for limiting our definition of oral proficiency in this way and present a detailed rendering of the construct lexical complexity.

The aim of this chapter is to explore how, if at all, the lexical complexity of learners' spoken output changes after studying literature. To do so, it follows on and expands Bredella and Delanoy's (1996) work, which argues that researching literature involves examining classroom dynamics beyond the literary text under analysis. By doing so, we aim first to widen understandings of how literary studies impact oral proficiency development in university-aged English as a Foreign Language (EFL) learners and, second, to advance research methods already aligned with similar teaching and learning contexts outside the umbrella of literature studies. The latter, we believe, is imperative if researchers wish to address Paran's call for more empirical studies in the area of literature studies and L2 learning. This chapter first provides an overview of how previous research characterises the relationship between studying literary texts and L2 oral proficiency. It then outlines the methods employed to capture the influence of literature studies on lexical complexity. After documenting the findings, this chapter then makes suggestions for how instructors can manage classrooms to use literary texts to advance students' oral proficiency and general L2 development. The chapter concludes by discussing and making suggestions for how future studies can re-orient their approaches to studying this and similar contexts.

Previous Research

As summarised in Chapter 1 (this volume), publications have examined the effect that studying literature has on L2 development across modes, including its usefulness for advancing language awareness (Lin 2010), academic writing (Fogal 2019), reading comprehension (Paesani 2006), reading proficiency (Beglar, Hunt and Kite 2012) and general academic performance (Badran 2012). However, limited studies – and with varying results – have explored the utility of studying literary texts for enhancing L2 oral proficiency. Below we review the research on this topic.

Several studies have argued for the efficacy of examining literary texts for advancing L2 oral competency. However, these studies consider oral proficiency as a single construct, and as many of these works lack convincing evidence to substantiate their claims. For example, on two occasions, Erkaya (2005, 2011) asserted that short stories facilitate L2 learners' oral language proficiency. However, no data were provided to substantiate these claims. Rather, claims were supported from inferences about what literature is supposed to do – or more accurately, its latent potential to foster fluency. Erkaya (2005: 4–5) suggested that reading short stories provides students with 'the opportunity to come up with their own insights, helping them to speak the language in a more imaginative way'. However, left unreported is whether learners' oral output actually improved. Similar claims about the effectiveness of using short stories to develop oral proficiency are made in Erkaya (2011), Pardede (2011), Babaee and Yahya (2014) and Arias Rodríguez (2017).

Pardede (2011: 21) argued that 'by interpreting what they [L2 learners] read, they can work toward speaking English more creatively' and that short stories 'can also be a powerful and motivating source for teaching both speaking and listening'. Hişmanoğlu (2005) and Babaee and Yahya (2014) make similar claims about using short stories (as well as other literary genres) to develop oral proficiency. However, the studies of Pardede (2011), Babaee and Yahya (2014) and Hişmanoğlu, like Erkaya's (2005, 2011) work, provided no evidence to substantiate these claims.

Informed by an action research method, Arias Rodríguez (2017) also focused on the utility of short stories in classroom studies for promoting L2 oral proficiency. In the language department of a Colombian university, Arias Rodríguez examined whether reading and listening to short stories in English improved learners' oral (and written) fluency. Sixteen participants focused on four short stories over one semester and prepared oral reports for each story. These reports were presented in English to the class. Guided by grounded theory, data were collected from artefacts that learners generated (e.g. written summaries of the short stories), the researcher's journal reflections and a survey administered to students individually at the end of the study. Based primarily on the survey results, Arias Rodríguez noted that learners believed their oral proficiency improved after studying the four short stories. The author credits this result to effective communicative activities in the classroom and extensive exposure to the target language (the target language was left undefined). However, no explicit measures of oral proficiency were documented in the report. Instead, changes in fluency were marked by impressionistic accounts of change. While such accounts begin to provide insight into the efficacy of short stories for developing oral proficiency, there remains an underreporting of data to verify or replicate Arias Rodríguez's findings.

Similar impressionistic accounts of how literature contributes to developing general oral proficiency also appear in Nasu (2015). Nasu's findings emerged from a qualitative analysis of seven adult participants' oral histories. The participants were described as accomplished learners of additional languages, including Chinese, English and Japanese. In their oral histories the participants described how reading and studying literature impacted their language development. While not all participants were explicit about the connection between literature and oral proficiency specifically, all participants underscored the effect reading or studying literature had on improving communicative competency. Given the nature of oral histories and their intended use, Nasu duly reported on no specific construct of oral proficiency nor did she document measures of verbal performance. Instead, Nasu provided a rich account of participants' engagement with literature and thus inferred that participant's oral proficiency developed to some important degree by engaging with literary works.

In a classroom-based study in a Japanese university EFL context that explored unique classroom settings, Sheehan (2015) focused on, among other interests, the influence of graded readers on improving the oral communication skills of first-year students in one class and the discussion skills of high-level learners in another class. Data were collected from classroom observations by Sheehan (the researcher-cum-instructor), multiple surveys and post-intervention interviews across the two classrooms. In the first class ($n = 26$) 50 per cent of learners believed that studying graded readers helped improve their oral proficiency. The remainder of the students were unsure or doubtful of any changes. In the class where Sheehan explored the discussion skills of high-level learners ($n = 18$), about 40 per cent of learners believed that using graded readers aided their oral proficiency abilities. Other students were unsure (35 per cent) or doubtful (24%) of any improvement. By shedding light on how learners interpreted the utility of graded readers, Sheehan's work provides some evidence for the role literature plays in advancing oral proficiency. Unclear, however, is exactly what elements of oral proficiency developed as a result of the interventions and what objective measure of proficiency gains are able to support learners' and Sheehan's impressions of linguistic improvements.

As noted, the studies documented thus far treat oral proficiency as a single construct, thus disguising the complex nuances that inform oral language development. A notable exception to this trend is Kim (2004). At a large American university, Kim examined nine international students from five different countries studying in a university preparatory English as a Second Language (ESL) class. As part of their studies, participants engaged in literature circles for almost four weeks. One facet of Kim's study explored what features of discussing literature facilitated changes in language use. Students prepared for their discussions in advance by reading and then responding in writing to questions she prepared about the literary text in question. Kim collected classroom observations of the ensuing discussions, fifteen hours of audio recordings, field notes and interviews with the students. Kim documented that participants improved the authenticity of their language use – defined as conversations characterised by open-ended questions, turn-taking and genuine interest in others' ideas. Other language gains were reported in uptake or high responsiveness – defined as learners' ability to form links between utterances of difference speakers during discussions. Kim's study primarily emphasised social interaction patterns that promote communicative competency. Her work is one of a limited number of studies that defines explicitly what constructs inform oral proficiency (i.e. authenticity and uptake); however, unclear from Kim's study is to what degree studying literature itself had an impact on development versus the dynamics operationalised in the classroom to facilitate discussion, a reservation also noted by the author.

While Kim's (2004) work is a notable exception, most studies to date rely on impressionistic accounts of oral proficiency development that are heavily informed by interviews and questionnaires. Singularly, these studies provide meaningful insights into how learners, for example, interpret changes in their oral proficiency in particular contexts. Such accounts, however, collectively underscore two concerns with previous research. The first concern is a consistent lack of clearly articulated constructs that can be used to measure oral proficiency. For example, changes in oral proficiency may be defined as acquiring a sense for turn-taking or developing an increased sensitivity to cultural nuances, or may be marked by changes in syntactic or lexical complexity. Because speech acts are complex events that are embedded and informed by numerous processes, studies may do well to unpack this multifaceted construct. Doing so may reveal how different components of oral proficiency mature. Such studies could benefit researchers, instructors and learners.

The second concern raised by this review is the consistent focus on interview and questionnaire data. Again, singularly these data provide meaningful insights into L2 development. However, studies are also needed that can quantify changes in unique constructs of oral proficiency, as Paran (2008) duly notes. Such research can complement present insights into how literature might positively impact L2 oral development.

To address these issues, this study operationalises oral proficiency as a measure of lexical complexity and examines said measures partly using quantitative analyses (we unpack lexical complexity and the analytic methods in the ensuing section). To aid with this investigation, the following research questions were devised:

RQ1: Does the lexical complexity of spontaneous oral production in L2 learners increase after a semester of studying English literature?

We also developed a second research question to understand how the teaching and studying of literature impressed upon lexical complexity:

RQ2: What classroom interactions inform the teaching and learning environment?

Methodology

As noted, to our knowledge only Kim (2004) has examined the effect of studying literature on a specific construct of oral proficiency. Accordingly, given this paucity of research and the resulting lack of a meaningfully relevant framework to follow, we decided to proceed cautiously and to examine only a single construct of oral language development. In doing so, this study hopes to contribute to laying a foundation for continued research that engages specific (and eventually multiple) constructs of oral proficiency across varying literature-based contexts. While a wide set of measures of oral proficiency are available – including fluency, accuracy, syntactic complexity and lexical complexity (see Koizumi 2005 for a rendering of each) – for this study lexical complexity was chosen to track changes in speaking performance. Tracking lexical complexity provides a reliable window into the variety of lexical items available to learners to communicate orally (Bulté and Housen 2012). To this end, tracking changes in learners' lexical complexity functions as a useful, singular measure of the impact studying literature has on L2 students' developing oral proficiency.

Teaching and Learning Context

This study focused on the teaching and learning context of Japanese learners in an EFL discussion and presentation class at a private university in Japan. This course is compulsory for first-year students in the Department of English

Literature and is the second of two discussion and presentation courses offered in successive semesters. The two courses are taught by different instructors, and the content and syllabus of each course is set independently following predetermined course guidelines. These guidelines focus on developing students' oral proficiency and ability to discuss topics related to literature.

To achieve said aims, these courses are motivated by three categories of discourse: conversation (speaking on topics for their own sake), discussion (speaking with specific aims, e.g. to answer a question) and presentation (speaking to an audience). Each class meeting (90-minutes and twice a week for one, fifteen-week semester) intended to improve learners' communicative competency in these areas. Generally, however, most classes focused on conversation and discussion, with those classes focused on presentations linked to assessment. To facilitate these competencies, the instructor (who is also the second author of this study) emphasized group work by providing discussion prompts based on readings of literary texts. The core literary texts employed over the semester were chosen by the instructor for their appropriateness to the students' English proficiency and their literary relevance to other works which students will encounter throughout their degree programme. The syllabus was divided into three major areas of study: poetry, short stories and children's literature. For example, students examined texts by William Wordsworth ('Daffodils'), Raymond Carver ('Little Things'), Allen Ginsberg ('Sunflower Sutra') and Maurice Sendak ('Where the Wild Things Are').

Following Ushioda's (2014) recommendations for facilitating greater autonomy and motivation, the instructor also focused on sharpening learners' metacognitive awareness. Specifically, learners were afforded opportunities to reflect on their learning (e.g. students submitted short written reflections related to classroom-based performances such as presentations) and were instructed on goal-setting techniques. To further reflect on their learning and for the purposes of this study, a self-assessment was also introduced based on the can-do statements for oral proficiency of the Common European Framework of Reference for Languages (CEFR 2016). Although mainly applied in Europe, the CEFR has been translated into Japanese (and named the CEFR-J) and has been adapted for Japanese learners (Tono 2010). A comparison of the CEFR and CEFR-J proficiency bands are documented in Table 9.1.

Participants

The instructor was a British male with a doctorate in applied linguistics and English language teaching. He has been working where this study occurred since 2011, and in that time has continually taught the discussion and presentation course. There were 23 Japanese, EFL university students in the course

Table 9.1 *Comparison of CEFR and CEFR-J proficiency bands*

	CEFR	CEFR-J[a]
Proficient user	C2	C2
	C1	C1
Independent user	B2	B2.2
		B2.1
	B1	B1.2
		B1.1
Basic user	A2	A2.2
		A2.1
	A1	A1.2
		A1.1

[a] based on Tono (2010).

(4 male and 19 female). With the exception of two females who were repeating the course, all of the students were in the second semester of their first year of university.

Towards the end of the study, we invited eight learners to act as focal participants who then received the main focus of our analysis. The focal participants consisted of two males and six females, all of whom were first-year students of 18 years of age whose proficiency level approximated B1 on the CEFR scale. Three participants had spent a year abroad as students in English-speaking countries and began studying English across a range of ages (3, 7 and 10). The remaining students had never studied overseas and began compulsory English studies at 12 years of age. All but one learner had some exposure to studying English literature during their secondary school studies. These eight participants students were invited because theirs were the most complete dataset available for analysis.

Data Collection and Analysis

To track the development of oral proficiency, defined as changes in lexical complexity, and to understand clearly the teaching and learning context of the participants in this study, this project took the following steps and collected the following data. To examine changes in lexical complexity a pre-test post-test research design was adapted. Prior to starting the semester, 4-minute audio recordings of learners engaged with a single prompt were collected (see Appendix 9A for a sample). After receiving the prompt, learners were left alone in a room to engage in a discussion. One week after the end of the semester, a comparable prompt was also used to trigger oral production. Both sets of recordings were later transcribed separately by both authors (discrepancies in the transcription were discussed and changes were made accordingly). The unit of transcription was the well-established utterance (Brown 1973).

To measure any changes in lexical complexity over time, this study followed Horst and Collins (2006) and Bulté and Housen (2012) who argue that tracking lexical complexity requires monitoring its development across a complementary set of variables. The variables employed in this study included lexical diversity, density and sophistication. Lexical diversity, interpreted as the 'learner's productive lexical knowledge' (Thériault 2015: 27), was measured using the type-token ratio (the number of unique words divided by the total number of words in a sample) (Bulté et al. 2008; Daller, van Hout and Treffers-Daller 2003). Lexical density was measured by categorising lexical words (nouns, verbs, adjectives and adverbs) and dividing them by the total number of words (Ishikawa 2007; Michel, Kuiken and Vedder 2007). Finally, lexical sophistication was tracked by developing a lexical profile for each participant using a standard set of measures (Laufer 1994, 1998; Laufer and Nation 1995; Horst and Collins 2006;). This profile comprises four unique measures of lexical sophistication that compare the words used in a sample with those occurring most in the target language. These measures include the following: words appearing in the 1,000 most frequent English word families (K1); words appearing in the 1,001–2,000 most frequent word families (K2); the academic word list (AWL) (Coxhead 2000); and words that do not appear in any of the three previous categories (off-list words). A freely available online lexical profiler was used (www.lextutor.ca) to help analyse how lexical diversity, density and sophistication, as measures of lexical complexity, changed over time. In order to run the analyses, pauses and sounds that did not form a word were removed from the transcripts.

Subsequent to the results of the online analyses, a Wilcoxon signed-rank test was used to compare changes in lexical complexity over time. A conventional significance level ($p = 0.05$) was set, and effect sizes were calculated using the following formula: $r = Z/\sqrt{N}$ (Rosenthal 1991; Field 2009). The r coefficient was also converted to the Cohen's d index using the Rosenthal transformation (Cohen 1988; Rosenthal 1994), a more standard report of effect sizes in applied linguistics research (Dörnyei 2007; Mackey and Gass 2015).

In addition to statistical analyses of change, learners were asked to self-assess changes in their language use. Participants scored changes in their proficiency using the Japanese translation of the CEFR-J can-do statements (Tono 2010) and conducted this self-assessment immediately before the pre-test, in the middle of the semester, and then again just prior to the post-test.

To examine the teaching and learning dynamic, classroom observations were conducted by the first author on four occasions (during weeks 1, 3, 7 and 8) and were audio-recorded. These observations were guided by an instrument developed by de Graaff et al. (2007) for use in contexts where content and language study overlap significantly. The first author also conducted post-intervention, semi-structured interviews with each of the participants. The interviews were audio-recorded, and along with a research assistant the first author coded the observations and the interviews using an open coding framework adopted from Braun and Clarke (2006). Where there were disagreements in the coding, discussions were had to resolve the concerns. Once the interviews were coded, both the observations and the interviews were analysed using a thematic analysis (Pavlenko 2007; Mackey and Gass 2015).

In addition, this study collected evidence-based reflections from the instructor (accounts compiled by an instructor or learner after the fact that address a classroom situation and that foregrounds experiences that are supported by data rather than affective or emotional responses to a situation – see Lachuk and Koellner 2015), drawn from trace data (Rodriguez and Ryave 2002) in the form of emails from focal participants, students' forum posts, grades and other pedagogic materials. The reflections also utilised field notes and reflective journal entries, all composed by the instructor. The evidence-based reflections were informed by three successive phases: (1) reflecting on the class from memory, which focused reflection on salient moments or critical incidents (Tripp 1993; Farrell 2008); (2) mining trace data for information that could help reveal factors and contexts informing the critical incidents; and (3) conducting a deeper layer of analysis based on re-examining the data from phase two. This final step resulted in fine-tuning and noting changes or alternative perspectives on the trace data specific to critical incidents. While focusing on classroom dynamics, the evidence-based reflections also attended to the development and performance of the eight focal participants.

Results

Initially a Wilcoxon signed-rank test was employed to examine changes in learners' lexical complexity after a semester of studying English literature. Table 9.2 summarises the results of the analysis.

The results show no statistically significant changes in learners' lexical complexity between the pre-test (Time 1) and the post-test (Time 2).

Table 9.3 documents participant self-assessments of changes in their language development and oral proficiency based on the CEFR-J bandwidths. Table 9.3 indicates that four participants noted no changes in their general language ability over time, including their oral proficiency.

One participant noted an improvement (from 1.1 to 2.1), while another participant documented a decrease in linguistic competency over time. Two remaining participants did not complete all of the assessment tasks; however,

Table 9.2 Summary of means, standard deviations and Wilcoxon signed-rank test for measures of lexical complexity over time (n = 8)

		Time 1			Time 2			z	r^b	Sig.[c]	d^d
		M	SD	Mdn	M	SD	Mdn				
Density		0.47	0.03	0.45	0.45	0.06	0.45	-0.91	-0.32	0.36	-0.74
Diversity		0.48	0.05	0.49	0.55	0.11	0.57	-1.57	-0.55	0.11	-1.4
Sophistication[a]	K1	86.78	4.49	88.4	85.54	5.05	85.95	-0.7	-0.24	0.48	-0.53
	K2	6.57	4.40	6.55	6.7	4.46	5.28	-0.14	-0.05	0.89	0.09
	AWL	0.61	0.66	0.54	0.53	0.66	0.18	-0.31	-0.11	0.75	-0.23
	Off-list	6.03	4.25	4.92	7.21	4.11	5.89	-0.7	-0.24	0.48	-0.53

[a] Expressed as a percentage.
[b] Effect size ($r = z/\sqrt{N}$).
[c] Asymp. sig. (2-tailed).
[d] Standardized effect size ($d = 2\,r \div \sqrt{1 - r^2}$).

Table 9.3 *Results of learner*
self-assessments based on CEFR-J

Participant	CEFR-based self-assessment		
	Time 1	Time 2	Time 3
1	B2.1	B2.1	B2.1
2	B2.1	B2.1	B2.1
3	B2.1	B2.1	B2.1
4	B2.2	B2.1	–
5	B1.1	–	B2.1
6	B2.1	B2.1	B1.2
7	B1.1	B2.1	B2.1
8	B2.1	B2.1	B2.1

based on what was completed one learner indicated a decrease over time (from 2.2 to 2.1), while the other learner noted an increase (from 1.1 to 2.1). Data from evidence-based reflections (discussed in detail below) also indicate that the instructor held similar impressions regarding limited changes in lexical complexity.

To summarise, non-parametric analyses show no statistically significant changes in learners' lexical complexity from the start of the semester to the end of the semester. Moreover, learners' self-assessment of linguistic development based on the CEFR-J scale suggests minimal, if any, changes in oral competency. These findings are also echoed in the evidence-based reflections. There is sufficient evidence from the dataset to suggest, then, that the lexical complexity of learners did not improve as a result of studying literature. To capture why this result was the case, findings from the second research question are documented next.

Research question 2 sought to understand the dynamics of the classroom from the perspective of learners and the instructor. To this end classroom observations, post-intervention interviews and evidence-based reflections compiled by the instructor were collected. Table 9.4 provides a summary of classroom engagement practices during the four classroom observations and suggests that learners engaged each other in their first language (L1) as a regular part of their classroom interactions and that a large portion of their time was spent listening to the instructor either lecture, model or provide instructions for task-based activities. Learners also spent no time listening to their peers provide sustained L2 input, nor did they spend considerable time producing the L2 orally. Moreover, writing activities informed by self-assessment forms comprised a significant amount of L2 output.

Table 9.5 summarises the activities learners engaged in during the observations. It documents that learners were afforded many possibilities to engage the

Table 9.4 *Summary of classroom observations (n = 4) of student engagement*

Observation (45 minutes[a])	Time engaged in English (minutes)				Time engaged in Japanese (minutes) listening and/or speaking[b]
	Listening primarily to instructor	primarily to peers	Speaking	Writing	
1 (Lesson 2)	17	0	^	0	21
2 (Lesson 6)	19	0	^	0	24
3 (Lesson 14)	16	0	6[c] + ^	16	4
4 (Lesson 15)	25	0	9 + ^	0	1

^Indicates periods of minimal engagement (e.g. the instructor interacted with different groups of learners for less than 3 minutes).
[a] Some observations do not add up to 45 minutes due to periods of silent engagement with a task.
[b] Indicates exclusive periods when learners engaged partners or a small group in discussion.
[c] Indicates a period of discussion where students moved freely between English and Japanese.

Table 9.5 *Summary of classroom activities common across all observations (n = 4)*

Activities students engaged in across all observations (*n* = 4)
• thinking/problem solving based on oral directions (individual and in pairs or small groups)
• thinking/problem solving based on artefact(s)[a] (individual and in pairs or small groups)
• discussing in pairs or small groups
• discussing with instructor in pairs or small groups
• responding orally to instructor's questions
• participating in classroom-wide discussions

[a] artefacts here include learning aids such as handouts, worksheets, slides and whiteboards.

target language across a variety of tasks designed to elicit discussion about literature in the L2. These opportunities involved activating a variety of cognitive processes known to aid L2 maturation, including, for example, languaging, i.e. 'the process of making meaning and shaping knowledge and experience through language' (Swain 2010). Table 9.5, then, emphasises that learners were provided with numerous meaningful opportunities to develop their oral proficiency. Data collected from post-intervention interviews and evidence-based reflections are also relevant to this finding.

The interview data reveal several salient themes. Firstly, regarding learners' impressions of their developing oral proficiency, only two learners thought their speaking abilities improved, while the other students noted that it remained static or decreased (all learners believed that their listening comprehension benefited the most from taking this course – a finding consistent with Table 9.4). Secondly, the participants believed that the instructor was responsible for ensuring learners stayed on task, primarily in the target language. For example, the participants noted a preference for a learning environment where the instructor explicitly promoted the use of and continued focus on English. Thirdly, and similarly, learners suggested that the in-class discussions lacked both a structure and a focus on the target language. The following comments, each from different learners, underscore these concerns:

• This class we did a lot of discussion, but no so much about literature. We talked about other things. So not so much I talked about literature in this semester;
• I tried to speak English as much as possible, but when I spoke with my friends [classmates] we spoke in Japanese [in class];
• I think every time the teacher said, 'Ask your partner' but after said that, we talked in Japanese so that's not good for us;
• At first I thought it was easier [to discuss in Japanese] but I found discussing in Japanese is not helpful to improve my English;
• If I had to do the course again I wish to ban the Japanese.

These issues are particularly relevant given the abundant opportunities learners had to discuss different literature-related issues in class (see Table 9.5). Moreover, learners emphasised that the class focus on discussion and presentation merited this extra attention to a strict policing of the discourse language environment. Of note, however, are three learners who suggested that expressing themselves in Japanese helped them to grasp the course content that focused on developing knowledge about English literature. Another student was unsure about this, while a different student did not think this was the case (the remaining students did not comment explicitly on this).

   Another salient theme to emerge from the interviews was learners' belief that the course lacked sufficient scaffolding to improve their oral proficiency. This scaffolding might have included, they cited, vocabulary lists, including register appropriate for studying English literature, and chunks or phrases similarly related. One particularly telling comment in this regard follows: 'The special word for English literature, like catharsis, and some words like that are really difficult to understand for us. So, before we start to read we should understand these specific words [used for analysing literature]. That makes it easier to analyze [the text]' (interview data, January 2018). The interviews reveal a degree of learner dissatisfaction, then, with how the course unfolded regarding language development, despite, as Table 9.5 suggests, ample opportunities for learners to engage in the L2. This tension is unpacked in the 'Discussion' section below.

While learners did not express a favourable overall view of their developing oral proficiency during the interviews, there was a strong, positive consensus regarding other aspects of the course: improving technical knowledge of presentation software; expanding the scope of English literature studies to include children's literature, short stories, and poetry; and, conducting self-assessment as a tool for goal setting and raising metacognitive awareness of learners' language competencies. All of these factors were repeatedly stressed as strengths that future iterations of this course should strive to repeat.

The evidence-based reflections primarily revealed a matter of miscommunication between the instructor and the students concerning the aims of the class (specifically where the study of literature was concerned) and the teaching approach relating to L2 practice, especially the balance between L1 and L2 usage. As explained in the 'Data Collection and Analysis' section, the evidence-based reflections formed over three distinct phases, each of which was structured around a set of critical incidents which the instructor identified as significant to the narrative of the class's development and his role within this inquiry. These incidents need to be explained within the narrative of the course to contextualise them, and thus they are briefly presented below in chronological order. Although there were numerous critical incidents identified, the three most relevant are presented here.

The first critical incident occurred two weeks into the course. The instructor commented on a voucher for a nearby restaurant on one student's desk and subsequently learned that almost the entire class had attended the restaurant together. This comment was consciously offered to personalise the learning environment and to invoke aspects of his and the learners' identities whenever possible – these forms of self-disclosure have been shown to be vital in forging a strong link between teacher and student motivation (Henry and Thorsen 2018a, 2018b). This degree of extracurricular socialising (near class-wide attendance at the restaurant) is quite unusual in Japan, especially for a relatively large class of first-year students. The instructor, being familiar with research on group dynamics, and after learning of the class's extracurricular engagement, began noticing other indicators of a strong group dynamic and began then incorporating this knowledge into his comments, telling the class, for example, that they were a 'good group' and 'special'. These comments were informed by the idea of a class legend which helps strengthen the social bonds in a group (Hadfield 1992; Dörnyei and Murphey 2003).

As the group dynamics became a strong part of this class's identity, several other episodes occurred, culminating in the second critical incident. As a monolingual class in an EFL context, it is quite normal that classroom discussions inevitably flow between the L1 and the L2. However, by Week 9, the class was becoming difficult to control: students were so focused on socialising (typically in the L1) that they failed to notice when the teacher was asking for their attention. As an experienced EFL teacher, this was particularly unusual for this instructor. This lack of focus on the teacher was perhaps indicative of learners frequently prioritising social experiences with their peers rather than classroom learning. At this point, although the group dynamics were clearly causing issues, the instructor did not appreciate their potential to disrupt learning.

The final critical incident surfaced after the course ended, when the instructor reviewed the observation data and students' interview responses. These data revealed how learners interpreted the instructor's role in the class. For example, comments from the interviews suggest that students held the instructor responsible for their lack of engagement with content knowledge: 'Teacher's lectures were not enough to learn about or enrich my knowledge about literature' (interview data, January 2018). In another instance, a different learner suggested that students were taking advantage of the instructor's kindness, suggesting that the instructor was not in control of the class, thus inadvertently providing a platform for students to address each other off topic and in their L1.

After recognising these three critical incidents and exploring them through the initial round of evidence-based reflection, an additional round of reflection began. What emerged most notably from this final reflection was a miscommunication concerning educational philosophies between the instructor and his students: the latter envisioned the instructor as an authority figure who should police learners and demand a predominately English-only environment while, in contrast, the instructor intentionally avoided doing so directly, wanting instead to promote an environment that took advantage of learners' multilingual competences and that built on efforts to promote learner autonomy and metacognitive strategies. However, the instructor failed to explicitly communicate his educational philosophy to the students, and so despite his best efforts, students still held the instructor accountable for their lack of linguistic and content-knowledge development.

Discussion

This study explored two research questions. Firstly, this work examined whether the lexical complexity of spontaneous oral production in L2 learners increased after a semester of studying English literature. Non-parametric analyses indicate no statistically significant changes in learners' lexical complexity over the indicated time period. In addition, learners' self-assessment of linguistic development based on the CEFR-J scale highlights minimal, if any, perceived changes in oral competency. These findings are mirrored in the evidence-based reflections that inform the results of question two, collectively suggesting that learners did not improve the lexical complexity of spontaneous oral output as a result of studying literature.

Research question 2 investigated classroom dynamics regarding the study of literature and asked, specifically, what classroom interactions informed the teaching and learning environment? The answer provided insight into why changes in oral proficiency were not recorded. To summarise, learners spent the greater part of their time during classroom observations listening to their instructor or discussing with peers in their L1 and often on topics unrelated to literature. Despite numerous meaningful classroom activities designed to promote oral proficiency, learners failed to engage these opportunities. This was primarily due to learners having bonded unusually well and having prioritised nurturing friendships over classroom learning goals, to a learning environment where learners were not compelled (to their disappointment) to use the target language, and to a lack of linguistic scaffolding to support L2 discussions about literature. Moreover, while the instructor grew increasingly aware of elements of this unfolding dynamic, he was less aware of the negative impact it was having on developing students' oral proficiency and on levels of dissatisfaction later expressed by learners. These events underscored a disconnect between the instructor's and learners' teaching and learning philosophies, respectively: the former favoured a multilingual approach to classroom learning and worked to foster learner autonomy (approaches widely supported by literature on L2 pedagogy), while learners expected and desired an English-only environment, although paradoxically they were unwilling to create this themselves.

While the findings appear to raise questions about the utility of studying literary texts for L2 learners, we discuss, rather, how the results pave a positive way forward that enables a principled approach to teaching and researching L2 development in the context of L2 literary studies. Given publishing constraints, we focus on three key features for discussion that prompt a range of diverse implications: the instructor, the learners and the research methods. We initially discuss the first two features and how various classroom interactions contributed to minimal language change over time. Despite the findings, we underscore this study's contribution to understanding how literature can be used effectively in L2 contexts to develop oral fluency. We also acknowledge that this study was not designed to explore how these variables interacted and so they are presented as relatively distinct features in the discussion below. Wherever possible, however, efforts have been made to highlight the overlapping nature of this dynamic learning context. Regarding the focus on research methods, we suggest improvements for researching such contexts to help capture the efficacy of literary studies on L2 oral proficiency and language development in general.

Firstly, relevant literature has emphasised for some time the importance of instructor's pedagogical content knowledge concerning the use of literary works in L2 contexts (Bredella and Delanoy 1996; Hişmanoğlu 2005; Paran

2017). As Hall (2005) notes, literary texts are still too often used by foreign language instructors as a tool for focusing on the text as an aesthetic experience, at the expense of focusing on linguistic elements. While the aim of the present course was to develop linguistic competency, students were often asked to engage with the text as a literary experience (sample discussion questions included, 'What do you think of the story?' 'Do you like it?' 'How did it make you feel?'), while attention to linguistic features was minimal. This inattention to linguistic forms, including lexical items, was a key concern expressed by learners in the interviews and echoes extensive literature on the importance of learners attending to language, form and meaning to develop the target language (Larsen-Freeman 2017; Verspoor 2017), including when employing literary texts (Hanaeur 1997; Carter 2003; Kim 2004). See also Chapter 4 (this volume) for an example of an approach to literary texts based on language awareness.

Interestingly, while the instructor did not focus on language per se, his attention was not exclusively on the literary experience either. He also focused on *preparing* students for improving their oral proficiency by attending to affective variables that inform learning – itself an important pedagogical undertaking. In this case, however, such attention came at the expense of providing learners with sufficient linguistic support (i.e. the instructor buttressed learners' metacognitive awareness and facilitated a comfortable learning space but failed to provide the necessary scaffolding to support positive changes in oral proficiency). Ideally, when learners stall linguistic support aids their engagement with the aesthetic, literary experience while developing their L2, or as Hall (2005: 47) describes, 'better balanced and better integrated approaches may have much to offer'. Another contribution of this study, then, underscores the negative impact of using literary texts on language development when a focus on literature, the learner and the language of the text is not merged in classroom teaching. This may be a particularly fruitful perspective in TESOL training contexts as getting this balance right – as others have suggested (Bredella and Delanoy 1996; Hişmanoğlu 2005; Hall 2015; Paran 2017) – may require that language teachers be trained explicitly in using literature in L2 contexts.

Although strong group dynamics are desirable, this study also suggests that such dynamics may not necessarily support L2 development if they detract from the pedagogic aims of the class. In this study, a strong group dynamic, rather than facilitating a positive L2 learning experience, hindered L2 use and development primarily because students had a common L1 and, more importantly, prioritised personal relations. Moreover, despite pedagogical shortcomings that did not explicitly address language-related learning features, the students themselves are accountable for failing to engage with the multiple opportunities provided by the instructor to use English, as noted in Table 9.5.

We suggest, then, that learners and the instructor, as described in the subsequent paragraph, contributed to the undesirable learning outcome.

As noted earlier, the instructor failed to explicitly outline to his students his underlying pedagogical principles and philosophy of practice, resulting in a miscommunication about the classroom ideals. The hindsight permitted by the evidence-based reflections suggest that the teacher afforded the students too much freedom without fully understanding how to turn this into autonomy and without the necessary linguistic scaffolding, the importance of which has been repeatedly asserted in the literature on autonomy (McDevitt 1997; Little 2007; Ushioda 2011). Moreover, despite the instructor's best efforts at providing metacognitive strategies and asking students to set meaningful goals, by the end of the course learning aims failed to materialise. To address these concerns about classroom teaching and learning, we suggest that instructors take time to explicitly outline their teaching philosophy to students, thus grounding learners theoretically and metacognitively to the pedagogic moves informing the class. This seems particularly important when the class goals are to develop spoken language, as learners may automatically assume literature simply involves reading. Such an approach is supported in the general applied linguistics literature (Gao 2007; Zhang 2010), and there is no reason to believe that L2 learners engaging with literary texts would react differently. To gain the most from studying literary texts, instructors may also negotiate class goals and pedagogical decisions with learners (including the setting of reading materials to boost interest and motivation) and follow up on seeing these decisions through. In this vein, this work also recommends that a measured degree of policing language use, particularly as a form of scaffolding, may be necessary, especially when group dynamics tilt the learning context in surprising ways or when the instructor loses a degree of control to the class. This is particularly relevant in the present L2 language and literature context (where the focus was on discussion and presentation), as Paran (2008: 475) highlights in an extensive review article: 'The more the focus is on literature rather than on language development, the more teachers (and researchers) seem to allow the use of the L1 in the class.' Instructors should also caution against favouring group dynamics at the expense of individuals and may consider a more balanced approach to classroom dynamics that emphasises individuals and that recognises 'individuals as fundamentally social and relational beings' (Mercer 2015: 74). For this reason, network theory and the creation of sociograms (Mercer 2015; Pinner 2019) may be useful for teachers to think about and gain a deeper appreciation of classroom group dynamics as the school year unfolds.

This discussion has thus far highlighted the integrated nature of language teaching and literature studies and the importance of considering both perspectives when teaching in similar contexts that focus on improving oral fluency, and beyond (i.e. ideally placed L2 pedagogical practices need to be balanced with similarly informed practices about using literary texts in L2 settings). The importance of balancing practices also needs addressing when considering how to examine the efficacy of literary studies for developing oral proficiency: commonplace research methods in this area of study may need to be rebalanced and thus refined. We discuss this possibility in the subsequent paragraphs.

The present study triangulated a series of data to understand how studying literature impacts changes in lexical complexity. Such mixed-methods approaches are underused in this context, yet they are valuable for exploring how literature studies interact with L2 learning. The methods employed in the present study allowed the researchers to quantify and statistically test for degrees of language change, while interviews, observations and evidence-based reflections provided a deep layer of information that underscored the dynamics and outcomes of the learning context. Each perspective complemented the other. We suggest that similar mixed-methods approaches should increasingly become the norm when trying to assess the impact of studying literature on oral proficiency, for two reasons.

Firstly, the proclivity of research on oral proficiency development (and beyond; see Hall 2007 and Fogal 2015) to employ qualitative methods almost exclusively (see the review of recent studies above) has produced little evidence to support the efficacy of literary studies for this purpose beyond impressionistic accounts of typically unstated linguistic constructs. While experimental research in this context is not without its drawbacks (see Hall 2005 for a thorough rendering of these concerns), as the review of the literature suggests an earlier call for 'ethnographic and qualitative studies of literature in language education' (Hall 2005: 189) has produced little verifiable evidence to support using literary texts to develop oral proficiency. Instead, studies with this focus may consider repeated calls in the wider field of applied linguistics to engage mixed-methods research.

Responding to these calls is particularly important for a second reason. In the present research context, isolating literary studies from sound L2 pedagogical practices as a causal variable is particularly problematic, as Paran (2008) and Fogal (2015) show and Kim's (2004) study highlights. While a lack of a control group is a limitation of this work, mixed-methods approaches allow for controlled studies and typically employ one or more statistical test, and such tests work best with clearly defined constructs. This approach would address a concern highlighted earlier, that oral proficiency has traditionally been employed as an umbrella term to cover a range of constructs that instead need to be closely examined for their unique contribution to advancing oral proficiency. A mixed-methods approach, then, enables researchers to isolate literature studies as a potential causal variable informing changes in discrete linguistic features and allows studies to continue to examine deeply the type of questions and interactions that qualitative approaches alone cannot address. Employing such methods may result in findings that can begin to ground firmly the pedagogical potential of literature to advance L2 oral proficiency and L2 development in general, a grounding that several researchers (Hall 2007; Paran 2008; Fogal 2015) have argued is long overdue.

Conclusion

This study describes an attempt to use literature to develop L2 oral proficiency, defined as linguistic complexity, in an EFL context in a Japanese university. While the results show that learners did not improve their oral proficiency over one semester, this work contributes to advancing how researchers and instructors can reframe their approaches to studying and teaching literature in L2 contexts, respectively. Specifically, this study calls on researchers to expand earlier calls to focus on qualitative and ethnographic studies by adapting a mixed-methods approach to investigating how literary studies develop L2 oral proficiency. This work also suggests that future studies adapt clearly defined constructs for operationalising oral proficiency. This study also recommends that instructors consider (a) outlining explicitly their pedagogical motives, (b) adapting, when required, to shifting learning dynamics that include regulating extensive use of the target language and (c) attending to individual learners as well as classroom dynamics, for which sociograms may be useful. This study also underscores how employing literary texts may lead to negative learning outcomes if a balanced focus on literature, the learner, and the language of the text is not sufficiently achieved. Considering these contributions, however, this study is not without its limitations. This work focused on only eight learners and one learning context. Future studies would do well to expand the number of participants and the learning environment. The former would allow for more powerful and thus more revealing statistical analyses, while collaborative research may be useful across research settings to capture a wider set of learning contexts. Moreover, as noted, employing a control group may better isolate literature studies as the primary cause of any improvements in oral proficiency. This approach might be considered in institutions where more than one section of a class is offered.

In outlining both the contributions and the limitations of this work, this chapter hopes to help shape relevant future studies to sharpen their focus and their tools of investigation in the service of instructors and, ultimately, learners. To this end, this work can point future studies and classroom contexts in a useful direction, one that has the capacity to transform and realize literature's oft-cited potential to develop learner's L2 oral proficiency.

Appendix 9A Sample Prompt and Transcription of Audio Recording

The unit of transcription was the utterance, determined by turn-taking, pauses and intonation patterns (Brown 1973). Partly or completely unintelligible utterances were excluded from the analysis.

Prompt: Discuss any aspect of the short video that you found interesting or uninteresting.

Transcription

Participant a. So what did you think about the video?

Participant b. I thought this.

    a. TV

    b. This TV's storyline is so simple and easy to understand but

    b. I don't know why people laughed so much.

    a. Yes.

    b. I don't think it is.

    b. I don't like it.

    a. Yes.

    b. How about you?

    a. I couldn't understand why people are laughing so much because

    a. He's ... the character. The main character is was saying nothing. And

    a. Of course it is easy to understand but

    a. It was not funny for me so I don't like it either.

    a. So what kind of TV drama do you like?

    b. I like

    b. variety.

    a. variety?

    b. variety.

    a. variety.

    b. I

    b. My favourite TV programme is (Japanese title).

    a. Oh.

    b. Do you. Do you know it?

    a. I know it. It's very famous one in here.

    a. Yes but I've I've never watched it so much.

    b. Oh really.

    a. I like drama. And I like comedy too.

    b. Oh really?

    a. And I like

    a. American TV drama. For example, I like

a. Gossip Girl. And Glee.

b. Oh Glee. Me too. Yes.

a. And do you do you often watch movie or not?

b. Sometimes so not so much but

b. Sometimes.

a. So is it Japanese movie or American movie or?

b. Mostly Japanese.

a. Is it romance or comedy or action?

b. Maybe fantasy like

a. Fantasy.

b. Harry Potter.

a. Harry Potter.

a. So

b. Do you often see movies?

a. Oh yes. I watch Japanese one and also American one. And I like romance

a. And comedy.

a. And I like Harry Potter too.

b. Oh really?

a. So what character do you like in Harry Potter?

b. I like Luna.

a. Luna? Oh. She is

a. She has blonde hair.

b. Yes.

a. And she's like

b. And she's a little strange but

b. She's important character so I like her.

a. And I think she can see what people can see. Like

b. Yes.

a. Because she. Her family died or something.

b. Which character do you like?

a. I like Hermione.

b. Hermione.

References

Arias Rodríguez, G. L. 2017. 'Students' language skills development through short stories', *Íkala, Revista de Lenguaje y Cultura* 22(1): 103–118.

Babaee, R. and Yahya, W. R. B. W. 2014. 'Significance of literature in foreign language teaching', *International Education Studies* 7(4): 80.

Badran, D. 2012. 'Metaphor as argument: A stylistic genre-based approach', *Language and Literature* 21(2): 119–135.

Beglar, D., Hunt, A. and Kite, Y. 2012. 'The effect of pleasure reading on Japanese university EFL learners' reading rates', *Language Learning* 62(3): 665–703.

Boyd, M. and Maloof, V. M. 2000. 'How teachers can build on student-proposed intertextual links to facilitate student talk in the ESL classroom', in Hall, J. K. and Verplaetse, L. S. (eds.), *Second and Foreign Language Learning through Classroom Interaction*. Mahwah, NJ: Erlbaum, 163–182.

Braun, V. and Clarke, V. 2006. 'Using thematic analysis in psychology', *Qualitative Research in Psychology* 3(2): 77–101.

Bredella, L. and Delanoy, W. 1996. *Challenges of Literary Texts in the Foreign Language Classroom*. Tübingen: Gunter Narr.

Brown, R. 1973. *A First Language: The Early Stages*. Cambridge, MA: Harvard University Press.

Bulté, B. and Housen, A. 2012. 'Defining and operationalising L2 complexity', in Housen, A., Kuiken, F. and Vedder, I. (eds.), *Dimensions of L2 Performance and Proficiency: Complexity, Accuracy and Fluency in SLA*. Amsterdam: John Benjamin, 21–46

Bulté, B., Housen, A., Pierrard, M. and Van Daele, S. 2008. 'Investigating lexical proficiency development over time: The case of Dutch-speaking learners of French in Brussels', *Journal of French Language Studies* 18(3): 277–298.

Carter, R. 2003. 'Language awareness', *ELT Journal* 57(1): 64–65.

2007. 'Foreword', in Watson, G. and Zyngier, S. (eds.), *Literature and Stylistics for Language Learners*. London: Palgrave Macmillan, vii–xi.

CEFR. 2016. *European Language Portfolio (ELP)*. Available at: www.coe.int/en/web/portfolio (Accessed 20 September 2017).

Cohen, J. 1988. *Statistical Power Analysis for the Behavioral Sciences* (2nd edn). Mahwah, NJ: Erlbaum.

Coxhead, A. 2000. 'A new academic word list', *TESOL Quarterly* 34(2): 213–238.

Daller, H., van Hout, R. and Treffers-Daller, J. 2003. 'Lexical richness in the spontaneous speech of bilinguals', *Applied Linguistics* 24: 197–222.

de Graaff, R., Jan Koopman, G., Anikina, Y. and Westhoff, G. 2007. 'An observation tool for effective L2 pedagogy in content and language integrated learning (CLIL)', *International Journal of Bilingual Education and Bilingualism* 10(5): 603–624.

Dörnyei, Z. 2007. *Research Methods in Applied Linguistics*. Oxford: Oxford University Press.

Dörnyei, Z. and Murphey, T. 2003. *Group Dynamics in the Language Classroom*. Cambridge: Cambridge University Press.

Erkaya, O. R. 2005. 'Benefits of using short stories in the EFL context', *Asian EFL Journal* 8: 1–13.

2011. 'Advantages of using translated stories from students' native language to teach EFL', *The Journal of Language Teaching and Learning* 1(2): 57–66.

Farrell, T. S. C. 2008. 'Critical incidents in ELT initial teacher training', *ELT Journal* 62 (1): 3–10.

Field, A. 2009. *Discovering Statistics Using SPSS* (3rd edn). London: Sage.

Fogal, G. G. 2015. 'Pedagogical stylistics in multiple foreign language and second language contexts: A synthesis of empirical research', *Language and Literature* 24 (1): 54–72.

2019. 'Tracking microgenetic changes in authorial voice development from a complexity theory perspective', *Applied Linguistics* 40(3): 432–455.

Gao, X. 2007. 'Has language learning strategy research come to an end? A response to Tseng et al. (2006)', *Applied Linguistics* 28: 615–620.

Hadfield, J. 1992. *Classroom Dynamics*. Oxford: Oxford University Press.

Hall, G. 2005. *Literature in Language Education*. London: Palgrave Macmillan.

2007. 'Stylistics in second language contexts: A critical perspective', in Watson G. and Zyngier S. (eds.), *Literature and Stylistics for Language Learners*. London: Palgrave Macmillan, 3–14.

2015. 'Recent developments in Uses of Literature in Language Teaching', in Teranishi, M., Saito, Y. and Wales, K. (eds.), *Literature and Language Learning in the EFL Classroom*. London: Palgrave Macmillan, 13–25.

Hanauer, D. 1997. 'Poetry reading in the second language classroom', *Language Awareness* 6: 1–15.

Henry, A. and Thorsen, C. 2018a. 'Teacher–student relationships and L2 motivation', *The Modern Language Journal* 102(1): 218–241.

2018b. 'Teachers' self-disclosures and influences on students' motivation: A relational perspective', *International Journal of Bilingual Education and Bilingualism*, 1–15.

Hişmanoğlu, M. 2005. 'Teaching English through literature', *Journal of Language and Linguistic Studies* 1(1): 53–66.

Horst, M. and Collins, L. 2006. 'From *faible* to strong: How does their vocabulary grow?', *The Canadian Modern Language Review / La Revue canadienne des langues vivantes* 63(1:) 83–106.

Housen, A., Kuiken, F. and Vedder, I. 2012. 'Complexity, accuracy and fluency: Definitions, measurement and research', in Housen, A., Kuiken, F. and Vedder, I. (eds.), *Dimensions of L2 Performance and Proficiency: Complexity, Accuracy and Fluency in SLA*. Amsterdam: John Benjamins, 1–20.

Ishikawa, T. 2007. 'The effect of manipulating task complexity along the [+ / – here-and -now] dimension on L2 written narrative discourse', in Garcia Mayo, M. d. P. (ed.), *Investigating Tasks in Formal Language Learning*. Clevedon: Multilingual Matters, 136–156.

Kim, M. 2004. 'Literature discussions in adult L2 learning', *Language and Education* 18(2): 145–166.

Koizumi, R. 2005. 'Speaking performance measures of fluency, accuracy, syntactic complexity, and lexical complexity', *JABAET (Japan-Britain Association for English Teaching) Journal* 9: 5–33.

Lachuk, A. J. and Koellner, K. 2015. 'Performance-based assessment for certification: Insights from edTPA implementation', *Language Arts* 93(2): 84–95.

Larsen-Freeman, D. 2017. 'Complexity theory: The lessons continue', in Ortega, L. and Han, Z. (eds.), *Complexity Theory and Language Development: In Celebration of Diane Larsen-Freeman*. Amsterdam: John Benjamins, 11–50.

Laufer, B. 1994. 'The lexical profile of second language writing: Does it change over time?', *RELC Journal* 25(2): 21–33.

1998. 'The development of passive and active vocabulary in a second language: Same or different?', *Applied Linguistics* 19(2): 255–271.

Laufer, B. and Nation, P. 1995. 'Vocabulary size and use: Lexical richness in L2 written production', *Applied Linguistics* 16(3): 307–322.

Lin, H. 2010. 'The taming of the immeasurable: An empirical assessment of language awareness', in Paran A. and Sercu L. (eds.), *Testing the Untestable in Language Education*. Toronto: Multilingual Matters, 91–216.

Little, D. 2007. 'Language learner autonomy: Some fundamental considerations revisited', *International Journal of Innovation in Language Learning and Teaching* 1 (1): 14–29.

Mackey, A. and Gass, S. M. 2015. *Second Language Research: Methodology and Design* (2nd edn). New York: Routledge.

McDevitt, B. 1997. 'Learner autonomy and the need for learner training', *The Language Learning Journal* 16(1): 34–39.

Mercer, S. 2015. 'Social network analysis and complex dynamic systems', in Dörnyei, Z., MacIntyre, P. and Henry A. (eds.), *Motivational Dynamics in Language Learning*. Bristol: Multilingual Matters, 73–82.

Michel, M. C., Kuiken, F. and Vedder, I. 2007. 'The influence of complexity in monologic versus dialogic tasks in Dutch L2', *IRAL – International Review of Applied Linguistics in Language Teaching* 45(3): 241–259.

Nasu, M. 2015. 'The role of literature in foreign language learning', in Teranishi, M., Saito, Y. and Wales, K. (eds.), in *Literature and Language Learning in the EFL Classroom*. London: Palgrave Macmillan, 229–247.

Paesani, K. 2006. '"Exercices de style": Developing multiple competencies through a writing portfolio', *Foreign Language Annals* 39(4): 618–639.

Paran, A. 2008. 'The role of literature in instructed foreign language learning and teaching: An evidence-based survey', *Language Teaching* 41(4): 465–496.

— 2017. 'Interview with Amos Paran, Specialist in L2 reading and literature in language teaching', *Language Teacher* 41: 16–19.

Pardede, P. 2011. Using short stories to teach language skills. *Journal of English Teaching* 1(1): 14–27.

Pavlenko, A. 2007. 'Autobiographic narratives as data in applied linguistics', *Applied Linguistics* 28: 163–188.

Pinner, R. S. 2019. *Social Authentication and Teacher–Student Motivational Synergy: A Narrative of Language Teaching*. London: Routledge.

Rodriguez, N. M. and Ryave, A. 2002. *Systematic Self-observation: A Method for Researching the Hidden and Elusive Features of Everyday Social Life* (Vol. 49). London: Sage.

Rosenthal, R. 1991. *Meta-analytic Procedures for Social Research* (2nd edn). Newbury Park, CA: Sage.

— 1994. 'Parametric measures of effect size', in Cooper H. and Hedges L. V. (eds.), *The Handbook of Research Synthesis*. New York: Sage, 231–244.

Sheehan, M. D. 2015. 'Increasing Motivation and Building Bridges to Content with Graded Readers', in Teranishi, M., Saito, Y. and Wales, K. (eds.), in *Literature and Language Learning in the EFL Classroom*. London: Palgrave Macmillan, 280–297.

Swain, M. 2010. '"Talking-it-through": Languaging as a source of learning', in Batstone R. (ed.), *Sociocognitive Perspectives on Second Language Learning and Use*. Oxford: Oxford University Press, 112–129.

Thériault, M. 2015. 'The development of lexical complexity in sixth-grade intensive English students', Master's thesis, Université Laval, Québec.

Tono, Y. 2010. *CEFR-J* を活用するための *'Can Do' Descriptor* リスト [CEFR-J oral proficiency 'Can Do' Descriptor List]. Tono Laboratory. Available at: www.cefr-j .org/ (Accessed 20 September 2017).

Tripp, D. 1993. *Critical Incidents in Teaching: Developing Professional Judgement* (Education Classic edn). London: Routledge.

Ushioda, E. 2011. 'Why autonomy? Insights from motivation theory and research', *Innovation in Language Learning and Teaching* 5(2): 221–232.

    2014. 'Motivation, autonomy and metacognition: Exploring their interactions', in Lasagabaster, D., Doiz, A. and Sierra J. M. (eds.), *Motivation and Foreign Language Learning: From Theory to Practice*. Amsterdam: John Benjamins, 31–49.

Verspoor, M. H. 2017. 'Complex dynamic systems theory and L2 pedagogy', in Ortega L. and Han Z. (eds.), *Complexity Theory and Language Development: In Celebration of Diane Larsen-Freeman*. Amsterdam: John Benjamins, 144–162.

Zhang, L. J. 2010. 'A dynamic metacognitive systems account of Chinese university students' knowledge about EFL reading', *TESOL Quarterly* 44(2): 320–353.

10   Conclusion: Implications for Pedagogy and Research

Christian Jones

This aim of this final chapter is to draw together the different threads and summarise what we can learn from the chapters in this volume and also attempt to identify ways forward in both research and teaching. The conclusions I draw aim to be instructive and reflective rather than didactic. The purpose of this volume has been to investigate the potential of using literature to develop awareness of spoken language or speaking skills and, as noted, there have only been a limited number of studies in this area. These findings then need to be developed by other researchers or taken forward and adapted by teachers in their own contexts. Despite these caveats, I feel there are some useful conclusions we can draw from the chapters presented.

This chapter takes the following form: it first lists and discusses five implications for teaching and then five for research. As each implication is discussed, explicit reference will be made to the chapters in this book and their findings, and it is hoped that these implications provide suggestions for teaching and research.

Five Implications for Teaching

1   Literature as a Model of Spoken Language

Several chapters have investigated the potential of literature to offer a useful model of spoken language. We know that conversations in literature are not identical to those we will find in spoken corpora. For example, rather than serving interpersonal goals, they will often serve an author's intention to develop a character or theme, or create atmosphere (see Chapter 2, this volume, for a more detailed discussion). Despite this, some of the chapters included here have shown that literature often contains many features which are common in spoken language. Chapter 2 shows that even in more dated literature, such as that of Dickens, features such as spoken discourse markers and vague language are frequent and often function in similar ways to data we find in corpora of spoken language. Chapter 5 (this volume) examined a corpus of learner-produced haiku poetry and shows that asking learners to compose short literary texts such as these can help to develop students' awareness of spoken forms such as contractions, common spoken verbs and vague language. The specific requirements of the haiku encourage the use of such spoken forms. In both cases, texts such as these have the potential to be used as models of spoken language. Learners could engage with such texts in extensive reading programmes outside of class time, and the spoken aspects of the texts would form part of the input learners receive. The importance of input in second language acquisition is well established (Ellis 2008), and the benefits of extensive reading have also been established in a number of studies (e.g. Waring 2006; Chen 2018). Learners could be given a range of texts and asked to choose those which most interest them. Classroom time could then be used to focus on the spoken language used in texts which have been read in order to develop learners' spoken language awareness. As discussed in Chapters 3 and 4 (this volume), the aim of such activities is to develop an 'enhanced consciousness of the forms and functions of language' (Carter 2003: 64) and in this case to focus learners on spoken language. Alternatively, if establishing extensive reading programmes is impossible, texts such as haiku can be used in class. For example, texts produced by learners (Chapter 5) can be read, understood and then explored in terms of the spoken forms they use before learners produce their own texts in class or in their own time.

2   Literature and Engagement

Related to the first point is the idea that literature offers real potential to provide learners with engaging texts to either talk about and/or discuss the spoken language within them. Chapter 3 explores the potential of literary dialogues, which could be used as part of a text-driven approach, whereby texts are chosen with the intention initially to engage the learners affectively and cognitively and then later as a source for discovery activities to help the learners to become aware of how a particular linguistic or discourse feature functions. Such texts can be used, as shown in this chapter, as the basis for units of materials, rather than starting from the basis of organising units around particular language forms. Clearly, once engaging texts have been found, teachers also need to consider the usefulness of the language in texts but as this chapter shows, this approach is one which teachers in a variety of teaching contexts were generally positive about. Other chapters in this volume also demonstrate the potential for developing awareness of spoken language or speaking skills. Chapters four and six show that dramatised literature and screenplays can engage and motivate learners, as well as help to develop awareness of spoken forms and functions, and Chapters 7 and 8 show the benefits of collaborative dialogue between learners when discussing texts. Such collaboration, it has been shown, can develop learners' ability to notice (taken here to mean as 'conscious registration of attended specific instances of language' (Schmidt 2010: 725)), negotiate meaning and develop interpersonal interaction skills in general. Put simply, a clear conclusion is that engaging literary texts can provide a motivation for learners to interact and make discoveries about the spoken language they contain. There are several reasons for this. One may be simply that literature is something that many learners will engage with in their first language and thus engaging with it in their second language interests them. Another is that literature contains what McRae(1991) has termed 'representational language', which is open to interpretation and discussion rather than being something which simply transmits information. This creates a natural opinion gap and hence, the motivation and interest in discussing such texts.

The chapters in this volume show that teachers have several options when using literary texts, each providing the various benefits outlined above. The first is to take a text-driven approach to creating units of materials. Chapter 3 gives a detailed explanation and rationale for such an approach. The second is to use literature circles as detailed in Chapter 8, whereby students make choices over texts they read outside of class time and later engage in group discussions guided by the roles they have prepared for this discussion, with the teacher in a supporting role to facilitate the organisation of the literature circles, over a longer period. A clear explanation of how to undertake this is given in this chapter.

Lastly, teachers can choose engaging texts to use in class, as shown in Chapters 4, 6, 7 and 9. The key to all of these options is, firstly, to choose texts which have the potential to engage and interest learners and then consider the usefulness of the spoken language they contain or their potential to provoke discussion. Such an approach is in preference to one where something is chosen on the basis that it has repeated examples of a particular language area.

3   *Literature as an Aid to Student Autonomy*

Related to points one and two is the notion that literature, as we have used it in these studies, can contribute to learner autonomy, something which is considered to be of importance in learners developing their L2 for themselves (Smith, Kucha and Lamb 2018)). Chapter 8, for example, demonstrates the benefits of giving learners a choice related to what they read and discuss in a literature circle. Asking learners to then take roles and develop the literature circles for themselves (with the teacher helping to facilitate the organisation of these) then adds to this autonomy and demonstrates the benefits of giving learning more control and choice over their own learning. In a similar way, using engaging texts related to students' cultural background as the focus of class work (see Chapter 7, for example) can make learners more aware of texts they can choose to engage with by themselves. It is easy to ask learners to simply undertake extensive reading or listening to dramatised literature outside of classes, but without some suggestions of possible choices, few will undertake this. Part of the role of a teacher must then be to help to guide students to useful, engaging choices available, which offer a plausible model of spoken language.

4   *Literature as an Aid to the Development of Communicative*
       Competence

Attempting to develop communicative competence (Hymes 1972) is generally seen as the central goal of communicative language teaching, however this may be realised in the many forms of this approach. Communicative competence can be broadly defined as consisting of linguistic (understanding and using forms), pragmatic (understanding and using appropriate language in context), strategic (understanding and using strategies to overcome communication difficulties) and discourse (understanding and using language as it connects in texts) competences (Jones, Byrne and Halenko 2017). These competences work together to help L2 speakers to communicate and understand what is communicated to them. The chapters in this volume show that literature is something teachers can use to develop aspects of this competence. Chapters 3 and 4, for example, show that engaging literature can be used to develop spoken language awareness, something which can potentially contribute to development of several competences. If a learner becomes more aware of language items in a literary text, then they are likely to understand their form and meaning (linguistic competence) and to notice how they are used appropriately in context (pragmatic competence) and how they link to other language used (discourse competence). While we cannot guarantee such awareness develops all these competences, it is more likely than if spoken language is examined in a de-contextualised fashion.

   Other chapters in this volume demonstrate that using literature as a discussion tool can also develop communicative competence. Chapter 6 shows that screenplays can help to develop metapragmatic awareness of speech acts, while Chapters 7 and 8 show that discussing literature in different ways can also help to develop strategic competence as leaners have to discuss and negotiate meaning with each other as they do so. What this implies for teaching is the importance of considering the aspects of communicative competence that literary texts might help us to develop in class and of questioning their use if they do not appear to lend themselves to this development. If this is considered as part of the normal business of lesson and course planning, it could help to alleviate teacher concerns about using literature in EFL/ESL classes, which can centre on how useful literature will be to learners (e.g. Jones and Carter 2011). As suggested earlier, a fruitful approach to choice of texts is, firstly, to assess the extent to which they might engage learners but then also to consider how the text and activities designed to be used with them might develop communicative competence. It is also important that such aims are communicated to learners so they can see how literature might develop their speaking skills or awareness of spoken language. As shown in Chapter 9, one reason that learners may not engage fully is if they are not clear about the potential benefits of discussing literature in classes.

5   *Literature within Communicative Methodology*

Related to point three, all chapters in this volume show that literature can be used with a communicative methodology to develop awareness of spoken language or speaking skills. We have shown that it can be used for many types of activities which are familiar in communicative classes, including imaginative, creative activities (Chapters 3 and 5) and discussion (Chapters 6, 7, 8 and 9). This demonstrates that if using literature to develop awareness of spoken language or speaking skills, teachers can use many familiar activities to engage learners with it, something which has been advocated by others for many years (e.g. Brumfit and Carter 1986; Carter and McRae 1996). It is not necessary to separate its use into 'the literature class' or adopt a methodology which treats literature entirely differently from other texts which we wish learners to engage with. Having noted this, it is also important that teaching takes into account the context in which it takes place. Chapters 6 and 9, for example, take place in a monolingual EFL context. These studies show the importance of a measured and principled approach to L1 use in classes, some-thing which Cook (2010) makes a sensible argument for. It can be very helpful, for example, to ask learners to undertake some language awareness discussion tasks in their L1 before asking them to report back or produce texts in L2. It is also important that learners are made aware of the purpose and benefits when teachers wish them to use the L2, as Chapter 9 shows. If this is not clear, learners may revert to using their L1 for the majority of classes and not gain the potential benefits of some discussion in the L2.

Five Implications for Research

1   *Investigating New Approaches*

Several chapters in this volume have investigated relatively new approaches to the use of literature. Chapter 3, for example, investigated teacher evaluation of literature materials designed to enhance spoken language awareness using a text-driven approach. Such an approach means a text is chosen for its potential to achieve affective and cognitive engagement for the target learners rather than because it contains a predetermined language point, skill, topic or theme. It was also noted in this chapter that there is a lack of empirical studies which have investigated such an approach. It would therefore be useful for future studies to investigate the effects of such as approach on the development of spoken language awareness and also how such materials impact on affective factors such as motivation. Logically, such studies could make comparisons with other materials which take a different approach to the use of literature. Chapter 8 explored the potential of literature circles in an EFL context. In these circles, students choose literary texts to read outside of class time and then undertake discussion of the texts in class time, with the teacher facilitating the discussion by helping to develop roles, organising and allocating time for the discussion but not playing an actual role in that discussion. Analysis of the discussions suggests that the conversations within the circles afford opportunities for language development and development of spoken output. However, although such circles have been used extensively in English L1 contexts, they are relatively new to L2 ELT and although studies have shown positive effects (e.g. Furr 2004; Kim 2004; Shelton-Strong 2012), more are clearly needed. It would be helpful to explore the effects in a variety of EFL contexts such as the one investigated in Chapter 8, where opportunities to speak may be limited outside of class time and thus often need to be maximised within class time. More work is also needed to investigate the potential in using literature to enhance awareness of features of spoken language such as ellipsis (Chapter 4). As Timmis (2012) and Carter and McCarthy (2017) note, there are still relatively few studies which have investigated the effects of different types of materials upon the acquisition of common features of spoken language such as discourse markers and vague language. Chapter 4 demonstrates the potential benefits of dramatised literature to raise awareness of such features, but further studies could investigate this in comparison to the effects of coursebook dialogues, as one example.

2   The Importance of a Variety of Research Designs

The studies in this volume underline the importance of examining the effect of literature on awareness of spoken language and development of speaking skills from both quantitative and qualitative angles. Chapters 3, 6, 7 and 8 show the potential of qualitative data for investigating this area. They show that we can gain clear insights via analysis of such data as classroom discussions. These allow us to see how the use of literature can impact upon areas such as noticing and metapragmatic awareness. Qualitative research of this type can offer real insight if undertaken in a principled way and for several aspects investigated in their volume, qualitative methods are likely to be the most effective. For example, if we seek to investigate how learners view the use of literature in class discussions (Chapter 9), one obvious option is to use some form of interview. We would encourage more studies of this type when researching the effects of literature on awareness of spoken language and development of speaking skills, and guidelines for qualitative research methods detailed by Richards (2003) offer helpful guidance. Several chapters have also shown the benefits of mixed-methods research. Chapters 2 and 5, for example, show the potential of using corpora to examine the language used in literature and its potential as a model of spoken language. Here, the benefits of using such quantitative measures as frequency counts are clear, but the benefits of close qualitative examination of language in context are also demonstrated. Such an approach is one often recommended when we explore corpus data (e.g. O'Keeffe, McCarthy and Carter 2007) as it allows us to discuss the frequency of form and also function. Chapters 4 and 9 also show the importance of combining data from pre- and post-tests with qualitative data from focus groups, interviews and lesson observations. Mixed-methods designs such as these allow us to understand the effects from several angles and thus give us a clearer picture of the effects of literature. We would recommend that future studies seeking to investigate the effects of literature employ mixed methods, as appropriate for the research questions being investigated (see Creswell and Plano Clark 2017 for a useful overview of this type of research). Such studies could investigate the kinds of areas outlined in point 1.

3   The Potential of Corpora

Two chapters in this volume (Chapters 2 and 5) have shown the potential which corpora have for helping us to analyse and use material based on such data. It has also been mentioned that work in the field of corpus stylistics (e.g. Mahlberg 2015) has done much to investigate how language is used in literature and how patterns contribute to the ways in which meaning is developed in texts. Such work continues to offer real insights into areas such as how authors use speech to develop characters (e.g. Mahlberg and Wiegand 2018). However, as also mentioned in Chapters 2 and 5, the use of such material has rarely been investigated in classroom research with English language learners as partici-pants. Such research could use corpus data to inform the type of work which Fogal (2015) describes in an overview of pedagogical stylistics. We might, for example, investigate the effects of using samples of corpus data as part of data-driven learning (Johns 1991), that is, using concordance lines as data to be discussed in order to raise awareness of features of spoken language. Such work has been found to have a positive effect on vocabulary learning in a recent meta-analysis (Lee, Warshauer and Lee 2018), and it would be helpful to know if similar positive effects can be found in regard to literature. The nature of literary corpora is that they do not contain very modern texts (for obvious reasons of copyright), but as argued in Chapter 2 there is no reason to auto-matically assume older texts will not interest learners, and they can contain many features of modern-day spoken English.

4   The Effects of Noticing

Several chapters in this volume (e.g. Chapter 4 and Chapter 8) suggest that literature can enhance the ability to notice features of language, either by exam-ining spoken language or producing it. As mentioned earlier in this chapter we can define noticing broadly as 'conscious registration of attended specific instances of language' (Schmidt 2010: 725). There is now a large body of research which demonstrates the benefits of noticing in general (see Bergsleithner, Frota and Yoshioka 2013 for a useful contribution), but more investigation is needed on how different forms of literature can aid noticing in relation to spoken language. For example, it would be useful to investigate the longer-term effects of noticing in terms of how it develops learners' language awareness (e.g. Lin 2010) in relation to the spoken language they encounter in face-to-face inter-action. We might also measure the extent to which reported noticing has an impact on other areas examined in this volume, such as lexical complexity (Chapter 9).

5   The Effects on Fluency

Several chapters in this volume (e.g. Chapters 6 and 7) show the benefits that discussing literature in class can have on aspects of spoken language develop-ment, such as developing the ability to manage conversations and to show listenership. More studies are needed in order to investigate this further. McCarthy and McCarten (2018) provide a useful analysis of conversation strategies which learners need to develop, and it would be helpful to investigate how such discussion can contribute to this development. Clearly, such ability can potentially develop through any conversation, but we have argued that the representational language (McRae 1991) in literature gives students something motivating to discuss because it is language which has to be interpreted and will be understood in different ways by different people. In addition, it would be helpful to investigate the extent to which discussing literature can help to develop fluency in the short and longer term. Such studies could usefully look at the development of lexical chunks, which have been shown to be a key aspect of fluent language use (e.g. Wray 2005; O'Keeffe et al. 2007; Wood 2009; McCarthy and McCarten 2018) and the ability to link turns effectively and respond well, which McCarthy (2010) has termed 'confluence'. These measures could be examined alongside common measures of fluency such as speed of delivery and undue pauses.

Conclusion

In this book, we have attempted to explore some of the effects of using literature to develop awareness of spoken language or speaking skills in second language learning. We have examined this in a number of different contexts and used different approaches to investigate it. We have shown that literature has real potential as a realistic, useful and motivating model of spoken language. It can develop spoken language awareness, and discussing literature can help to develop important speaking skills such as managing conversations. These findings link to several theories of second language acquisition, including the importance of noticing (Schmidt 1990) and interaction (Long 1996) as well as more individual affective factors such as motivation (Dörnyei 2012).

We have undertaken these investigations in the belief that it is worth understanding how literature can impact upon awareness of spoken language and speaking skills development. However, as stated in the introduction to this chapter, it is important to stress that the results here are instructive and should be developed further by teachers and researchers, in ways I have suggested. Once more studies are available in this area, further meta-analysis, such as Fogal (2015), can be undertaken, and we can then show more authoritative results gained from a number of studies. The chapters offered here thus give indications of the effects of literature in several different contexts, with several different types of focus. We would hope that these studies will encourage teachers to use literature to develop awareness of spoken language or speaking skills in their own teaching contexts and for other researchers to develop this area further.

References

Bergsleithner, J. H., Frota, S. N. and Yoshioka, J. K. (eds.) 2013. *Noticing and Second Language Acquisition: Studies in Honour of Richard Schmidt*. Hawaii: National Foreign language Resource Center.

Brumfit, C. and Carter, R. 1986. *Literature and Language Teaching*. Oxford: Oxford University Press.

Carter, R. 2003. 'Language awareness', *ELT Journal* 57(1): 64–65.

Carter, R. and McCarthy, M. 2017. 'Spoken grammar: Where we are and where we are going'?, *Applied Linguistics* 38(1): 1–20.

Carter, R. and McRae, J. 1996. *Language, Literature and the Learner: Creative Classroom Practice*. London: Longman.

Chen, Chen-I. 2018. 'Incorporating task-based learning in an extensive reading programme', *ELT Journal* 72(4): 405–414.

Cook, G. 2010. *Translation in Language Teaching.* Oxford: Oxford University Press.

Creswell, J. W. and Plano Clark, V. L. 2017. *Designing and Conducting Mixed Methods Research* (3rd edn). London: Sage Publications.

Dörnyei, Z. 2012. *Motivation in Language Learning.* Shanghai: Shanghai Foreign Language Education Press.

Ellis, R. 2008. *The Study of Second Language Acquisition (2nd edn).* Oxford: Oxford University Press.

Fogal, G. G. 2015. 'Pedagogical stylistics in multiple foreign language and second language contexts: A synthesis of empirical research', *Language and Literature* 24 (1): 54–72.

Furr, M. 2004. 'Literature circles for the EFL classroom'. Available at: www .eflliteraturecircles.com/litcirclesforEFL.pdf (Accessed 8 November 2018).

Hymes, D. 1972. 'On communicative competence', in Pride, J. B. and Holmes, J. (eds.), *Sociolinguistics.* Harmondsworth: Penguin, 269–293.

Johns, T. 1991. 'Should you be persuaded: Two examples of data-driven learning', *English Language Research Journal* 4: 1–16.

Jones, C ., Byrne, S. and Halenko, N. 2017. *Successful Spoken English: Findings from Learner Corpora.* London: Routledge.

Jones, C. and Carter, R. 2011.'Literature and language awareness: Using literature to achieve CEFR outcomes', *Journal of Second Language Teaching and Research* 1 (1): 69–82.

Kim, M. 2004. 'Literature discussions in adult L2 learning', *Language and Education* 18(2): 145–166. doi.org/10.1080/09500780408666872

Lee, H., Warshauer, M. and Lee, J. H. 2018.'The effects of corpus use on second language vocabulary learning: A multilevel meta-analysis', *Applied Linguistics* (Advanced Online Access). doi.org/10.1093/applin/amy012

Lin, H. W. 2010. 'The taming of the immeasurable: An empirical assessment of language awareness', in Paran, A. and Sercu, L. (eds.), *Testing the Untestable in Language Education.* Bristol: Multilingual Matters, 191–216.

Long, M. 1996. 'The role of the linguistic environment in second language acquisition', in Richie, W. and Bhatia, T. K. (eds.), *Handbook of Second Language Acquisition.* San Diego: Academic Press, 413–468.

Mahlberg, M. 2015. *Corpus Stylistics and Dickens's Fiction.* London: Routledge.

Mahlberg, M. and Wiegand, V. 2018. 'Corpus stylistics, norms and comparsion: Studying speech in Great Expectations', in Page, R., Busse, B. and Nørgard, N. (eds.), *Rethinking Language, Text and Context: Interdisciplinary Research in Stylistics in Honour of Michael Toolan.* London: Routledge, 123–143.

McCarthy, M. 2010. 'Spoken fluency revisited', *English Profile Journal.* Available at: http://journals.cambridge.org/action/displayJournal?jid=EPJ.

McCarthy, M. and McCarten, J. 2018. 'Now you're talking! Practising conversation in second language learning', in Jones, C. (ed.) *Practice in Second Language Learning.* Cambridge: Cambridge University Press, 7–29.

McRae, J. 1991. *Literature with a Small 'l'.* London: Macmillan.

O'Keeffe, A., McCarthy, M. and Carter, R. 2007. *From Corpus to Classroom.* Cambridge: Cambridge University Press.

Richards, K. 2003. *Qualitative Inquiry in TESOL*. Basingstoke: Palgrave Macmillan.

Schmidt, R. 1990. 'The role of consciousness in second language learning XE "language learning"', *Applied Linguistics* 11: 129–158.

      2010. 'Attention, awareness and individual differences in language learning', in Chan, W. M., Chi, S., Cin, K. N., Istanto, J., Nagami, M., Sew, J. W., Suthiwan, T. and Walker, I. (eds.), *Proceeding of ClaScc 2010 Singapore December 2–4*. Singapore: University of Singapore Center for Language Studies, 721–737.

Shelton-Strong, S. J. 2012. 'Literature circles in ELT', *ELT Journal* 66(2): 214–223.

Smith, R., Kuchah, K. and Lamb, M. 2018. 'Learner autonomy in developing countries', in Chik, A., Naoki, N. and Smith, R. (eds.), *Autonomy in Language Learning and Teaching*. London: Palgrave, 7–27.

Timmis, I. 2012. 'Spoken language research and ELT: Where are we now?', *ELT Journal* 66(4): 514–522.

Waring, R. 2006. 'Why extensive reading should be an indispensable part of all language programs', *The Language Teacher* 30(7): 44–47.

Wood, D. 2009. 'Effects of focused instruction of formulaic sequences on fluent expression in second language narratives: A case study', *Canadian Journal of Applied Linguistics* 12(1): 39–57.

Wray, A. 2005. *Formulaic Language and the Lexicon*. Cambridge: Cambridge University Press.

Index

Lightning Source UK Ltd.
Milton Keynes UK
UKHW021226010322
399316UK00015B/349

9 781108 460798